John Foster

Essays, in a Series of Letters, on the Following Subjects

1. On a man's writing memoirs of himself. 2. On decision of character. 3. On the application of the epithet romantic. 4. On some of the causes by which evangelical religion has been rendered

John Foster

Essays, in a Series of Letters, on the Following Subjects
1. On a man's writing memoirs of himself. 2. On decision of character. 3. On the application of the epithet romantic. 4. On some of the causes by which evangelical religion has been rendered

ISBN/EAN: 9783337038106

Printed in Europe, USA, Canada, Australia, Japan

Cover: Foto ©Thomas Meinert / pixelio.de

More available books at **www.hansebooks.com**

ESSAYS,

IN A SERIES OF LETTERS,

ON THE FOLLOWING SUBJECTS:

I.
ON A MAN'S WRITING MEMOIRS OF HIMSELF

II.
ON DECISION OF CHARACTER.

III.
ON THE APPLICATION OF THE EPITHET ROMANTIC.

IV.
ON SOME OF THE CAUSES BY WHICH EVANGELICAL RELIGION HAS BEEN RENDERED LESS ACCEPTABLE TO PERSONS OF CULTIVATED TASTE.

BY JOHN FOSTER.

LONDON: GEORGE BELL & SONS, YORK STREET
COVENT GARDEN
1876.

ADVERTISEMENT.

Perhaps it will be thought that pieces written so much in the manner of set compositions as the following, should not have been denominated Letters; it may therefore be proper to say, that they are so called because they were actually addressed to a friend. They were written however with an intention to put them in print, if, when they were finished, the writer could persuade himself that they deserved it; and the temper of even the most inconsiderable pretenders to literature in these times is too well known for any one to be surprised that he *could* so persuade himself.

When he began these letters, his intention was to confine himself within such limits, that essays on twelve or fifteen subjects might be comprised in a volume. But he soon found that so narrow a space would exclude many illustrations not less appropriate or useful than any which would be introduced.

It will not seem a very natural manner of commencing a course of letters to a friend, to enter formally on a subject in the first sentence. In excuse for this abruptness it may be mentioned, that there was an introductory letter; but as it was written in the presumption that a considerable variety of subjects would be treated in the compass of a moderate number of letters, it is omitted, as not being adapted to precede what is executed in a manner so different from the design.

When writing which has occupied a considerable length, and has been interrupted by considerable intervals, of time, which is also on very different subjects, and was perhaps meditated under the influence of different circumstances, is at last all gone over in one short course of perusal, this immediate succession and close comparison make the writer sensible of some things of which he was not aware in the slow separate stages of the progress. On thus bringing the following essays under one review, the writer perceives some reason to apprehend, that the spirit of the third may appear so different from that of the second, as to give an impression of something like inconsistency. The second may be thought to have an appearance of representing that a man may effect almost every thing, the third that he can effect scarcely any thing. But the writer would say, that the one does not assert the efficacy of human resolution and effort under the same conditions under which the other asserts their inefficacy; and that therefore there is no real contrariety between the principles of the two essays. From the evidence of history and familiar experience we know that, under certain conditions, and within certain limits, (strait ones indeed,) an enlightened and resolute human spirit has great power, this greatness being relative to the measures of things within a small sphere; while it is equally obvious that this enlightened and resolute spirit, if disregarding these conditions, and attempting to extend its agency over a much wider sphere, shall find its power baffled and annihilated, till it draws back within the boundary. Now the great power of the human mind within the narrow limit being forcibly and largely insisted on at one time, and its impotence beyond that limit, at another, the assemblage of sentiments and exemplifications most adapted to illustrate, (and without real or considerable exaggeration,) that power alone, will form apparently so strong a contrast with the assemblage of thoughts and facts proper for illustrating that imbecility alone, that on a superficial view the two representations may appear contradictory. The author appeals to the experience of such thinking men as are accustomed to commit their thoughts to writing, whether sometimes, on comparing the pages in which they had endeavoured to place one truth in the strongest light, with those in which they have endeavoured a strong but yet not extravagant exhibition of another, they have not felt a momentary difficulty to reconcile them, even while satisfied of the substantial justness of both. The whole doctrine on any extensive moral subject necessarily includes two views which may be considered as its extremes; and if these are strongly stated quite apart from their relations to each other, both the representations may be perfectly true, and yet may require, in order to the reader's perceiving their consistency, a recollection of many intermediate ideas.

In the fourth essay, it was not intended to take a comprehensive or systematic view of the causes contributing to prevent the candid attention and the cordial admission due to evangelical religion, but simply to select a few which had particularly attracted the writer's observation. One or two more would have been specified and slightly illustrated, if the essay had not been already too long.

ADVERTISEMENT

TO THE NINTH EDITION.

As it is signified in the title-page that the book is corrected in this edition, it may not be impertinent to indicate by a few sentences the nature and amount of the correction. After a revisal which introduced a number of small verbal alterations in one of the later of the preceding editions, the writer had been willing to believe himself excused from any repetition of that kind of task. But when it was becoming probable that the new edition now printed would be called for, an acute literary friend strongly recommended one more and a final revisal; enforcing his recommendation by pointing out, in various places, what the writer readily acknowledged to be faults in the composition. This determined him to try the effect of a careful inspection throughout with a view to such an abatement of the imperfections of the book, as might make him decidedly content to let it go without any future revision.

In this operation there has been no attempt at novelty beyond such slight changes and diminutive additions as appeared necessary in order to give a more exact or full expression of the sense. There is not, probably, more of any thing that could properly be called new, than might be contained in half-a-dozen pages. *Correction*, in the strict sense, has been the object. Sentences, of ill-ordered construction, or loose or inconsequential in their connexion, have been attempted to be reformed. In some instances a sentence has been abbreviated, in others a little extended by the insertion of an explanatory or qualifying clause. Here and there a sentence has been substituted for one that was not easily reducible to the exact direction of the line of thought, or appeared feeble in expression. In several instances some modification has been required to obviate a seeming or real inconsistency with what is said in other places. This part of the process may have taken off in such instances somewhat of the cast of force and spirit, exhibited or attempted in the former mode of expression; and might have been objected to as a deterioration, by a person not aware of the reason for the change. Here and there an epithet, or a combination of words, bordering on extravagance, has yielded to the dictate of the maturer judgment, or more fastidious taste, or less stimulated feelings, of advanced life, and given place to a somewhat moderated language. The general course of thought is not affected by these minute alterations; except that, (as the writer would persuade himself,) it is in parts a little more distinctly and palpably brought out. The endeavour has been to disperse any mists that appeared to lie on the pages, that the ideas might present themselves in as defined a form as the writer could give to any of them which had seemed obscure, and ineffective to their object, from indeterminate or involved enunciation. In the revised diction, as in the original writing, he has designedly and constantly avoided certain artificial forms of phraseology, much in conventional use among even good writers; and aimed at falling on the words most immediately, naturally, and simply appropriate to the thoughts.

If his book be of a quality to impart any useful instruction, he will hope that the benefit may be conveyed with perhaps a little more clearness and facility, in consequence of these last corrections it will receive from his hand.

January, 1820.

CONTENTS.

ESSAY I.
ON A MAN'S WRITING MEMOIRS OF HIMSELF.

LETTER I.
Affectionate interest with which we revert to our past life....It deserves a brief record for our own use....Very few things to be noted of the multitude that have occurred....Direction and use of such a review as would be required for writing a Memoir....Importance of our past life considered as the beginning of an endless duration of existence....General deficiency of self-observation....Oblivion of the greatest number of our past feelings.... Occasional glimpses of vivid recollection....Associations with things and places....The different and unknown associations of different persons with the same places ....PAGE 1

LETTER II.
All past life an education....Discipline and influence from...direct instruction ...companionship...books...scenes of nature...and the state of society. p. 10

LETTER III.
Very powerful impressions sometimes from particular facts, tending to form discriminated characters....Yet very few strongly discriminated and individual characters found....Most persons belong to general classes of character....Immense number and diversity of impressions, of indefinitely various tendency, which the moral being has undergone in the course of life....Might be expected that such a confusion of influences would not permit the formation of any settled character....That such a character is, nevertheless, acquired and maintained, is owing to some one leading determination, given by whatever means, to the mind, generally in early life....Common self-deceptive belief that we have maintained moral rectitude, and the exercise of sound reason, under the impressions that have been forming our characters ....p. 18

LETTER IV.
Most of the influences under which the characters of men are forming un favourable to wisdom, virtue, and happiness....Proof of this if a number of persons, suppose a hundred, were to give a clear account of the circumstances that have most effected the state of their minds....A few examples ...a misanthropist...a lazy prejudiced thinker...a man fancying himself a genius...a projector...an antiquary in excess...a petty tyrant...............p. 28

LETTER V.
An Atheist....Slight sketch of the process by which a man in the humbler order of abilities and attainments may become one................................p. 34

LETTER VI.
The influence of Religion counteracted by almost all other influences.... Pensive reflections on the imperfect manifestation of the Supreme Being... on the inefficacy of the belief of such a being...on the strangeness of that inefficacy...and on the debasement and infelicity consequent on it....Happiness of a devout man ....p. 42

LETTER VII.

Self-knowledge being supposed the principal object in writing the memoir, the train of exterior fortunes and actions will claim but a subordinate notice in it....If it were intended for the amusement of the public, the writer would do well to fill it rather with incident and action....Yet the mere mental history of some men would be interesting to reflecting readers ...of a man, for example, of a speculative disposition, who has passed through many changes of opinion....Influences that warp opinion....Effects of time and experience on the notions and feelings cherished in early life. ...Feelings of a sensible old man on viewing a picture of his own mind, drawn by himself when he was young....Failure of excellent designs; disappointment of sanguine hopes....Degree of explicitness required in the record....Conscience....Impudence and canting false pretences of many writers of "confessions."...Rousseau ....p. 51

ESSAY II.

ON DECISION OF CHARACTER.

LETTER I.

Examples of the distress and humiliation incident to an irresolute mind.... Such a mind cannot be said to belong to itself....Manner in which a man of decisive spirit deliberates, and passes into action....Cæsar....Such a spirit prevents the fretting away, in harassing alternations of will, of the ani mated feelings required for sustaining the vigour of action....Averts im pertinent interference....Acquires, if free from harshness of manner, an undisputed and beneficial ascendency over associates....Its last resource inflexible pertinacity....Instance in a man on a jury ....p. 67

LETTER II.

Brief inquiry into the constituents of this commanding quality....Physical constitution....Possibility, nevertheless, of a firm mind in a feeble body.... Confidence in a man's own judgment....This an uncommon distinction.... Picture of a man who wants it....This confidence distinguished from obstinacy....Partly founded on experience....Takes a high tone of inde- pendence in devising schemes....Distressing dilemmas ....p. 77

LETTER III.

Energy of feeling as necessary as confidence of opinion....Conduct that results from their combination....Effect and value of a ruling passion.... Great decision of character invests even wicked beings with something which we are tempted to admire....Satan....Zanga....A Spanish assassin.... Remarkable example of this quality in a man who was a prodigal and became poor, but turned miser and became rich....Howard....Whitefield.... Christian missionaries ....p. 86

LETTER IV.

Courage a chief constituent of the character....Effect of this in encountering censure and ridicule....Almagro, Pizarro, and De Luques....Defiance of danger....Luther....Daniel....Another indispensable requisite to decision is the full agreement of all the powers of the mind....Lady Macbeth.... Richard III....Cromwell....A father who had the opportunity of saving one of two sons from death..p. 94

LETTER V.

Formidable power of mischief which this high quality gives to bad men.... Care required to prevent its rendering good men unconciliating and overbearing....Independence and overruling manner in consultation....Lord Chatham....Decision of character not incompatible with sensibility and mild manners....But probably the majority of the most eminent examples of it deficient in the kinder affections....King of Prussia....Situations in which it may be an absolute duty to act in opposition to the promptings of those affections...p. 104

LETTER VI.

Circumstances tending to consolidate this Character....Opposition....Desertion. ...Marius....Satan....Charles de Moor....Success has the same tendency.... Cæsar....Habit of associating with inferiors....Voluntary means of forming or conforming this character....The acquisition of perfect knowledge in the department in which we are to act....The cultivation of a connected and conclusive manner of reasoning....The resolute commencement of action, in a manner to commit ourselves irretrievably....Ledyard....The choice of a dignified order of concerns....The approbation of conscience....Yet melancholy to consider how many of the most distinguished possessors of the quality have been wicked..p. 111

ESSAY III.

ON THE APPLICATION OF THE EPITHET ROMANTIC.

LETTER I.

Great convenience of having a number of words that will answer the purposes of ridicule or reprobation without having any precise meaning....Puritan. ...Methodist....Jacobin....The word Romantic of the greatest service to persons, who, wanting to show their scorn, have not wherewithal in the way of sense or wit....Whenever this epithet is applied, let the exact meaning be demanded....Does it attribute, to what it is applied to, the kind of absurdity prevalent in the works called Romances?...That absurdity was from the predominance, in various modes, of imagination over judgment....Mental character of the early Romance writers....Opposite character of Cervantes....Delightful, delusive, and mischievous operation of a predominant imagination....Yet desirable, for several reasons, that the imagination should have this ascendency in early life ....p. 127

LETTER II.

One of the modes of this ascendency justly called Romantic, is, the unfounded persuasion of something peculiar and extraordinary in a person's destiny ...This vain expectation may be relative to great talent and achievement, or to great felicity....Things ardently anticipated which not only cannot be attained, but would be unadapted to the nature and condition of man if they could....A person that hoped to out-do rather than imitate Gregory Lopez, the hermit....Absurd expectations of parents....Utopian anticipations of philosophers....Practical absurdity of the age of chivalry....The extravagant and exclusive passion for what is grand ....p. 140

LETTER III.

The epithet applicable to hopes and projects inconsistent with the known relations between ends and means....Reckoning on happy casualties.... Musing on instances of good luck....Novels go more than half the length of the older Romance in promoting this pernicious tendency of the mind. ...Specimen of what they do in this way....Fancy magnifies the smallest means into an apparent competence to the greatest ends....This delusive calculation apt to be admitted in schemes of benevolence....Projects for civilizing savage nations....Extravagant expectations of the efficacy of direct instruction, in the lessons of education, and in preaching....Reformers apt to overrate the power of means....The fancy about the omnipotence of truth....Our expectations ought to be limited by what we actually see and know of human nature....Estimate of that nature....Prevalence of passion and appetite against conviction..p. 150

LETTER IV.

Christianity the grand appointed mean of reforming the world....But though the religion itself be a communication from heaven, the administration of it by human agents is to be considered as a merely human mean, excepting so far as a special divine energy is made to accompany it....Its comparatively small success proves in what an extremely limited measure that energy, as yet, accompanies it....Impotence of man to do what it leaves undone.... Irrational to expect from its progressive administration a measure of success indefinitely surpassing the present state of its operations, till we see some signs of a great change in the Divine Government of the world....Folly of projects to reform mankind which disclaim Religion....Nothing in human nature to meet and give effect to the schemes and expedients of the moral revolutionist....Wretched state of that nature....Sample of the absurd estimates of its condition by the irreligious menders of society ....p. 166

LETTER V.

Melancholy reflections....No consolation amidst the mysterious economy but in an assurance that an infinitely good Being presides, and will at length open out a new moral world....Yet many moral projectors are solicitous to keep their schemes for the amendment of the world clear of any reference to the Almighty....Even good men are guilty of placing too much dependence on subordinate powers and agents....The representations in this Essay not intended to depreciate to nothing the worth and use of the whole stock of means, but to reduce them, and the effects to be expected from them, to a sober estimate....A humble thing to be a man....Inculcation of devout submission, and diligence, and prayer....Sublime quality and indefinite efficacy of this last, as a mean....Conclusion; briefly marking out a few general characters of sentiment and action to which, though very uncommon, the epithet Romantic is unjustly applied...............................p. 175

ESSAY IV.

ON SOME OF THE CAUSES BY WHICH EVANGELICAL RELIGION HAS BEEN RENDERED UNACCEPTABLE TO PERSONS OF CULTIVATED TASTE.

LETTER I.

Nature of the displacency with which some of the most peculiar features of Christianity are regarded by many cultivated men, who do not deny or doubt the divine authority of the religion....Brief notice of the term Evangelical ....p. 188

LETTER II.

One of the causes of the displacency is, that Christianity, being the religion of a great number of persons of weak and uncultivated minds, presents its doctrines to the view of men of taste associated with the characteristics of those minds; and though some parts of the religion instantaneously redeem themselves from that association by their philosophic dignity, other parts may require a considerable effort to detach them from it....This easily done if the men of taste were powerfully pre-occupied and affected by the religion....Reflections of one of them in this case....But the men of taste now in question are not in this case....Several specific causes of injurious impression, from this association of evangelical doctrines and sentiments with the intellectual littleness of the persons entertaining them....Their deficiency and dislike of all strictly intellectual exercise on religion....Their reducing the whole of religion to one or two favourite notions, and continually dwelling on them....The perfect indifference of some of them to general knowledge, even when not destitute of means of acquiring it; and the consequent voluntary and contented poverty of their religious ideas and language....Their admiration of things in a literary sense utterly bad.... Their complacency in their deficiencies....Their injudicious habits and ceremonies....Their unfortunate metaphors and similes....Suggestion to religious teachers, that they should not run to its last possible extent the parallel between the pleasures of piety, and those of eating and drinking. ....Mischief of such practices....Effect of the ungracious collision between uncultivated seniors and a young person of literary and philosophic taste. ...Expostulation with this intellectual young person, on the folly and guilt of suffering his mind to take the impression of evangelical religion from any thing which he knows to be inferior to that religion itself, as exhibited by the New Testament, and by the most elevated of its disciples......p. 195

LETTER III.

Another cause, the Peculiarity of Language adopted in religious discourse and writing....Classical standard of language....The theological deviation from it barbarous....Surprise and perplexity of a sensible heathen foreigner who, having learnt our language according to its best standard alone, should be introduced to hear a public evangelical discourse....Distinctive characters of this Theological Dialect....Reasons against employing it....Competence of our language to express all religious ideas without the aid of this uncouth peculiarity....Advantages that would attend the use of the language of mere general intelligence, with the addition of an extremely small number of words that may be considered as necessary technical terms in theology ......p. 218

LETTER IV.

Answer to the plea, in behalf of the dialect in question, that it is formed from the language of the Bible....Description of the manner in which it is so formed....This way of employing biblical language very different from simple quotation....Grace and utility with which brief forms of words, whether sentences or single phrases, may be introduced from the Bible, if they are brought in as pure pieces and particles of the sacred composition, *set in* our own composition as something distinct from it and foreign to it. ...But the biblical phraseology in the Theological Dialect, instead of thus appearing in distinct bright points and gems, is modified and mixed up throughout the whole consistence of the diction, so as at once to lose its own venerable character, and to give a pervading uncouthness, without dignity, to the whole composition....Let the scripture language be quoted often, but not degraded into a barbarous compound phraseology....Even if it were advisable to construct the language of theological instruction in some kind of resemblance to that of the Bible, it would not follow that it should be constructed in imitation of the phraseology of an antique version....License to very old theologians to retain in a great degree this peculiar dialect.... Young ones recommended to learn to employ in religion the language in which cultivated men talk and write on general subjects....The vast mass of writing in a comprehensive literary sense bad, on the subjects of evangelical theology, one great cause of the distaste felt by men of intellectual refinement....Several kinds of this bad writing specified ....p. 239

LETTER V.

A grand cause of displacency encountered by evangelical religion among men of taste is, that the great school in which that taste is formed, that of polite literature, taken in the widest sense of the phrase, is hostile to that religion....Modern literature intended principally to be animadverted on.... Brief notice of the ancient....Heathen theology, metaphysics, and morality. ...Harmlessness of the two former; deceptiveness of the last....But the chief influence is from so much of the history as may be called Biography, and from the Poetry....Homer....Manner in which the interest he excites is hostile to the spirit of the Christian religion....Virgil ....p. 254

LETTER VI.

Lucan....Influence of the moral sublimity of his heroes....Plutarch....The Historians....Antichristian effect of admiring the moral greatness of the eminent heathens....Points of essential difference between excellence according to Christian principles, and the most elevated excellence of the Heathens....An unqualified complacency in the latter produces an alienation of affection and admiration from the former..................................p. 269

LETTER VII.

When a communication, declaring the true theory of both religion and morals, was admitted as coming from heaven, it was reasonable to expect that, from the time of this revelation to the end of the world, all by whom it was so admitted would be religiously careful to maintain, in whatever they taught on subjects within its cognizance, a systematic and punctilious conformity to its principles....Absurdity, impiety, and pernicious effect, of disregarding this sovereign claim to conformity....The greatest number of our fine writers have incurred this guilt, and done this mischief....They are antichristian, in the first place, by omission; they exclude from their moral sentiments the modifying interference of the Christian principles.... Extended illustration of the fact, and of its consequences ....p. 281

LETTER VIII.

More specific forms of their contrariety to the principles of Revelation.... Their *good man* not a Christian....Contrasted with St. Paul....Their theory of happiness essentially different from the evangelical.....Short statement of both....In moralizing on life, they do not habitually consider, and they prevent their readers from considering, the present state as introductory to another. Their consolations for distress, old age, and death, widely different, on the whole, from those which constitute so much of the value of the Gospel....The grandeur and heroism in death, which they have represented with irresistible eloquence, emphatically and perniciously opposite to the Christian doctrine and examples of sublimity and happiness in death....Examples from tragedy ....p. 391

LETTER IX.

The estimate of the depraved moral condition of human nature is quite different in revelation and polite literature....Consequently, the Redemption by Jesus Christ, which appears with such momentous importance in the one, is, in comparison, a trifle in the other....Our fine writers employ and justify antichristian motives to action, especially the love of fame....The morality of this passion argued....The earnest repression of it shown to be a duty....Some of the lighter order of our popular writers have aided the counteraction of literature to evangelical religion by careless or malignant ridicule of things associated with it....Brief notice of the several classes of fine writers, as lying under the charge of contributing to alienate men of taste from the doctrines and moral spirit of the New Testament....Moral philosophers....Historians....Essayists....Addison....Johnson....The Poets.... Exception in favour of Milton, &c....Pope....Antichristian quality of his Essay on Man....Novels....Melancholy reflections on the Review....Conclusion...p. 314

ESSAY I.

ON A MAN'S WRITING MEMOIRS OF HIMSELF.

LETTER I.

MY DEAR FRIEND,

EVERY one knows with what interest it is natural to retrace the course of our own lives. The past states and periods of a man's being are retained in a connexion with the present by that principle of self-love, which is unwilling to relinquish its hold on what has once been his. Though he cannot but be sensible of how little consequence his life can have been in the creation, compared with many other trains of events, yet he has felt it more important to himself than all other trains together; and you will very rarely find him tired of narrating again the little history, or at least the favourite parts of the little history, of himself.

To turn this partiality to some account, I recollect having proposed to two or three of my friends, that they should write, each principally however for his own use, memoirs of their own lives, endeavouring not so much to enumerate the mere facts and events of life, as to discriminate the successive states of the mind, and so trace the progress of what may be called the character In this progress consists the chief importance of life; but even on an inferior account also to this of what the character has become, and regarded merely as supplying a constant series of interests to the affections and passions, we have all accounted our life an inestimable possession which it deserved incessant cares and labours to retain, and which continues in most cases to be still held with anxious attachment. What has been the object of so much partiality, and has been delighted and pained by so many emotions, might claim, even if the highest interest were out of the question, that a short memorial should be retained by him who has possessed it, has seen it all to this moment depart, and can never recall it.

To write memoirs of many years, as twenty, thirty, or forty, seems, at the first glance, a very onerous task. To reap the products of so many acres of earth indeed might, to one person, be an undertaking of mighty toil. But the materials of any value that all past life can supply to a recording pen, would be reduced by a discerning selection to a very small and modest amount. Would as much as one page of moderate size be deemed by any man's self-importance to be due, on an average, to each of the days that he has lived? No man would judge more than one in ten thousand of all his thoughts, sayings, and actions, worthy to be mentioned, if memory were capable of recalling them.* Necessarily a very large portion of what has occupied the successive years of life was of a kind to be utterly useless for a history of it; being merely for the accommodation of the time. Perhaps in the space of forty or fifty years, millions of sentences are proper to be uttered, and many thousands of affairs requisite to be transacted, or of journeys to

---

* An exception may be admitted for the few individuals whose daily deliberations, discourses and proceedings, affect the interests of mankind on a grand scale.

be performed, which it would be ridiculous to record. They are a kind of material for the common expenditure and waste of the day. Yet it is often by a detail of this subordinate economy of life, that the works of fiction, the narratives of age, the journals of travellers, and even grave biographical accounts, are made so unreasonably long. As well might a chronicle of the coats that a man has worn, with the colour and date of each, be called his life, for any important uses of relating its history. As well might a man, of whom I inquire the dimensions, the internal divisions, and the use, of some remarkable building, begin to tell me how much wood was employed in the scaffolding, where the mortar was prepared, or how often it rained while the work was proceeding.

But, in a deliberate review of all that we can remember of past life, it will be possible to select a certain proportion which may with the most propriety be regarded as the history of the man. What I am recommending is, to follow the order of time, and reduce your recollections, from the earliest period to the present, into as simple a statement and explanation as you can, of your feelings, opinions, and habits, and of the principal circumstances through each stage that have influenced them, till they have become at last what they now are.

Whatever tendencies nature may justly be deemed to have imparted in the first instance, you would probably find the greater part of the moral constitution of your being composed of the contributions of many years and events, consolidated by degrees into what we call character; and by investigating the progress of the accumulation, you would be assisted to judge more clearly how far the materials are valuable, the mixture congruous, and the whole conformation worthy to remain unaltered. With respect to any friend who greatly interests us, we have a curiosity to obtain an accurate account of the past train of his life and feelings: and whatever other reasons there may be for such a wish, it partly springs from a consciousness how much this retrospective knowledge would assist to complete our estimate of that friend; but our estimate of ourselves is of more serious consequence.

The elapsed periods of life acquire importance too from the prospect of its continuance. The smallest thing rises into consequence when regarded as the commencement of what has advanced, or is advancing into magnificence. The first rude settlement of Romulus would have been an insignificant circumstance, and might justly have sunk into oblivion, if Rome had not at length commanded the world. The little rill near the source of one of the great American rivers, is an interesting object to the traveller, who is apprised, as he steps across it, or walks a few miles along its bank, that this is the stream which runs so far, and which gradually swells into so vast a flood. So, while I anticipate the endless progress of life, and wonder through what unknown scenes it is to take its course, its past years lose that character of vanity which would seem to belong to a train of fleeting, perishing moments, and I see them assuming the dignity of a commencing eternity. In them I have *begun* to be that conscious existence which I *am* to be through endless duration; and I feel a strange emotion of curiosity about this little life, in which I am setting out on such a progress; I cannot be content without an accurate sketch of the windings thus far of a stream which is to bear me on for ever. I try to imagine how it will be to recollect, at a far distant point of my era, what I was when here; nd wish if it were possible to retain, as I advance, some clear trace of the whole course of my existence within the scope of reflection; to fix in my mind so strong an idea of what I have been in this original period of my time, that I may possess this idea in ages too remote for calculation.

The review becomes still more important, when I learn the influence which this first part of the progress will have on the happiness or misery of the next.

One of the greatest difficulties in the way of executing the proposed task will have been caused by the extreme deficiency of that self-observation, which is of no common habit either of youth or any later age. Men are content to have no more intimate sense of their existence than what they feel in the exercise of their faculties on extraneous objects. The vital being, with all its agency and emotions, is so blended and absorbed in these its exterior interests, that it is very rarely collected and concentrated in the consciousness of its own absolute *self*, so as to be recognised as a thing internal, apart and alone, for its own inspection and knowledge. Men carry their minds as for the most part they carry their watches, content to be ignorant of the constitution and action within, and attentive only to the little exterior circle of things, to which the passions, like indexes, are pointing. It is surprising to see how little self-knowledge a person not watchfully observant of himself may have gained, in the whole course of an active, or even an inquisitive life. He may have lived almost an age, and traversed a continent, minutely examining its curiosities, and interpreting the half-obliterated characters on its monuments, unconscious the while of a process operating on his own mind, to impress or to erase characteristics of much more importance to him than all the figured brass or marble that Europe contains. After having explored many a cavern or dark ruinous avenue, he may have left undetected a darker recess within where there would be much more striking discoveries. He may have conversed with many people, in different languages, on numberless subjects; but, having neglected those conversations with himself by which his whole moral being should have been kept continually disclosed to his view, he is better qualified perhaps to describe the intrigues of a foreign court, or the progress of a foreign trade; to depict the manners of the Italians, or the Turks; to narrate the proceedings of the Jesuits, or the adventures of the gypsies; than to write the history of his own mind.

If we had practised habitual self-observation, we could not have failed to be made aware of much that it had been well for us to know. There have been thousands of feelings, each of which, if strongly seized upon, and made the subject of reflection, would have shown us what our character was, and what it was likely to be become. There have been numerous incidents, which operated on us as tests, and so fully brought out our prevailing quality, that another person, who should have been discriminatively observing us, would speedily have formed a decided estimate. But unfortunately the mind is generally too much occupied by the feeling or the incident itself, to have the slightest care or consciousness that any thing *could* be learnt, or *is* disclosed. In very early youth it is almost inevitable for it to be thus lost to itself even amidst its own feelings, and the external objects of attention; but it seems a contemptible thing, and certainly is a criminal and dangerous thing, for a man in mature life to allow himself this thoughtless escape from self-examination.

We have not only neglected to observe what our feelings indicated, but have also in a very great degree ceased to remember what they were. We may wonder how we could pass away successively from so many scenes and conjunctures, each in its time of no trifling moment in our apprehension, and retain so light an impression, that we have now nothing distinctly to tell about what once excited our utmost emotion. As to my own mind, I perceive that it is becoming uncertain of the exact nature of many feelings of considerable interest, even of comparatively recent date; and that the remembrance of what was felt in very early life has nearly faded away. I have just been observing several children of eight or ten years old, in all the active vivacity which enjoys the plenitude of the moment without "looking before or after;" and while observing, I attempted, but without success, to recollect what I was at that age. I can indeed remember the principal events of the period, and the actions and projects to which my feelings impelled me; but the feelings themselves, in their own pure juvenility, cannot be revived so as to be described and placed in comparison with those of later life. What is become of all those vernal fancies which had so much power to touch the heart? What a number of sentiments have lived and revelled in the soul that are now irrevocably gone! They died like the singing birds of that time, which sing no more. The life we then had, now seems almost as if it could not have been our own. We are like a man returning, after the absence of many years, to visit the embowered cottage where he passed the morning of his life, and finding only a relic of its ruins.

Thus an oblivious shade is spread over that early tract of our time, where some of the acquired propensities which remain in force to this hour may have had their origin, in a manner of which we had then no thought or consciousness. When we met with the incident, or heard the conversation, or saw the spectacle, or felt the emotion, which were the first causes or occasions of some of the chief permanent tendencies of future life, how little could we think that long afterwards we might be curiously and in vain desirous to investigate those tendencies back to their origin.

In some occasional states of the mind, we can look back much more clearly, and much further, than at other times. I would advise to seize those short intervals of illumination which sometimes occur without our knowing the cause, and in which the genuine aspect of some remote event, or long-forgotten image, is recovered with extreme distinctness in spontaneous glimpses of thought, such as no effort could have commanded; as the sombre features and minute objects of a distant ridge of hills become strikingly visible in the strong gleams of light which transiently fall on them. An instance of this kind occurred to me but a few hours since, while reading what had no perceptible connexion with a circumstance of my early youth, which probably I have not recollected for many years, and which was of no unusual interest at the time it happened. That circumstance came suddenly to my mind with a clearness of representation which I was not able to retain to the end of an hour, and which I could not at this instant renew by the strongest effort. I seemed almost to *see* the walls and windows of a particular room, with four or five persons in it, who were so perfectly restored to my imagination, that I could recognise not only the features, but even the momentary expressions, of their countenances, and the tones of their voices.

According to different states of the mind too, retrospect appears longer or shorter. It may happen that some memorable circumstance of very early life shall be so powerfully recalled, as to contract the wide intervening space, by banishing from the view, a little while, all the series of intermediate remembrances, but when this one object of memory retires again to its remoteness and indifference, and all the others resume their proper places and distances, the retrospect appears long.

Places and things which have an association with any of the events or feelings of past life, will greatly assist the recollection of them. A man of strong associations finds memorials of himself already traced on the places where he has conversed with happiness or misery. If an old man wished to animate for a moment the languid and faded ideas which he retains of his youth, he might walk with his crutch across the green, where he once played with companions who are now laid to repose probably in another green spot not far off. An aged saint may meet again some of the affecting ideas of his early piety, in the place where he first found it happy to pray. A walk in a meadow, the sight of a bank of flowers, perhaps even of some one flower, a landscape with the tints of autumn, the descent into a valley, the brow of a mountain, the house where a friend has been met, or has resided, or has died, have often produced a much more lively recollection of our past feelings, and of the objects and events which caused them, than the most perfect description could have done; and we have lingered a considerable time for the pensive luxury of thus resuming the long-departed state.

But there are many to whom local associations present images which they fervently wish they could exorcise; images which haunt the places where crimes had been perpetrated, and which seem to approach and glare on the criminal as he hastily passes by, especially if in the evening or the night. No local associations are so impressive as those of guilt. It may here be observed that as each one has his own separate remembrances, giving to some places an aspect and a significance which he alone can perceive, there must be an unknown number of pleasing, or mournful, or dreadful associations, spread over the scenes inhabited or visited by men. *We* pass without any awakened consciousness by the bridge, or the wood, or the house, where there is something to excite the most painful or frightful ideas in another man if he were to go that way, or it may be in the companion who walks along with us. How much there is in a thousand spots of the earth, that is invisible and silent to all but the conscious individual!

>I hear a voice you cannot hear;
>I see a hand you cannot see.

LETTER II.

We may regard our past life as a continued though irregular course of education, through an order, or rather disorder of means, consisting of instruction, companionship, reading, and the diversified influences of the world. The young mind, in the mere natural impulse of its activity, and innocently unthinking of any process it was about to undergo, came forward to meet the operation of some or all of these plastic circumstances. It would be worth while to examine in what manner and measure they have respectively had their influence on us.

Few persons can look back to the early period when they were most directly the subjects of instruction, without a regret for themselves, (which may be extended to the human race,) that the result of instruction, excepting that which leads to evil, bears so small a proportion to its compass and repetition. Yet *some* good consequence must follow the diligent inculcation of truth and precept on the youthful mind; and our consciousness of possessing certain advantages derived from it will be a partial consolation, in the review which will comprise so many proofs of its comparative inefficacy. You can recollect, perhaps, the instructions to which you feel yourself permanently the most indebted, and some of those which produced the greatest effect at the time, those which surprised, delighted, or mortified you. You can partially remember the facility or difficulty of understanding, the facility or difficulty of believing, and the practical inferences which you drew from principles, on the strength of your own reason, and sometimes in variance with those made by your instructors. You can remember what views of truth and duty were most frequently and cogently presented, what passions were appealed to, what arguments were employed, and which had the greatest influence. Perhaps your present idea of the most convincing and persuasive mode of instruction, may be derived from your early experience of the manner of those persons with whose opinions you felt it the most easy and delightful to harmonize, who gave you the most agreeable consciousness of your faculties expanding to the light, like morning flowers, and who, assuming the least of dictation, exerted the greatest degree of power. You can recollect the submissiveness with which your mind yielded to instructions as from an oracle, or the hardihood with which you dared to examine and oppose them. You can remember how far they became, as to your own conduct, an internal authority of reason and conscience, when you were not under the inspection of those who inculcated them; and what classes of persons or things around you they contributed to make you dislike or approve. And you can perhaps imperfectly trace the manner and the particulars in which they sometimes aided, or sometimes counteracted, those other influences which have a far stronger efficacy on the character than instruction can boast.

Some persons can recollect certain particular sentences or conversations which made so deep an impression, perhaps in some instances they can scarcely tell why, that they have been thousands of times recalled, while innumerable others have been forgotten or they can revert to some striking incident, coming in aid of instruction, or being of itself a forcible instruction, which they seem even now to see as plainly as when it happened, and of which they will retain a perfect idea to the end of life. The most remarkable circumstances of this kind deserve to be recorded in the supposed memoirs. In some instances, to recollect the instructions of a former period will be to recollect too the excellence, the affection, and the death, of the persons who gave them. Amidst the sadness of such a remembrance, it will be a consolation that they are not entirely lost to us. Wise monitions, when they return on us with this melancholy charm, have more pathetic cogency than when they were first uttered by the voice of a living friend. It will be an interesting occupation of the pensive hour, to recount the advantages which we have received from the beings who have left the world, and to reinforce our virtues from the dust of those who first taught them.

In our review, we shall find that the companions of our childhood, and of each succeeding period, have had a great influence on our characters. A creature so prone to conformity as man, and at the same time so capable of being moulded into partial dissimilarity by social antipathies, cannot have conversed with his fellow beings thousands of hours, walked with them thousands of miles, undertaken with them numberless enterprises, smaller and greater, and had every passion, by turns, awakened in their company, without being immensely affected by all this association. A large share, indeed, of the social interest may have been of so common a kind, and with persons of so common an order, that the effect on the character has been too little peculiar to be perceptible during the progress. We were not sensible of it, till we came to some of those circumstances and changes in life, which make us aware of the state of our minds by the manner in which new objects are acceptable or repulsive to them. On removing into a new circle of society, for instance, we could perceive, by the number of things in which we found ourselves uncomplacent and unconformable with the new acquaintance, the modification which our sentiments had received in the preceding social intercourse. But in some instances we have been in a short time sensible of a powerful force operating on our opinions, tastes, and habits, and reducing them to a greatly altered cast. This effect is inevitable, if a young susceptible mind happens to become familiarly acquainted with a person in whom a strongly individual character is sustained and dignified by uncommon mental resources; and it may be found that, generally, the greatest measure of effect has been produced by the influence of a very small number of persons; often of one only, whose master-spirit had more power to surround and assimilate a young ingenuous being, than the collective influence of a multitude of the persons, whose characters were moulded in the manufactory of custom, and sent forth like images of clay of kindred shape and varnish from a pottery.—I am supposing, all along, that the person who writes memoirs of himself, is conscious of something more peculiar than a mere dull resemblance of that ordinary form and insignificance of character, which it strangely depreciates our nature to see such a multitude exemplifying. As to the crowd of those who are faithfully stamped, like bank notes, with the same marks, with the difference only of being worth more guineas or fewer, they are mere particles of a class, mere pieces and bits of the great vulgar or the small; *they* need not write their history, it may be found in the newspaper chronicle, or the gossip's or the sexton's narrative.

It is obvious, in what I have suggested respecting the research through past life, that all the persons who are recalled to the mind, as having had an influence on us, must stand before it in judgment. It is impossible to examine our moral and intellectual growth without forming an estimate, as we proceed, of those who retarded, advanced, or perverted it. Our dearest relations and friends cannot be exempted. There will be in some instances the necessity of blaming where we would wish to give entire praise; though perhaps some worthy motives and generous feelings may, at the same time, be discovered in the conduct, where they had hardly been perceived or allowed before. But, at any rate, it is important that in no instance the judgment be duped into delusive estimates, amidst the examination, and so as to compromise the principles of the examination, by which we mean to bring ourselves to rigorous justice. For if any indulgent partiality, or mistaken idea, of that duty which requires a kind and candid feeling to accompany the clearest discernment of defects, may be permitted to beguile our judgment out of the decisions of justice in favour of others, self-love, a still more indulgent and partial feeling, will not fail to practise the same beguilement in favour of ourselves. But indeed it would seem impossible, besides being absurd, to apply one set of principles to judge of ourselves, an another to judge of those with whom we have associated.

Every person of tolerable education has been considerably influenced by the books he has read; and remembers with a kind of gratitude several of those that made without injury the earliest and the strongest impression. It is pleasing at a more advanced period to look again into the early favourites; though the mature person may wonder how some of them had once power to absorb his passions, make him retire into a lonely wood in order to read unmolested, repel the approaches of sleep, or, when it came, infect it with visions. A capital part of the proposed task would be to recollect the books that have been read with the greatest interest, the periods when they were read, the partiality which any of them inspired to a particular mode of life, to a study, to a system of opinions, or to a class of human characters; to note the counteraction of later ones (where we have been sensible of it) to the effect produced by the former; and then to endeavour to estimate the whole and ultimate influence.

Considering the multitude of facts, sentiments, and characters, which have been contemplated by a person who has read much, the effect, one should think, must have been very great. Still, however, it is probable that a very small number of books will have the pre-eminence in our mental history. Perhaps your memory will promptly recur to six or ten that have contributed more to your present habits of feeling and thought than all the rest together.—It may be observed here, that when a few books of the same kind have pleased us emphatically, it is a possible ill consequence that they may create an almost exclusive taste, which is carried through all future reading, and is pleased only with books of that kind.

It might be supposed that the scenes of nature, an amazing assemblage of phenomena if their effect were not lost through familiarity, would have a powerful influence on opening minds, and transfuse into the internal economy of ideas and sentiment something of a character and a colour correspondent to the beauty, vicissitude, and grandeur, which press on the senses. They have this effect on minds of genius; and Beattie's Minstrel may be as just as it is a captivating description of the perceptions and emotions of such a spirit. But on the greatest number this influence operates feebly; you will not see the process in children, nor the result in mature persons. That significance is unfelt, which belongs to the beauties of nature as something more than their being merely objects of the senses. And in many instances even the senses themselves are so deficient in attention, so idly passive, and therefore apprehend these objects so slightly, undefinedly, and transiently, that it is no wonder the impressions do not go so much deeper than the senses as to infuse a mood of sentiment, awaken the mind to thoughtful and imaginative action, and form in it an order of feelings and ideas congenial with what is fair and great in external nature. This defect of sensibility and fancy is unfortunate amidst a creation infinitely rich with grand and beautiful objects, which can impart to a mind adapted and habituated to converse with nature an exquisite sentiment, that seems to come as by an emanation from a spirit dwelling in those objects. It is unfortunate I have thought within these few minutes —while looking out on one of the most enchanting nights of the most interesting season of the year, and hearing the voices of a company of persons, to whom I can perceive that this soft and solemn shade over the earth, the calm sky, the beautiful stripes of cloud, the stars, the waning moon just risen, are things not in the least more interesting than the walls, ceiling, and candle-light of a room. I feel no vanity in this instance; for perhaps a thousand aspects of night not less striking than this, have appeared before my eyes and departed, not only without awaking emotion, but almost without attracting notice.

If minds in general are not made to be strongly affected by the phenomena of the earth and heavens, they are however all subject to be powerfully influenced by the appearances and character of the *human* world. I suppose a child in Switzerland, growing up to a man, would have acquired incomparably more of the cast of his mind from the events, manners, and actions of the next village, though its inhabitants were but his occasional companions, than from all the mountain scenes, the cataracts, and every circumstance of beauty or sublimity in nature around him. We are all true to our species, and very soon feel its importance to us, (though benevolence be not the basis of the interest,) far beyond the importance of any thing that we see besides. Beginning your observation with children, you may have noted how instantly they will turn their attention away from any of the aspects of nature, however rare or striking, if human objects present themselves to view in any active manner. This " leaning to our kind" brings each individual not only under the influence attending immediate association with a few, but under the operation of numberless influences, from all the moral diversities of which he is a spectator in the living world; a complicated though insensible tyranny, of which every fashion, folly, and vice, may exercise its part.

Some persons would be able to recollect very strong and influential impressions made, in almost the first years of life, by some of the events and appearances which they witnessed in surrounding society. But whether the operation on us of the formative power of the community began with impressions of extraordinary force or not, it has been prolonged through the whole course of our acquaintance with mankind. It is no little effect for the living world to have had on us, that very many of our present *opinions* are owing to what we have seen and experienced in it. That thinking which has involuntarily been kept in exercise on it, however remiss and desultory, could not fail to result in a number of settled notions, which may be said to be shaped upon its facts and practices. We could not be in sight of it, and in intercourse with it, without the formation of opinions adjusted to what we found in it; and thus far it has been the creator of our mental economy. But its operation has not stopped here. It will not confine itself to occupying the understanding, and yield to be a mere subject for judgments to be formed upon; but all the while that the observer is directing on it the exercise of his judicial capacity, it is reactively throwing on him various moral influences and infections.

LETTER III.

A PERSON capable of being deeply interested, and accustomed to reflect on his feelings, will have observed in himself this subjection to the influences of what has been presented to him in society. Their force may have been sufficient in some instances to go far toward new-modelling the habit of the mind. Recollect your own experience. After witnessing some remarkable transaction, or some new and strange department of life and manners, or some striking disclosure of character, or after listening to some extraordinary conversation, or impressive recital of facts, you may have been conscious that what you have heard or seen has given your mind some one strong determination of a nature resulting from the quality of that which has made the impression. It is true, that your receiving the effect in this one manner implies the existence of an adapted predisposition, for many other persons might not have been similarly affected; yet the newly acquired impulse might be so different from the former action of your mind, and at the same time so strong, as to give you the consciousness of a greatly altered moral being. In the state thus suddenly formed, some of the previously existing dispositions had sunk subordinate, while others, which had been hitherto inert, were grown into an imperious prevalence: or even a new one appeared to have been originated.* While this state continues, a man is in character another man; and if the moral tendency thus excited or created, could be prolonged into the sequel of his life, the difference might be such, that it would be by means only of his person that he would be recognised for the same; while an observer ignorant of the cause would be perplexed and surprised at the change. Now this permanence of the new moral direction might be effected, if the impression which causes it were so intensely powerful as to haunt him ever after; or if he were subjected to a long succession of impressions of the same tendency, without

* So great an effect, however, as this last, is perhaps rarely experienced from even the most powerful causes, except in early life.

any powerfully opposite ones intervening to break the process.

You have witnessed perhaps a scene of injustice and oppression, and have retired with an indignation which has imprecated vengeance. Now supposing that the image of this scene were to be revived in your mind in all its odiousness, as often as any iniquitous circumstance in society should present itself to your notice, and that you had an entire persuasion that your feeling was the pure indignation of virtue; or, supposing that you were repeatedly to witness similar instances, without diminution of the abhorrence by familiarity with them; the consequence might be that you would acquire the spirit of Draco or Minos.

It is easy to imagine the impression of a few atrocious facts on an ardent constitution, converting a humane horror of cruelty into the vindictive fanaticism of Montbar, the Buccaneer.* A person of gentler sensibility, by accidentally witnessing a scene of distress, of which none of the circumstances caused disgust toward the sufferers, or indignation against others as the cause of the suffering, having once tasted the pleasure of soothing woes which perhaps death alone can terminate, might be led to seek other instances of distress, acquire both an aptitude and a partiality for the charitable office, and become a pensive philanthropist. The repulsion which has struck the observer of some extravagance of ostentatious wealth, or some excess of frivolity and dissipation, and acted on him again at sight of every succeeding and inferior instance of the same kind, with a greater force than would have been felt in these inferior instances, if the offensive effect did not run into the vestiges of the first indelible

* Abbé Raynal's History of the Indies.

impression, may produce a cynic or a miser, a recluse or a philosopher. Numberless other illustrations might be brought to shew how much the characters of human beings, entering on life with unwarned carelessness of heart, are at the mercy of the incalculable influences which may strike them from any point of the surrounding world.

It is true that, notwithstanding so many influences are acting on men, and some of them apparently of a kind and of a force to produce in their subjects a notable peculiarity, comparatively few characters determinately marked from all around them are found to arise. In looking on a large company of persons whose dispositions and pursuits are substantially alike, we cannot doubt that several of them have met with circumstances, of which the natural tendency must have been to give them a determination of mind extremely dissimilar to the character of those whom they now so much resemble. And why does the influence of such circumstances fail to produce such a result? Partly, because the influences which are of a more peculiar and specific operation are overborne and lost in that wide general influence, which accumulates and conforms each individual to the crowd; and partly, because even were there no such general influence to steal away the impressions of a more peculiar tendency, few minds are of so fixed and faithful a consistence as to retain, in continued efficacy, impressions of a kind which the common course of life is not adapted to reinforce, nor prevailing example to confirm. The mind of the greater proportion of human beings, if attempted to be wrought into any boldly specific form, proves like a half-fluid substance, in which angles or circles, or any other figures may be cut, but which recovers, while you are looking, its former state, and closes them up; or like a quantity of dust, which may be raised into momentary reluctant shapes, but which is relapsing, amidst the operation, towards its undefined mass.

But if characters of strong individual peculiarity are somewhat rare, such as are marked with the respective distinctions which discriminate moral *classes* are very numerous; the decidedly avaricious for instance; the devoted slaves of fashion; and the eager aspirers to power, in however confined a sphere, the little Alexanders of a mole-hill, quite as ambitious, in their way, as the great Alexander of a world. It is observable here, how much more largely the worse prominences of human character meet our attention than the better. And it is a melancholy illustration of the final basis of character, human nature itself, that both the distinctions which designate a bad class, and those which constitute a bad individual peculiarity, are attained with far the greatest frequency and facility. While, however, I have the most entire conviction of this mighty inclination to evil, which is the grand cause of all the diversified forms of evil; and while, at the same time, I hold the vulgar belief of a great native difference between men, in the original temperament of those principles, which are to be unfolded by the progress of time into intellectual powers and moral dispositions; I yet cannot but perceive that the *immediate* and occasional causes of the greater portion of the prominent actual character of human beings, are to be found in those moral elements through which they pass. And if one might be pardoned for putting in words so fantastic an idea, as that of its being possible for a man to live back again to his infancy, through all the scenes of his life, and to give back from his mind and character, at each time and circumstance, as he repassed it, exactly that which he took from it, when he was there before, it would be most curious to see the fragments and *exuviæ* of the moral man lying here and there along the retrograde path, and to find what he was in the beginning of this train of modifications and acquisitions. Nor can it be doubted that any man, whose native tendencies were ever so determinate, and who has passed through a course of events and interests adapted to develope and confirm them according to their determination, might, by being led through a different train, counteractive to those native tendencies, have been an extremely different man from what he now is.—I am supposing his mind to be in either case equally cultivated, and referring to another kind of difference than that which would in any case be made by the different measure or quantity, if I may express it so, of intellectual attainment.

Here a person of your age might pause, and look back with great interest on the world of circumstances through which life has been drawn. Consider what thousands of situations, appearances, incidents, persons, you have been present with, each in its time. The review would carry you over something like a chaos, with all the moral, and all other elements, confounded together; and you may reflect till you begin almost to wonder how an individual retains the same essence through all the diversities, vicissitudes, and counteractions of influence, that operate on it during its progress through the confusion. While the essential being might, however, defy a universe to extinguish, absorb, or transmute it, you will find it has come out with dispositions and habits which will shew where it has been, and what it has undergone. You may descry in it the marks and colours of many of the things by which it has, in passing, been touched or arrested.

Consider the number of meetings with acquaintance,

friends, or strangers; the number of conversations you have held or heard; the number of exhibitions of good or evil, virtue or vice; the number of occasions on which you have been disgusted or pleased, moved to admiration or to abhorrence; the number of times that you have conter plated the town, the rural cottage, or verdant fields; the number of volumes you have read; the times that you have looked over the present state of the world, or gone by means of history into past ages; the number of comparisons of yourself with other persons, alive or dead, and comparisons of them with one another; the number of solitary musings, of solemn contemplations of night, of the successive subjects of thought, and of animated sentiments that have been kindled and extinguished. Add all the hours and causes of sorrow which you have known. Through this lengthened, and, if the number could be told, stupendous multiplicity of things, you have advanced, while all their heterogeneous myriads have darted influences upon you, each one of them having some definable tendency. A traveller round the globe would not meet a greater variety of seasons, prospects, and winds, than you might have recorded of the circumstance capable of affecting your character, during your journey of life. You could not wish to have drawn to yourself the agency of a vaster diversity of causes; you could not wish, on the supposition that you had gained advantage from all these, to wear the spoils of a greater number of regions. The formation of the character from so many materials reminds one of that mighty appropriating attraction, which, on the fanciful hypothesis that the resurrection should reassemble the same particles which composed the body before, must draw them from dust, and trees, and animals, from ocean, and winds.

It would scarcely be expected that a being which should be conducted through such anarchy of discipline, in which the endless crowd of influential powers seem waiting, each to take away what the last had given, should be permitted to acquire, or to retain, any settled form of qualities at all. The more probable result would be, either several qualities disagreeing with one another, or a blank neutrality. And in fact, a great number of nearly such neutralities are found every where; persons, who, unless their sharing of the general properties of human nature, a little modified by the insignificant distinction of some large class, can be called character, have no character. It is therefore somewhat strange, if you, and if other individuals, have come forth with moral features of a strongly marked and consistently combined cast, from the infinity of miscellaneous impressions. If the process has been so complex, how comes the result to be apparently so simple? How has it happened that the *collective* effect of these numerous and jarring operations on your mind, is that which only a *few* of these operations would have seemed adapted to produce, and quite different from that which many others of them should naturally have produced, and do actually produce in many other persons? Here you will perceive that some one capital determination must long since have been by some means established in your mind, and that, during your progress, this predominant determination has kept you susceptible of the effect of some influences, and fortified against many others. Now, what was the prevailing determination, whence did it come, how did it acquire its power? Was it an original tendency and insuppressible impulse of your nature; or the result of your earliest impressions; or of some one class of impressions repeated oftener than any other; or of one single impression of extreme force? What was it, and whence did it come? This is the great secret in the history of character; for, it is scarcely necessary to observe, that as soon as the mind is under the power of a predominant tendency, the difficulty of growing into the maturity of that form of character, which this tendency promotes or creates, is substantially over. Because, when a determined principle is become ascendant, it not only produces a partial insensibility to all impressions that would counteract it, but also continually augments its own ascendency, by means of a faculty or fatality of finding out every thing, and attracting to itself every cause of impression, that is adapted to coalesce with it and strengthen it; like the instinct of animals, which instantly selects from the greatest variety of substances those which are fit for their nutriment. Let a man have some leading and decided propensity, and it will be surprising to see how many more things he will find, and how many more events will happen, than any one could have imagined, of a nature to reinforce it. And sometimes even circumstances which seemed of an entirely counteractive order, are strangely seduced by this predominant principle into an operation that confirms it; just in the same manner as polemics most self-complacently avow their opinions to be more firmly established by the strongest objections of the opponent.

It would be easy to enlarge without end on the influences of the surrounding world in forming the character of each individual. Yet while there is no denying that such influences are effectively operating, a man may be unwilling to allow that he has been quite so servilely passive, as he would probably find that he has been, if it were possible for him to make a complete examination. He may be disposed to think that his reason has been an independent power, has kept a strict watch, and passed a right judgment on his moral progress, has met the circumstances of the external world on terms of examination and authority, and has *permitted* only such impressions to be received, or at least only such consequences to follow from them, as it wisely approved. But I would tell him, that he has been a very extraordinary man, if the greater part of his time has not been spent entirely without a thought of reflecting what impressions were made on him, or what their tendency might be ; and even without a consciousness that the effect of any impressions was of importance to his moral habits. He may be assured that he has been subjected to many gentle gradual processes, and has met many critical occasions, on which, and on the consequences of which to himself, he exercised no attention or opinion. And again, it is unfortunately true, that even should attention be awake, and opinions be formed, the faculty which forms them is very servile to the other parts of the human constitution. If it could be extrinsic to the man, a kind of domestic Pythia, or an attendant genius, like the demon of Socrates, it might then be a dignified regulator of the influences which are acting on his character, to decide what should or should not be permitted to affect him, and in what manner; though even then its disapproving dictates might fail against some extremely powerful impression which might give a temporary bias, and such repetitions of that impression as should confirm it. But the case is, that this faculty, though mocked with imperial names, being condemned to dwell in the company of far more active powers than itself, and earlier exercised, becomes humbly obsequious to them. The passio easily beguile this majestic reason, or judgment, into neglect, or bribe it into acquiescence, or repress it into silence, while *they* receive the impressions, and while *they* acquire from those impressions that determinate direction, which will constitute the character. If, after thus much is done during the weakness, or without the notice, or without the leave, or under the connivance or corruption of the judgment, it be called upon to perform its part in estimating the quality and actual effect of the modifying influences, it has to perform this judicial work with just that degree of rectitude which it can have acquired and maintained under the operation of those very influences. In acting the judge, it is itself in subjection to the effect of those impressions of which its office was, to have previously decided whether they should not be strenuously repelled. Thus its opinions will unconsciously be perverted; like the answers of the ancient oracles, dictated for the imaginary god by beings of a very terrestrial sort, though the sly intervention could not be perceived. It is quite a vulgar observation, how pleased a man may be with the formation of his own character, though *you* smile at the gravity of his persuasion, that his tastes, preferences, and qualities, have on the whole grown up under the sacred and faithful guardianship of judgment, while, in fact, his judgment has accepted every bribe that has been offered to betray him.

LETTER IV.

You will agree with me, that in a comprehensive view of the influences which have formed, and are forming, the characters of men, we shall find, religion excepted, but little cause to felicitate our species. Make the supposition that any assortment of persons, of sufficient number to comprise the most remarkable distinctions of character, should write memoirs of themselves, so exactly and honestly telling the story, and exhibiting so clearly the most effective circumstances, as to explain, to your discernment at least, if not to their own consciousness, the main process by which their minds have attained their present state. If they were to read these memoirs to you in succession, and if your benevolence could so long be maintained in full exercise, and your rules for estimating lost nothing of their determinate principle in their application to such a confusion of subjects, you would often, during the disclosure, regret to observe how many things may be the causes of irretrievable mischief. Why is the path of life, you would say, so haunted as if with evil spirits of every diversity of noxious agency, some of which may patiently accompany, or others of which may suddenly cross, the unfortunate wanderer? And you would regret to observe into how many forms of intellectual and moral perversion the human mind readily yields itself to be modified.

As *one* of the number concluded the account of himself, your observation would be, I perceive with compassion the process under which you have become a misanthropist. If your juvenile ingenuous ardour had not been chilled on your entrance into society, where your most favourite sentiments were not at all comprehended by some, and by others deemed wise and proper enough—perhaps for the people of the millennium; if you had not felt the mortification of relations being uncongenial, of persons whom you were anxious to render happy being indifferent to your kindness, or of apparent friendships proving treacherous or transitory; if you had not met with such striking instances of hopeless stupidity in the vulgar, or of vain self-importance in the learned, or of the coarse or supercilious arrogance of the persons whose manners were always regulated by the consideration of the proportion of gold and silver by which they were better than you; if your mortifications had not given you a keen faculty of perceiving the all-pervading selfishness of mankind, while, in addition, you had perhaps a peculiar opportunity to observe the apparatus of systematic villany, by which combinations of men are able to arm their selfishness to oppress or ravage the world—you might even now, perhaps, have been the persuasive instructor of beings, concerning whom you are wondering why they should have been made in the form of rationals; you might have conciliated to yourself and to goodness, where you repel and are repelled; you might have been the apostle and pattern of benevolence, instead of envying the powers and vocation of a destroying angel. Yet not that the world should bear all the blame. Frail and changeable in virtue, you *might* perhaps have been good under a series of auspicious circumstances; but the glory had been to be victoriously good against malignant ones. Moses lost none of his generous concern for a people, on whom *you* would have invoked the waters of Noah or the fires of Sodom to return; and that Greater than Moses, who endured from men such a matchless excess of injustice, while for their sake alone he sojourned and suffered on earth, was not alienated to misanthropy, in his life, or at his death.

A *second* sketch might exhibit external circumstances not producing any effect more serious than an intellectual stagnation. When it was concluded, your reflection might be, if I did not know that mental freedom is a dangerous thing, peculiarly in situations where the possessor would feel it a singular attainment;

and if I did not prefer even the quiescence of un-examining belief, when tolerably right in the most material points, to the indifference or scepticism which feels no assurance or no importance in any belief, or to the weak presumption that darts into the newest and most daring opinions as *therefore* true—I should deplore that your life was destined to preserve its sedate course so entirely unanimated by the intellectual novelties of the age, the agitations of ever-moving opinion; and under the habitual and exclusive influence of one individual, worthy perhaps and in a certain degree sensible, but of contracted views, whom you have been taught and accustomed to regard as the comprehensive repository of all the truth requisite for you to know, and from whom you have derived, as some of your chief acquisitions, a contented assurance that the trouble of inquiry is needless, and a superstitious horror of innovation, without even knowing what points are threatened by it.

At the end of *another's* disclosure, you would say, How unfortunate, that you could not believe there might be respectable and valuable men, who were not born to be wits or poets. And how unfortunate were those first evenings that you were privileged to listen to a company of men, who could *say* more fine things in an hour than their biographers will be able, even with the customary aid of laudatory fiction, to record them to have *done* in the whole space of life. It was then you discovered that *you* too were of the progeny of Apollo, and that you had been iniquitously transferred at your nativity into the hands of ignorant foster-parents, who had endeavoured to degrade and confine you to the sphere of regular employments and sober satisfactions. But, you would "tower up to the region of your sire." You saw what wonderful things might be found to be said on all subjects; you found it not so very difficult yourself to say *different* things from other people: and every thing that was not *common* dulness, was therefore pointed,—every thing that was not sense by any *vulgar* rule, was therefore sublime. You adopted a certain vastitude of phrase, mistaking extravagance of expression for greatness of thought. You set yourself to dogmatize on books, and the abilities of men, but especially on their prejudices; and perhaps to demolish, with the air of an exploit, some of the trite observations and maxims current in society. You awakened and surprised your imagination, by imposing on it a strange new tax of colours and metaphors; a tax reluctantly and uncouthly paid, but perhaps in some one instance so luckily, as to gain the applause of the gifted (if they were not merely eccentric) men, into whose company you had been elated by admittance. This was to you the proof and recognition of fraternity: and it has since been the chief question that has interested you with each acquaintance and in each company, whether they too could perceive what you were so happy to have discovered, yet so anxious that the acknowledgment of others should confirm. Your own persuasion, however, became as pertinacious as ivy climbing a wall. It was almost of course to attend to necessary pursuits with reluctant irregularity, though suffering by the consequences of neglecting them, and to feel indignant that *genius* should be reproached for the disregard of these ordinary duties and employments to which it ought never to have been subjected.

During a *projector's* story of life and misfortunes, you might regret that he should ever have heard of Harrison's time-piece, the perpetual motion, or the Greek fire.

After an *antiquary's* history, you might be allowed to congratulate yourself on not having fallen under the spell which confines a human soul to inhabit, like a spider in one of the corners, a dusty room, consecrated with religious solemnity to old coins, rusty knives, illuminated mass books, swords and spurs of forgotten kings, and slippers of their queens; with perhaps a Roman helmet, the acquisition of which was the first cause of the collection and of the passion, elevated imperially over the relics of kings and queens and the whole museum, as the eagle was once in "proud eminence" over subjugated kingdoms. And you might be inclined to say, I wish that helmet had been a pan for charcoal, or had been put on the head of one of the quiet equestrian warriors in the Tower, or had aided the rattlings of Sir Godfrey, haunting the baron's castle where he was murdered, or had been worn by Don Quixote, instead of the barber's basin, or had been the cauldron of Macbeth's witches, or had been in any other shape, place, or use, rather than dug up an antiquity, in a luckless hour, in a bank near your garden.

I compassionate you, would, in a *very* benevolent hour, be your language to the wealthy unfeeling *tyrant of a family and a neighbourhood,* who seeks, in the overawed timidity and unretaliated injuries of the unfortunate beings within his power, the gratification that should have been sought in their happiness. Unless you had brought into the world some extraordinary refractoriness to the influence of evil, the process that you have undergone could not fail of being efficacious. If your parents idolized their own importance in their son so much, that they never themselves opposed your inclinations, nor permitted it to be done by any subject to their authority; if the humble companion, sometimes summoned to the honour of amusing you, bore your caprices and insolence with the meekness without which he had lost his privilege; if you could despoil the garden of some harmless dependent neighbour of the carefully reared flowers, and torment his little dog or cat, without his daring to punish you or to appeal to your infatuated parents; if aged men addressed you in a submissive tone, and with the appellation of "Sir," and their aged wives uttered their wonder at your condescension, and pushed their grandchildren away from around the fire for your sake, if you happened, though with the strut of supercilious pertness, and your hat on your head, to enter one of their cottages, perhaps to express your contempt of the homely dwelling, furniture, and fare; if, in maturer life, you associated with vile persons, who would forego the contest of equality, to be your allies in trampling on inferiors; and if, both then and since, you have been suffered to deem your wealth the compendium or equivalent of every ability, and every good quality—it would indeed be immensely strange if you had not become, in due time, the miscreant, who may thank the power of the laws in civilized society, that he is not assaulted with clubs and stones; to whom one could cordially wish the opportunity and the consequences of attempting his tyranny among some such people as those *submissive* sons of nature in the forests of North America; and whose dependents and domestic relations may be almost forgiven when they shall one day rejoice at his funeral.

LETTER V.

I will imagine only one case more, on which you would emphatically express your compassion, though for one of the most daring beings in the creation, a *contemner of God*, who explodes his laws by denying

If you were so unacquainted with mankind, that such a being might be announced to you as a rare or singular phenomenon, your conjectures, till you saw and heard the man, at the nature and the extent of the discipline through which he must have advanced, would be led toward something extraordinary. And you might think that the term of that discipline must have been very long; since a quick train of impressions, a short series of mental gradations, within the little space of a few months and years, would not seem enough to have matured such a portentous heroism. Surely the creature that thus lifts his voice, and defies all invisible power within the possibilities of infinity, challenging whatever unknown being may hear him, and may appropriate that title of Almighty which is pronounced in scorn, to evince his existence, if he will, by his vengeance, was not as yesterday a little child that would tremble and cry at the approach of a diminutive reptile.

But indeed it is heroism no longer, if he *know* that there is no God. The wonder then turns on the great process, by which a man could grow to the immense intelligence which can know that there is no God. What ages and what lights are requisite for THIS attainment! This intelligence involves the very attributes of Divinity, while a God is denied. For unless this man is omnipresent, unless he is at this moment in every place in the universe, he cannot know but there may be in some place manifestations of a Deity, by which even *he* would be overpowered. If he does not know absolutely every agent in the universe, the one that he does not know may be God. If he is not himself the chief agent in the universe, and does not know what is so, that which is so may be God. If he is not in absolute possession of all the propositions that constitute universal truth, the one which he wants may be, that there is a God. If he cannot with certainty assign the cause of all that he perceives to exist, that cause may be a God. If he does not know every thing that has been done in the immeasurable ages that are past, some things may have been done by a God. Thus, unless he knows all things, that is, precludes all other divine existence by being Deity himself, he cannot know that the Being whose existence he rejects, does not exist. But he must *know* that he does not exist, else he deserves equal contempt and compassion for the temerity with which he firmly avows his rejection and acts accordingly. And yet a man of ordinary age and intelligence may present himself to you with the avowal of being thus distinguished from the crowd; and if he would describe the manner in which he has attained this eminence, you would feel a melancholy interest in contemplating that process of which the result is so prodigious.

If you did not know that there are more than a few such examples, you would say, in viewing this result, I *should* hope this is the consequence of some malignant intervention so occasional that ages may pass away before it return among men; some peculiar conjunction of disastrous influences must have lighted on your selected soul; you have been struck by that energy of evil which acted upon the spirits of Pharao and Epiphanes. But give your own description of what you have met with, in a world which has been deemed to present in every part the indications of a Deity. Tell of the mysterious voices which have spoken to you from the deeps of the creation, falsifying the expressions marked on its face. Tell of the new ideas, which, like meteors passing over the solitary wanderer, gave you the first glimpses of truth while benighted in the common belief of the Divine existence. Describe the whole train of causes which have operated to create and consolidate that state of mind, which you carry forward to the great experiment of futurity under a different kind of hazard from all other classes of men.

It would be found, however, that those circumstances, by which even a man who had been presented from his infancy with the ideas of religion, could be elated into a contempt of its great object, were far from being extraordinary. They might have been incident to any man, whose mind had been cultivated and exercised enough to feel interested about holding any system of opinions at all; whose pride had been gratified in the consciousness of having the liberty of selecting and changing opinions; and whose habitual assent to the principles of religion, had neither the firmness resulting from decisive arguments, nor the warmth of pious affection.* Such a person had only, in the first place, to come into intimate acquaintance with a man, who had the art of alluding to a sacred subject in a manner which, without appearing like intentional

* It will be obvious that I am describing the progress of one of the humbler order of aliens from all religion, and not that by which the great philosophic leaders have ascended the dreary eminence where they look with so much complacency up to a vacant heaven, and down to the gulf of annihilation. *Their* progress undoubtedly is much more systematic and deliberate, and accompanied often by a laborious speculation, which, though in ever so perverted a train, the mind is easily persuaded to identify, because it *is* laborious, with the search after truth and the love of it. While, however, it is in a persevering train of thought, and not by the hasty movements of a more vulgar mind, that they pursue their deviation from some of the principles of religion into a final abandonment of it all, they are very greatly mistaken if they assure themselves that the moral causes which contribute to guide and animate their progress are all of a sublime order: and if they could be fully revealed to their own view, they might perhaps be severely mortified to find what vulgar

contempt, divested it of its solemnity: and who had possessed himself of a few acute observations or plausible maxims, not explicitly hostile to revealed religion, but which, when opportunely brought into view in connexion with some points of it, tended to throw a degree of doubt on their truth and authority. Especially if either or both of these men had any decided moral tendencies and pursuits of a kind which christianity condemned, the friend of intellectual and moral freedom was assiduous to insinuate, that, according to the principles of reason and nature at least, it would be difficult to prove the wisdom or the necessity of some of those dictates of religion, which must, however, be admitted, be respected, because divine. Let the mind have once acquired a feeling, as if the sacred system might in some points be invalidated, and the involuntary inference would be rapidly extended to other parts, and to the whole. Nor was it long probably before this new instructor plainly avowed his own entire emancipation from a popular prejudice, to which he was kindly sorry to find a *sensible* young man still in captivity. But he had no doubt that the deductions

motives, while they were despising vulgar men, have ruled their intellectual career. Pride, which idolizes self, which revolts at every thing that comes in the form of *dictates*, and exults to find that there is a possibility of controverting whether any dictates come from a greater than mortal source; repugnance as well to the severe and comprehensive morality of the laws reputed of divine appointment, as to the feeling of accountableness to an all-powerful Authority, that will not leave moral laws to be enforced solely by their own sanctions; contempt of inferior men; the attraction of a few brilliant examples; the fashion of a class; the ambition of showing what ability can do, and what boldness can dare—if such things as these, after all, have excited and directed the efforts of a philosophic spirit, the unbelieving philosopher must be content to acknowledge plenty of companions and rivals among little men, who are quite as capable of being actuated by such elevated principles as himself.

of enlightened reason would successfully appeal to every liberal mind. And accordingly, after perhaps a few months of frequent intercourse, with the addition of two or three books, and the ready aid of all the recollected vices of pretended christians, and pretended christian churches, the whole venerable magnificence of revelation was annihilated. Its illuminations respecting the Divinity, its miracles, its Messiah, its authority of moral legislation, its regions of immortality and retribution, the sublime virtues and devotion of its prophets, apostles, and martyrs, together with the reasonings of so many accomplished advocates, and the credibility of history itself, were vanished all away; while the convert, exulting in his disenchantment, felt a strange pleasure to behold nothing but a dreary train of impostures and credulity stretching over those past ages which lately appeared a scene of divine government; and the thickest Egyptian shades fallen on that total vast futurity toward which the spirit of inspiration had thrown some grand though partial gleams.

Nothing tempts the mind so powerfully on, as to have successfully begun to demolish what has been long regarded as most sacred. The soldiers of Cæsar probably had never felt themselves so brave, as after they had cut down the Massilian grove; nor the Philistines, as when the ark of the God of Israel was among their spoils : the mind is proud of its triumphs in proportion to the reputed greatness of what it has overcome. And many examples would seem to indicate, that the first proud triumphs over religious faith, involve some fatality of advancing, however formidable the mass of arguments which may obstruct the progress, to further victories. But perhaps the intellectual difficulty of the progress might be less than a zealous believer would be apt to imagine. As the ideas which give the greatest distinctness to our conception of a Divine Being are imparted by revelation, and rest on its authority, the rejection of that revelation would in a great measure banish those ideas, and destroy that distinctness. We have but to advert to pure heathenism, to perceive what a faint conception of this Being could be formed by the strongest intellect in the absence of revelation; and after the *rejection* of it, the mind would naturally be carried very far back toward that darkness; so that some of the attributes of the Deity would immediately become, as they were with the heathens, subjects of doubtful conjecture and hopeless speculation. But from this state of thought it is perhaps no vast transition to that, in which his being also shall begin to appear a subject of doubt; since the reality of a being is with difficulty apprehended, in proportion as its attributes are undefinable. And when the mind is brought into doubt, we know it easily advances to disbelief, if to the smallest plausibility of arguments be added any powerful moral cause for wishing such a conclusion. In the present case, there *might* be a very powerful cause, besides that pride of victory which I have just noticed. The progress in guilt, which generally follows a rejection of revelation, makes it still more and more desirable that no object should remain to be feared. It was not strange, therefore, if this man read with avidity, or even strange if he read with something which his wishes completed into conviction, a few of the writers, who have attempted the last achievement of presumptuous man. After inspecting these pages awhile, he raised his eyes, and the Great Spirit was gone. Mighty transformation of all things! The luminaries of heaven no longer shone with his splendour; the adorned earth no longer looked fair with his beauty

the darkness of night had ceased to be rendered solemn
by his majesty; life and thought were not an effect of
his all-pervading energy; it was not his providence
that supported an infinite charge of dependent beings;
his empire of justice no longer spread over the universe;
nor had even that universe sprung from his all-creating
power. Yet when you saw the intellectual course
brought to this signal conclusion, though aware of the
force of each preceding and predisposing circumstance,
you might nevertheless be somewhat struck with the
suddenness of the final decision, and might be curious
to know what kind of argument and eloquence could
so quickly finish the work. You would examine those
pages with the expectation probably of something more
powerful than subtlety attenuated into inanity, and, in
that invisible and impalpable state, mistaken by the
writer, and willingly admitted by the perverted reader,
for profundity of reasoning; than attempts to destroy
the certainty, or preclude the application, of some of
those great familiar principles which must be taken as
the basis of human reasoning, or it can have no basis·
than suppositions which attribute the order of the
universe to such causes as it would be felt ridiculous
to pronounce adequate to produce the most trifling
piece of mechanism; than mystical jargon which,
under the name of *nature*, alternately exalts almost
into the properties of a god, and reduces far below
those of a man, some imaginary and undefinable agent
or agency, which performs the most amazing works
without power, and displays the most amazing wisdom
without intelligence; than a zealous preference of that
part of every great dilemma which merely confounds
and sinks the mind to that which elevates while it
overwhelms it; than a constant endeavour to degrade
as far as possible every thing that is sublime in our

speculations and feelings; or than monstrous parallels between religion and mythology. You would be still more unprepared to expect on so solemn a subject the occasional wit, or affectation of wit, which would seem rather prematurely expressive of exultation that the grand Foe is retiring.

A feeling of complete certainty would hardly be thus rapidly attained; but a slight degree of remaining doubt, and of consequent apprehension, would not prevent this disciple of darkness from accepting the invitation to pledge himself to the cause in some associated band, where profaneness and vice would consolidate impious opinions without the aid of augmented conviction; and where the fraternity, having been elated by the spirit of social daring to say, What is the Almighty that *we* should serve him? the individuals might acquire each a firmer boldness to exclaim, Who is the Lord that *I* should obey his voice? Thus easy it is, my friend, for a man to meet that train of influences which may seduce him to live an infidel, though it may betray him to die a terrified believer; of which the infatuation, while it promises him the impunity of non-existence, and degrades him to desire it, impels him to fill the measure of his iniquity, till the divine wrath come upon him to the uttermost.

LETTER VI.

In recounting so many influences that operate on man, it is grievous to observe that the incomparably noblest of all, religion, is counteracted with a fatal success by a perpetual conspiracy of almost all the rest, aided by the intrinsic predisposition of this our perverted nature, which yields itself with such consenting facility, to every impression tending to estrange it still further from God.

It is a cause for wonder and sorrow, to see millions of rational creatures growing into their permanent habits, under the conforming efficacy of every thing which it were good for them to resist, and receiving no part of those habits from impressions of the Supreme Object. They are content that a narrow scene of a diminutive world, with its atoms and evils, should usurp and deprave and finish their education for endless existence, while the Infinite Spirit is here, whose sacred energy, received on their minds, might create the most excellent condition of their nature, and, in defiance of a thousand malignant forces attempting to stamp on them an opposite image, convey them into eternity in his likeness. Oh, why is it so possible that this greatest inhabitant of every place where men are living, should be the last to whose society they are attracted, or of whose continual presence they feel the importance? Why is it possible to be surrounded with the intelligent Reality, which exists wherever we are, with attributes that are infinite, and not feel respecting all other things which may be attempting to press on our minds and affect their character, as if they retained with difficulty their shadows of existence, and were continually on the point of vanishing into nothing? Why is this stupendous Power so unperceived and silent, while present, over all the scenes of the earth, and in all the paths and abodes of men? Why does he keep his glory veiled behind the shades and visions of the material world? Why does not this latent glory sometimes beam forth with such a manifestation as could never be forgotten, nor could ever be remembered without an emotion of religious awe? And why, in contempt of all that he *has* displayed to excite either fear or love, is it still possible for a rational creature so to live, that it must finally come to an interview with him in a character completed by the full assemblage of those acquisitions, which have separately been disapproved by him through every stage of the accumulation? Why is it possible for feeble creatures to maintain their little dependent beings fortified and invincible in sin, amidst the presence of essential purity? Why does not the apprehension of such a Being strike through the mind with such intense antipathy to evil, as to blast with death every active principle that is beginning to pervert it, and render gradual additions of depravity, growing into the solidity of habit, as impossible as for perishable materials to be raised into structures amidst the fires of the last day? How is it possible to escape the solicitude, which should be inseparable from the knowledge that the beams of all-searching intelligence are continually darting on us, and pervading us; that we are exposed to the piercing inspection, compared to which the concentrated attention of all the beings in the universe besides, would be but as the powerless gaze of an infant? Why is faith, that faculty of spiritual apprehension, so absent, or so incomparably less perceptive of the grandest of its objects, than the senses are of theirs? While there is a Spirit in infinite energy through the universe, why have the few particles of dust which enclose *our* spirits the power to intercept all sensible communication with him, and to place them as in a vacuity, where the sovereign Essence had been precluded or extinguished?

The reverential submission, with which you contemplate the mystery of omnipotent benevolence forbearing to exert the agency, which could assume a

instantaneous ascendancy in every mind over the causes
f depravation and ruin, will not avert your compassion
from the unhappy persons who are practically "without
God in the world." And if your intellect could be
enlarged to a capacity for comprehending the whole
measure and depth of disaster contained in this exclusion, (an exclusion under which a human being
having the full and fearful truth of his situation revealed
to him would behold, as relatively to *his* happiness, the
whole resources of the creation sunk as into dust and
ashes, and all the causes of joy and hope reduced to
insipidity and lost in despair,) you would feel a distressing emotion at each recital of a life in which
religion had no share; and you would be tempted to
wish that some spirit from the other world, empowered
with an eloquence that might threaten to alarm the
slumbers of the dead, would throw himself in the way
of this one mortal, and this one more, to protest, in
sentences of lightning and thunder, against the infatuation that can at once acknowledge there is a God,
and be content to forego every connexion with him, but
that of danger. You would wish they should rather
be assailed by the "terror of the Lord," in whatever
were its most appalling form, than retain the satisfaction
of carelessness till the day of his mercy be past.

But you will need no such enlargement of comprehension, in order to compassionate the situation of
persons who, with reason sound to think, and hearts
not strangers to feeling, have advanced far into life,
perhaps near to its close, without having felt the influence of religion. If there is such a Being as we
mean by the term God, the ordinary intelligence of a
serious mind will be quite enough to see that it must
be a melancholy thing to pass through life, and quit it,
just as if there were not. And sometimes it will appear

as strange as it is melancholy; especially to a person who has been pious from his youth. He would be inclined to say, to a person who has nearly finished an irreligious life, What would have been justly thought of you, if you could have been habitually in the society of the wisest and best men on earth, and have acquired no degree of conformity; much more, if you could all the while have acquired progressively the meanness, prejudices, follies, and vices, of the lowest society, with which you might have been at intervals thrown in unavoidable contact? You might have been asked how *that* was possible. But then through what fatality have you been able, during so many years spent in the presence of a God, to continue even to this hour as clear of all signs of assimilation or impression as if the Deity were but a poetical fiction, or an idol in some temple of Asia?—Evidently, as the immediate cause, through want of thought concerning him.

And why did you not think of him? Did a most solemn thought of him never *once* penetrate your soul, while admitting it true that there is such a Being? If it never did, what is reason, what is mind, what is man? If it did once, how could its effects stop there? How could a deep thought on so transcendent a subject, fail to impose on the mind a permanent necessity of frequently recalling it; as some awful or magnificent spectacle would haunt you with a long recurrence of its image, even were the spectacle itself seen no more?

Why did you not think of him? How could you estimate so meanly your mind with all its capacities, as to feel no regret that an endless series of trifles should seize, and occupy as their right, all your thoughts, and deny them both the liberty and the ambition of going on to the greatest Object? How, while called to the contemplations which absorb the spirits of Heaven, could you be so patient of the task of counting the flies of a summer's day?

Why did you not think of him? You knew yourself to be in the hands of some Being from whose power you could not be withdrawn; was it not an equal defect of curiosity and prudence to indulge a careless confidence that sought no acquaintance with his nature, as regarded in itself and in its aspect on his creatures; nor ever anxiously inquired what conduct should be observed toward him, and what expectations might be entertained from him? You would have been alarmed to have felt yourself in the power of a mysterious stranger, of your own feeble species; but let the stranger be omnipotent, and you cared no more.

Why did you not think of him? One would deem that the thought of him must, to a serious mind, come second to almost every thought. The thought of virtue would suggest the thought of both a lawgiver and a rewarder; the thought of crime, of an avenger; the thought of sorrow, of a consoler; the thought of an inscrutable mystery, of an intelligence that understands it; the thought of that ever-moving activity which prevails in the system of the universe, of a supreme agent; the thought of the human family, of a great father; the thought of all being not necessary and self-existent, of a creator; the thought of life, of a preserver; and the thought of death, of an uncontrollable disposer. By what dexterity, therefore, of irreligious caution, did you avoid precisely every track where the idea of him would have met you, or elude that idea if it came? And what must sound reason pronounce of a mind which, in the train of millions of thoughts, has wandered to all things under the sun, to all the permanent objects or vanishing appearances in the creation, but never fixed its thought on the Supreme Reality never approached, like Moses, "to see this great sight?"

If it were a thing which we might be allowed to imagine, that the Divine Being were to manifest himself in some striking manner to the senses, as by some resplendent appearance at the midnight hour, or by rekindling on an elevated mountain the long extinguished fires of Sinai, and uttering voices from those fires; would he not compel from you an attention which you now refuse? Yes, you will say, he would then seize the mind with irresistible force, and religion would become its most absolute sentiment; but he only presents himself to faith. Well, and is it a worthy reason for disregarding him, that you *only believe* him to be present and infinitely glorious? Is it the office of faith to veil, to frustrate, to annihilate in effect, its object? Cannot you reflect, that the grandest representation of a spiritual and divine Being to the senses would bear not only no proportion to his glory, but no relation to his nature; and could be adapted only to an inferior dispensation of religion, and to a people who, with the exception of a most extremely small number of men, had been totally untaught to carry their thoughts beyond the objects of sense? Are you not aware, that such a representation would considerably tend to restrict you in your contemplation to a defined image, and therefore a most inadequate and subordinate idea of the divine Being? while the idea admitted by faith, though less immediately striking, is capable of an illimitable expansion, by the addition of all that progressive thought can accumulate, under the continual certainty that all is still infinitely short of the reality.

On the review of a character thus grown, in the exclusion of the religious influences, to the nature and perhaps ultimate state, the sentiment of pious benevolence would be,—I regard you as an object of great compassion, unless there can be no felicity in friendship with the Almighty, unless there be no glory in being assimilated to his excellence, unless there be no eternal rewards for his devoted servants, unless there be no danger in meeting him, at length, after a life estranged equally from his love and his fear. I deplore, at every period and crisis in the review of your life, that religion was not there. If that had been there, your youthful animation would neither have been dissipated in the frivolity which, in the morning of the short day of life, fairly and formally sets aside all serious business for *that* day, nor would have sprung forward into the emulation of vice, or the bravery of profaneness. If religion had been there, that one despicable companion, and that other malignant one, would not have seduced you into their society, or would not have retained you to share their degradation. And if religion had accompanied the subsequent progress of your life, it would have elevated you to rank, at this hour, with those saints who will soon be added to " the spirits of the just." Instead of which, what are you now, and what are your expectations as looking to that world, where piety alone can hope to find such a sequel of existence, as will inspire exultation in the retrospect of this introductory life, in which the spirit took its impress for eternity from communication with God?

On the other hand, it would be interesting to record, or to hear, the history of a character which has received its form, and reached its maturity, under the strongest efficacy of religion. We do not know that there is a more beneficent or a more direct mode of the divine agency in any part of the creation than that which "apprehends" a man, (as apostolic language expresses it,) amidst the unthinking crowd, constrains him to serious reflection, subdues him under persuasive conviction, elevates him to devotion, and matures him in progressive virtue, in order to his passing finally to a nobler state of existence. When he has long been commanded by this influence, he will be happy to look back to its first operations, whether they were mingled in early life almost insensibly with his feelings, or came on him with mighty force at some particular time, and in connexion with some assignable and memorable circumstance which was apparently the instrumental cause. He will trace the progress of this his better life, with grateful acknowledgment to the sacred power that has wrought him to a confirmation of religious habit which puts the final seal on his character. In the great majority of things, habit is a greater plague than ever afflicted Egypt: in religious character, it is eminently a felicity. The devout man exults to feel that in aid of the *simple* force of the divine principles within him, there has grown by time an accessional power, which has almost taken place of his will, and holds a firm though quiet domination through the general action of his mind. He feels this confirmed habit as the grasp of the hand of God, which will never let him go. From this advanced state he looks with confidence on futurity, and says, I carry the indelible mark upon me that I belong to God; by being devoted to him I am free of the universe; and I am ready to go to any world to which he shall please to transmit me, certain that every where, in height or depth, he will acknowledge me for ever.

LETTER VII.

The preceding letters have attempted to exhibit only general views of the influences, by which a reflective man may perceive the moral condition of his mind to have been determined.

In descending into more particular illustrations, there would have been no end of enumerating the local circumstances, the relationships of life, the professions and employments, and the accidental events, which may have affected the character. A person who feels any interest, in reviewing what has formed thus far his education for futurity, may carry his own examination into the most distinct particularity.— A few miscellaneous observations will conclude the essay.

You will have observed that I have said comparatively little of that which forms the exterior, and in general account the main substance, of the history of a man's life —the train of his fortunes and actions. If an adventurer or a soldier writes memoirs of himself for the information or amusement of the public, he may do well to keep his narrative alive by a constant crowded course of facts; for the greater part of his readers will excuse him the trouble of investigating, and he might occasionally feel it a convenience to be excused from disclosing, if he had investigated, the history and merits of his internal principles. Nor can this ingenuousness be any part of his duty, any more than it is that of an exhibiter in a public show, as long as he tells all that probably he professes to tell—where he has been, what he has witnessed, and the more reputable portion of what he has done. Let him go on with his lively anecdotes, or his legends of the marvellous, or his gazettes of marches, stratagems and skirmishes, and there is no obligation for him to turn either penitent or philosopher on our hands.—But I am supposing a man to retrace himself through his past life, in order to acquire a deep self-knowledge, and to record the investigation for his own instruction. Through such a retrospective examination, the exterior life will hold but the second place in attention, as being the imperfect offspring of that internal state, which it is the primary and more difficult object to review. From an effectual inquisition into this inner man, the investigator may proceed outward, to the course of his actions; of which he will thus have become qualified to form a much juster estimate, than he could by any exercise of judgment upon them regarded merely as exterior facts. No doubt that sometimes also, in a contrary process, the judgment will be directed upon the dispositions and principles within by a consideration of the actions without, which will serve as a partial explication of the interior character. Still it is that interior character, whether displayed in actions or not, which forms the leading object of inquiry. The chief circumstances of his practical life will, however, require to be noted, both for the purpose of so much illustration as they will afford of the state of his mind, and because they mark the points, and distinguish the stages, of his progress.

Though in memoirs intended for publication, a large share of incident and action would generally be necessary, yet there are some men whose mental history alone might be very interesting to reflective readers; as, for instance, that of a thinking man, remarkable for a number of complete changes of his speculative system. From observing the usual tenacity of views once deliberately adopted in mature life, we regard as a curious phenomenon the man whose mind has been a kind of caravansera of opinions, entertained awhile, and then sent on pilgrimage; a man who has admired and dismissed systems with the same facility with which John Buncle found, adored, married, and interred, his succession of wives, each one being, for the time, not only better than all that went before, but the best in the world. You admire the versatile aptitude of a mind, sliding into successive forms of belief, in this intellectual metempsychosis by which it animates so many new bodies of doctrines in their turn. And as none of those dying pangs which hurt you in a tale of India, attend the desertion of each of these speculative forms which the soul has awhile inhabited, you are extremely amused by the number of transmigrations, and curious to see what is to be the next; for you never reckon on the present state of such a man's views, as to be for permanence, unless perhaps when he has terminated his course of believing every thing, in ultimately believing nothing. Even then, unless he be very old, or feel more pride in being a sceptic, the conqueror of all systems, than he ever felt in being the champion of one, even then, it is very possible he may spring up again, like an igneous vapour from a bog, and glimmer through new mazes, or retrace his course through half of those he went errant through before. You will observe, that no respect is attached to this Proteus of opinion, after his changes have been multiplied; as no party expect him to remain with them, or account him much of an acquisition if he should. One, or perhaps two, considerable changes, will be regarded as signs of a liberal inquirer, and therefore the party to which his first or his second intellectual conversion may assign him, will receive him gladly. But he will be deemed to have abdicated the dignity of reason, when it is found that he can adopt no principles but to betray them; and it will be perhaps justly suspected that there is something extremely infirm in the structure of that mind, whatever vigour may mark some of its operations, to which a series of very different and sometimes contrasted theories, can appear in succession demonstratively true, and which imitates sincerely the perverseness which Petruchio only affected, declaring that which was yesterday, to a certainty, the sun, to be to-day, as certainly, the moon.

It would be curious to observe in a man who should make such an exhibition of the course of his mind, the sly deceit of self-love. While he despises the system which he has rejected, it must not imply so great a want of sense in *him* once to have embraced it, as in the rest, who were then or are now its adherents and advocates. No, in *him* it was no debility of intellect, it was at most but its immaturity or temporary lapse; and probably he is prepared to explain to you that such peculiar circumstances, as might warp a very strong and liberal mind, attended his consideration of the subject, and misled him to admit the belief of what others prove themselves fools by believing.

Another thing apparent in a record of changed opinions would be, what I have noticed before, that there is scarcely any such thing in the world as simple conviction. It would be amusing to observe how the judgment had, in one instance, been overruled into acquiescence by the admiration of a celebrated name, or in another, into opposition by the envy of it; how most opportunely judgment discovered the truth just at the time that interest could be essentially served by avowing it; how easily the impartial examiner could be induced to adopt some part of another man's opinions, after that other had zealously approved some favourite, especially if unpopular part of his; as the Pharisees almost became partial even to Christ, at the moment that he defended one of their doctrines against the Sadducees. It would be curious to see how a respectful estimate of a man's character and talents might be changed, in consequence of some personal inattention experienced from him, into depreciating invective against him or his intellectual performances, and yet the railer, though actuated solely by petty revenge, account himself, all the while, the model of equity and sound judgment.* It might be seen how the patronage of power could elevate miserable prejudices into revered wisdom, while poor old Experience was mocked with thanks for her instruction; and how the vicinity and society of the rich, and as they are termed, great, could perhaps transmute a mind that seemed to be of the stern consistence of the early Roman republic, into the gentlest wax on which Corruption could wish to imprint the venerable creed, " The right divine of kings to govern wrong," with the pious and loyal inference of the flagrant iniquity of expelling Tarquin. I am supposing the *observer* to perceive all these accommodating dexterities of reason; for it were probably absurd to expect that any mind should itself be able, in its review, to detect all its own obliquities, after having been so long beguiled, like the mariners in a story which I remember to have read, who followed the direction of their compass, infallibly right as they could have no doubt, till they arrived at an enemy's port, where they were seized and made slaves. It happened that the wicked captain, in order to betray the ship, had concealed a large loadstone at a little distance on one side of the needle.

On the notions and expectations of one stage **of life,**

* I remember several remarkable instances of this.

I suppose most reflecting men look back with a kind of compassionate contempt, though it may be often with a mingling wish that some of its enthusiasm of feeling could be recovered, I mean the period between childhood and maturity. They are prompted to exclaim, What fools we have been—while they recollect how sincerely they entertained and advanced the most ridiculous speculations on the interests of life, and the questions of truth; how regretfully astonished they were to find the mature sense of some of those around them so completely wrong; yet in other instances what veneration they felt for authorities for which they have since lost all their respect; what a fantastic importance they attached to some most trivial things;* what complaints against their fate were uttered on account of disappointments which they have since recollected with gaiety or self-congratulation; what happiness or Elysium they expected from sources which would soon have failed to impart even common satisfaction; and how sure they were that the feelings and opinions then predominant would continue through life.

If a reflective aged man were to find at the bottom of an old chest, where it had lain forgotten fifty years, a record which he had written of himself when he was young, simply and vividly describing his whole heart and pursuits, and reciting verbatim many recent passages of the language sincerely uttered to his favourite companions; would he not read it with more wonder than almost any other writing could at his age excite? His consciousness would be strangely confused in the attempt to verify his identity with such a being. He

---

* I recollect a youth of some acquirements, who earnestly wished the time might one day arrive, when his name should be adorned with the addition of D.D., which he deemed one of the sublimest of human distinctions.

would feel the young man, thus introduced to him, separated by so wide a distance as to render all congenial communion impossible. At every sentence, he might repeat, Foolish youth! I have no sympathy with your feelings, I can hold no converse with your understanding. Thus you see that in the course of a long life a man may be several moral persons, so dissimilar, that if you could find a real individual that should nearly exemplify the character in one of these stages, and another that should exemplify it in the next, and so on to the last, and then bring these several persons together into one company, which would thus be a representation of the successive states of one man, they would feel themselves a most heterogeneous party, would oppose and probably despise one another, and soon separate, not caring if they were never to meet again. The dissimilarity in mind between the two extremes, the youth of seventeen and the sage of seventy, might perhaps be little less than that in countenance; and as the one of these contrasts might be contemplated by an old man, if he had a true portrait for which he sat in the bloom of life, and should hold it beside a mirror in which he looks at his present countenance, the other would be powerfully felt if he had such a genuine and detailed memoir as I have supposed. Might it not be worth while for a self-observant person in early life, to preserve, for the inspection of the old man, if he should live so long, such a mental likeness of the young one? If it be not drawn near the time, it can never be drawn with sufficient accuracy.*

* It is to be acknowledged that the above representation of the changes and the contrast is given in the strongest colouring it will admit. Many men, perhaps the majority, retain through life so much of the chief characteristic quality of the dispositions developed

If this sketch of life were not written till a very mature or an advanced period of it, a somewhat interesting point would be, to distinguish the periods during which the mind made its greatest progress in the enlargement of its faculties, and the time when they appear to have reached their insuperable limits.

And if there have been vernal seasons, (if I may so express it,) of goodness also, periods separated off from the latter course of life by some point of time subsequent to which the christian virtues have had a less generous growth, this is a circumstance still more worthy to be strongly marked. No doubt it will be with a reluctant hand that a man marks either of these circumstances; for he could not reflect, without regret, that many children have grown into maturity and great talent, and many unformed or defective characters into established excellence, since the period when he ceased to become abler or better. Pope, at the age of fifty, would have been incomparably more mortified than, as Johnson says, his readers are, at the fact, if he had perceived it, that he could not then write materially better than he had written at the age of twenty.—And the consciousness of having passed many years without any moral and religious progress, ought to be not merely the regret for an infelicity, but the remorse of guilt; since, though natural causes must somewhere have circumscribed and fixed the extent of the intellectual power, an advancement in the nobler distinctions has still continued to be possible, and will be possible till the evening of rational life. The instruction resulting from a clear

or acquired in youth, and of the order of notions then taken in, that they remain *radically* of the same character, notwithstanding very great modifications effected by time and events; so that, in a general account of men, the mental difference between the two extremes of life may be less than the physical.

estimate of what has been effected or not in this capital concern, is the chief advantage to be derived from recording the stages of life, comparing one part with another, and bringing the whole into a comparison with the standard of perfection, and the illustrious human examples which have approached that standard the nearest. In forming this estimate, we shall keep in view the vast series of advantages and monitions, which has run parallel to the train of years; and it will be inevitable to recollect, with severe mortification, the sanguine calculations of improvement of the best kind, which at various periods the mind delighted itself in making for other given future periods, should life be protracted till then, and promised itself most *certainly* to realize by the time of their arrival. The mortification will be still more grievous, if there was at those past seasons something more hopeful than mere confident presumptions, if there were actual favourable omens, which partly justified while they raised, in ourselves and others, anticipations that have mournfully failed. My dear friend, it is very melancholy that EVIL must be so palpable, so hatefully conspicuous to an enlightened conscience, in every retrospect of a human life.

If the supposed memoirs be to be carried forward as life advances, each period being recorded as soon as it has elapsed, they should not be composed by small daily or weekly accumulations, (though this practice may have its use, in keeping a man observant of himself,) but at certain considerable intervals, as at the end of each year, or any other measure of time that is ample enough for some definable alteration to have taken place in the character or attainments.

It is needless to say that the *style* should be as simple as possible—unless indeed the writer accounts the theme worthy of being bedecked with brilliants and flowers.

If he idolize his own image so much as to think it deserves to be enshrined in a frame or cabinet of gold, why, let him enshrine it.

Should it be asked what degree of explicitness ought to prevail through this review, in reference to those particulars on which conscience has fixed the most condemning mark; I answer, that if a man writes it exclusively for his own use, he ought to signify the quality and measure of the delinquency, so far explicitly, as to secure to his mind a defined recollection of the verdict pronounced by conscience before its emotions were quelled by time; and so far as, in default of an adequate sentence *then*, to constrain him to pronounce it *now*. Such honest distinctness is necessary, because this will be the most useful part of his record for reflection to dwell upon; because this is the part which self-love is most willing to diminish and memory to dismiss; because mere general terms or allusions of censure will but little aid the cultivation of his humility; and because this license of saying so much about himself in the character of a biographer may become only a temptation to the indulgence of vanity, and a protection from the shame of it, unless he can maintain the feeling in earnest that it is really at a confessional, a severe one, that he is giving his account.

But perhaps he wishes to hold this record open to an intimate relation or friend; perhaps even thinks it might supply some interest and some lessons to his children. And what then? Why then it is perhaps too probable that though he could readily confess some of his faults, there may have been certain states of his mind, and certain circumstances in his conduct, which he cannot persuade himself to present to such inspection. Such a difficulty of being quite ingenuous, when it is actually guilt, and not merely some propriety of discretion or good taste, that creates it, is in every instance a cause for deep regret. Should not a man tremble to feel himself not daring to confide to an equal and a mortal, what has been all observed by the Supreme Witness and Judge? And the consideration of the large proportion of men constituting such instances, throws a melancholy hue over the general human character. It has several times, in writing this essay, occurred to me what strangers men may be to one another, whether as to the influences which have determined their characters, or as to the less obvious parts of their conduct. What strangers too we may be, with persons who have the art of concealment, to the principles which are at this moment prevailing in the heart. Each mind has an interior apartment of its own, into which none but itself and the Divinity can enter. In this secluded place the passions mingle and fluctuate in unknown agitations. Here all the fantastic and all the tragic shapes of imagination have a haunt, where they can neither be invaded nor descried. Here the surrounding human beings, while quite insensible of it, are made the subjects of deliberate thought, and many of the designs respecting them revolved in silence. Here projects, convictions, vows, are confusedly scattered, and the records of past life are laid. Here in solitary state sits Conscience, surrounded by her own thunders, which sometimes sleep, and sometimes roar, while the world does not know. The secrets of this apartment, could they have been even but very partially brought forth, might have been fatal to that eulogy and splendour with which many a piece of biography has been exhibited by a partial and ignorant friend. If, in a man's own account of himself, written on the supposition of being seen by any other person, the substance of the secrets of this apartment be brought forth, he throws open the last asylum of his character, where it is well if there be nothing found that will distress and irritate his most partial friend, who may thus become the ally of his conscience to condemn, without the leniency which even conscience acquires from self-love. And if it be not brought forth, where is the integrity or value of the history, supposing it pretend to afford a full and faithful estimate; and what ingenuous man could bear to give a delusive assurance of his being, or having been, so much more worthy of applause or affection than conscience all the while pronounces? It s obvious then that a man whose sentiments and designs, or the undisclosed parts of whose conduct, have been deeply criminal, must keep his record sacred to himself; unless he feels such an unsupportable longing to relieve his heart by confiding its painful consciousness, that he can be content to hold the regard of his friend on the strength of his penitence and recovered virtue. As to those, whose memory of the past is sullied by shades if not by stains, they must either in the same manner retain the delineation for solitary use, or limit themselves in writing it, to a deliberate and strong expression of the *measure* of conscious culpabilities, and their effect in the general character, with a certain, not deceptive but partially reserved explanation, that shall equally avoid particularity and mystery; or else they must consent to meet their friends, who share the human frailty and have had their deviations, on terms of mutual ingenuous acknowledgment. In this confidential communication, each will learn to behold the other's transgressions fully as much in that light in which they certainly are infelicities to be commiserated, as in that in which they are also faults or vices to be condemned; while both earnestly endeavour to improve by their remembered errors.

But I shall find myself in danger of becoming ridiculous, amidst these scruples about an entire ingenuousness to a confidential friend or two, while I glance into the literary world, and observe the number of historians of their own lives, who magnanimously throw the complete cargo, both of their vanities and their vices, before the whole public. Men who can gaily laugh at themselves for ever having even pretended to goodness; who can tell of having sought consolation for the sorrows of bereaved tenderness, in the recesses of debauchery; whose language betrays that they deem a spirited course of profligate adventures a much finer thing than the stupidity of vulgar virtues, and who seem to claim the sentiments with which we regard an unfortunate hero, for the disasters into which these adventures led them; venal partisans whose talents would hardly have been bought, if their venom had not made up the deficiency; profane travelling coxcombs; players, and the makers of immoral plays — all can narrate the course of a contaminated life with the most ingenuous hardihood. Even courtezans, grieved at the excess of modesty with which the age is afflicted, have endeavoured to diminish the evil, by presenting themselves before the public in their narratives, in a manner very analogous to that in which the Lady Godiva is said to have consented, from a most generous inducement, to pass through the city of Coventry. They can gravely relate, perhaps with intermingled paragraphs and verses of plaintive sensibility, (a kind of weeds in which sentiment without principle apes and mocks mourning virtue,) the whole nauseous detail of their transitions from proprietor to proprietor. They can tell of the precautions for meeting some "illustrious personage," accomplished in depravity even in his early youth, with the proper adjustment of time and circumstances to save him the scandal of such a meeting; the hour when they crossed the river in a boat; the arrangements about money; the kindness of the "personage" at one time, his contemptuous neglect at another; and every thing else that can turn the compassion with which we deplore their first misfortunes and errors, into detestation of the effrontery which can take to itself a merit in proclaiming the commencement sequel, and all, to the wide world.

With regard to all the classes of self-describers who thus think the publication of their vices necessary to crown their fame, one should wish there were some public special mark and brand of emphatic reprobation, to reward this tribute to public morals. Men that court the pillory for the pleasure of it, ought to receive the honour of it too, in all those contumelious salutations which suit the merits of vice grown proud of its impudence. They who "glory in their shame" should, like other distinguished personages, "pay a tax for being eminent." Yet I own the public itself is to be consulted in this case; for if the public welcomes such productions, it shows there are readers who feel themselves akin to the writers, and it would be hard to deprive congenial souls of the luxury of their appropriate sympathies. If such is the taste, it proves that a considerable portion of the public deserves just that kind of respect for its virtue, which is very significantly implied in this confidence of its favour.

One is indignant at the cant pretence and title of Confessions, sometimes adopted by these exhibiters of their own disgrace; as if it were to be believed, that penitence and humiliation would ever excite men to call thousands to witness a needless disclosure of what oppresses them with grief and shame. If they would be mortified that only a few readers should think it worth while to see them thus performing the work of self-degradation, like the fetid heroes of the Dunciad in a ditch, would it be because they are desirous that the greatest possible number should have the benefit of being averted from vice through disgust and contempt of them as its example? No, this title of Confessions is only a nominal deference to morality, necessary indeed to be paid, because mankind never forget to insist, that the *name* of virtue shall be respected, even while vice obtains from them that practical favour on which these writers place their reliance for toleration or applause. This slight homage being duly rendered and occasionally repeated, they trust in the character of the community that they shall not meet the kind of condemnation, and they have no desire for the kind of pity, which would strictly belong to criminals: nor is it any part or effect of their penitence, to wish that society may be made better by seeing in them how odious are folly and vice. They are glad the age continues such, that even *they* may have claims to be praised; and honour of some kind, and from some quarter, is the object to which they aspire, and the consequence which they promise themselves. Let them once be convinced, that they make such exhibitions under the absolute condition of subjecting themselves irredeemably to opprobrium, as in Miletus the persons infected with a rage for destroying themselves were by a solemn decree assured of being exposed in naked ignominy after the perpetration of the deed—and these literary suicides will be heard of no more.

Rousseau has given a memorable example of this voluntary humiliation. And he has very honestly assigned the degree of contrition which accompanied the self-inflicted penance, in the declaration that this document with all its dishonours, shall be presented in his justification before the Eternal Judge. If we could, in any case, pardon the kind of ingenuousness which he has displayed, it would certainly be in the disclosure of a mind so wonderfully singular as his.* We are almost willing to have such a being preserved to all the unsightly minutiæ and anomalies of its form, to be placed, as an unique in the moral museum of the world

Rousseau's impious reference to the Divine Judge, leads me to suggest, as I conclude the consideration, that the history of each man's life, though it should not be written by himself or by any mortal hand, is thus far unerringly recorded, will one day be finished in truth, and one other day yet to come, will be brought to a final estimate. A mind accustomed to grave reflections is sometimes led involuntarily into a curiosity of awful conjecture, which asks, What are those words which I should read this night, if, as to Belshazzar, a hand of prophetic shade were sent to write before me the identical expression, or the momentous import, of the sentence in which that final estimate will be declared?

* There is indeed one case in which this kind of honesty would be so signally useful to mankind, that it would deserve almost to be canonized into a virtue. If statesmen, including monarchs, courtiers, ministers, senators, popular leaders, ambassadors, &c., would publish, before they go in the triumph of virtue, to the " last audit," or leave to be published after they are gone, each a frank exposition of motives, intrigues, cabals, and manœuvres, the worship which mankind have rendered to power and rank would cease to be, what it has always been, a mere blind *superstition*, when such rational grounds should come to be shown for the homage. It might contribute to a happy exorcism of that spirit which has never suffered nations to be at peace; while it would give an altered and less delusive character to history. Great service in this way, but unfortunately late, is in the course of being rendered in our times, by the publication of private memoirs, written by persons connected or acquainted with those of the highest order. Let any one look at the exhibition of the very centre of the dignity and power of a great nation, as given in Pepys's Memoirs, though with the omission in that publication, as I am informed on the best authority, of sundry passages contained in the manuscript, of such a colour that their production would have exceeded the very utmost license allowable by public decorum. I need not revert to works now comparatively ancient, such as Lord Melbourn's Diary.

ESSAY II.

ON DECISION OF CHARACTER.

LETTER I.

MY DEAR FRIEND,

WE have several times talked of this bold quality, and acknowledged its great importance. Without it, a human being, with powers at best but feeble and surrounded by innumerable things tending to perplex, to divert, and to frustrate, their operations, is indeed a pitiable atom, the sport of divers and casual impulses. It is a poor and disgraceful thing, not to be able to reply, with some degree of certainty, to the simple questions, What will you be? What will you do?

A little acquaintance with mankind will supply numberless illustrations of the importance of this qualification. You will often see a person anxiously hesitating a long time between different, or opposite determinations, though impatient of the pain of such a state, and ashamed of the debility. A faint impulse of preference alternates toward the one, and toward the other; and the mind, while thus held in a trembling balance, is vexed that it cannot get some new thought, or feeling, or motive; that it has not more sense, more resolution, more of any thing that would save it from envying even the decisive instinct of brutes. It wishes that any circumstance might happen, or any person might appear, that could deliver it from the miserable suspense.

In many instances, when a determination *is* adopted, it is frustrated by this temperament. A man, for example, resolves on a journey to-morrow, which he is not under an absolute necessity to undertake, but the inducements appear, this evening, so strong, that he does not think it possible he can hesitate in the morning. In the morning, however, these inducements have unaccountably lost much of their force. Like the sun that is rising at the same time, they appear dim through a mist; and the sky lowers, or he fancies that it does, and almost wishes to see darker clouds than there actually are; recollections of toils and fatigues ill repaid in past expeditions rise and pass into anticipation; and he lingers, uncertain, till an advanced hour determines the question for him, by the certainty that it is now too late to go.

Perhaps a man has conclusive reasons for wishing to remove to another place of residence. But when he is going to take the first actual step towards executing his purpose, he is met by a new train of ideas, presenting the possible and magnifying the unquestionable, disadvantages and uncertainties of a new situation; awakening the natural reluctance to quit a place to which habit has accommodated his feelings, and which has grown *warm* to him, (if I may so express it,) by his having been in it so long; giving a new impulse to his affection for the friends whom he must leave; and so detaining him still lingering, long after his judgment may have dictated to him to be gone.

A man may think of some desirable alteration in his plan of the; perhaps in the arrangements of his family, or in the mode of his intercourse with society,—

Would it be a good thing? He thinks it would be a good thing. It certainly would be a very good thing. He wishes it were done. He will attempt it *almost* immediately. The following day, he doubts whether it would be quite prudent. Many things are to be considered. May there not be in tne change some evil of which he is not aware? Is this a proper time? What will people say?—And thus, thouhg he does not formally renounce his purpose, he shrinks out of it, with an irksome wish that he could be fully satisfied of the propriety of renouncing it. Perhaps he wishes that the thought had never occurred to him, since it has diminished his self-complacency, without promoting his virtue. But next week, his conviction of the wisdom and advantage of such a reform comes again with great force. Then, Is it so practicable as I was at first willing to imagine? Why not? Other men have done much greater things; a resolute mind may brave and accomplish every thing; difficulty is a stimulus and a triumph to a strong spirit; " the joys of conquest are the joys of man." What need I care for people's opinion? It shall be done.—He makes the first attempt. But some unexpected obstacle presents itself; he feels the awkwardness of attempting an unaccustomed manner of acting; the questions or the ridicule of his friends disconcert him; his ardour abates and expires. He again begins to question. whether it be wise, whether it be necessary, whether it be possible; and at last surrenders his purpose to be perhaps resumed when the same feelings return, and to be in the same manner again relinquished.

While animated by some magnanimous sentiments which he has heard or read, or while musing on some great example, a man may conceive the design, and partly sketch the plan, of a generous enterprise; and his imagination revels in the felicity, to others and himself, that would follow from its accomplishment. The splendid representation always centres in himself as the hero who is to realize it.

In a moment of remitted excitement, a faint whisper from within may doubtfully ask, Is this more than a dream; or am I really destined to achieve such an enterprise? Destined!—and why are not this conviction of its excellence, this conscious duty of performing the noblest things that are possible, and this passionate ardour, enough to constitute a destiny?— He feels indignant that there should be a failing part of his nature to defraud the nobler, and cast him below the ideal model and the actual examples which he is admiring; and this feeling assists him to resolve, that he will undertake this enterprise, that he certainly will, though the Alps or the Ocean lie between him and the object. Again, his ardour slackens; distrustful of himself, he wishes to know how the design would appear to other minds; and when he speaks of it to his associates, one of them wonders, another laughs, and another frowns. His pride, while with them, attempts a manful defence; but his resolution gradually crumbles down toward their level; he becomes in a little while ashamed to entertain a visionary project, which therefore, like a rejected friend, desists from intruding on him or following him, except at lingering distance; and he subsides, at'last, into what he labours to believe a man too rational for the schemes of ill-calculating enthusiasm. And it were strange if the effort to make out this favourable estimate of himself did not succeed, while it is so much more pleasant to attribute one's defect of enterprise to wisdom, which on maturer thought disapproves it, than to imbecility which shrinks from it.

A person of undecisive character wonders how all the embarrassments in the world happened to meet exactly in *his* way, to place him just in that one situation for which he is peculiarly unadapted, but in which he is also willing to think no other man could have acted with facility or confidence. Incapable of setting up a firm purpose on the basis of things as they are, he is often employed in vain speculations on some different supposable state of things, which would have saved him from all this perplexity and irresolution. He thinks what a determined course he could have pursued, *if* his talents, his health, his age, had been different; if he had been acquainted with some one person sooner; if his friends were, in this or the other point, different from what they are; or if fortune had showered her favours on him. And he gives himself as much license to complain, as if all these advantages had been among the rights of his nativity, but refused, by a malignant or capricious fate, to his life. Thus he is occupied—instead of marking with a vigilant eye, and seizing with a strong hand, all the possibilities of his actual situation.

A man without decision can never be said to belong to himself; since, if he dared to assert that he did, the puny force of some cause, about as powerful, you would have supposed, as a spider, may make a seizure of the hapless boaster the very next moment, and contemptuously exhibit the futility of the determinations by which he was to have proved the independence of his understanding and his will. He belongs to whatever can make capture of him; and one thing after another vindicates its right to him, by arresting him while he is trying to go on; as twigs and chips, floating near the edge of a river, are intercepted by every weed, and whirled in every little eddy. Having concluded on a design, he may pledge himself to accomplish it—*if* the hundred diversities of feeling which may come within the week, will let him. His character precluding all foresight of his conduct, he may sit and wonder what form and direction his views and actions are destined to take to-morrow; as a farmer has often to acknowledge that next day's proceedings are at the disposal of its winds and clouds.

This man's notions and determinations always depend very much on other human beings; and what chance for consistency and stability, while the persons with whom he may converse, or transact, are so various? This very evening, he may talk with a man whose sentiments will melt away the present form and outline of his purposes, however firm and defined he may have fancied them to be. A succession of persons whose faculties were stronger than his own, might, in spite of his irresolute re-action, take him and dispose of him as they pleased. Such infirmity of spirit practically confesses him made for subjection, and he passes, like a slave, from owner to owner. Sometimes indeed it happens, that a person so constituted falls into the train, and under the permanent ascendency, of some one stronger mind, which thus becomes through life the oracle and guide, and gives the inferior a steady will and plan. This, when the governing spirit is wise and virtuous, is a fortunate relief to the feeling, and an advantage gained to the utility, of the subordinate, and as it were, appended mind.

The regulation of every man's plan must greatly depend on the course of events, which come in an order not to be foreseen or prevented. But in accommodating the plans of conduct to the train of events, the difference between two men may be no less than that, in the one instance, the man is subservient to the events, and in the other, the events are made subservient to the man. Some men seem to have been taken along by a succession of events, and, as it were, handed forward in helpless passiveness from one to another; having no determined principle in their own characters, by which they could constrain those events to serve a design formed antecedently to them, or apparently in defiance of them. The events seized them as a neutral material, not they the events. Others, advancing through life with an internal invincible determination, have seemed to make the train of circumstances, whatever they were, conduce as much to their chief design as if they had, by some directing interposition, been brought about on purpose. It is wonderful how even the casualties of life seem to bow to a spirit that will not bow to them, and yield to subserve a design which they may, in their first apparent tendency, threaten to frustrate.

You may have known such examples, though they are comparatively not numerous. You may have seen a man of this vigorous character in a state of indecision concerning some affair in which it was necessary for him to determine, because it was necessary for him to act. But in this case, his manner would assure you that he would not remain long undecided; you would wonder if you found him still balancing and hesitating the next day. If he explained his thoughts, you would perceive that their clear process, evidently at each effort gaining something toward the result, must certainly reach it ere long. The deliberation of such a mind is a very different thing from the fluctuation of one whose second thinking only upsets the first, and whose third confounds both. To *know how* to obtain a determination, is one of the first requisites and indications of a rationally decisive character.

When the decision was arrived at, and a plan of

action approved, you would feel an assurance that something would absolutely be done. It is characteristic of such a mind, to think for effect; and the pleasure of escaping from temporary doubt gives an additional impulse to the force with which it is carried into action. The man will not re-examine his conclusions with endless repetition, and he will not be delayed long by consulting other persons, after he had ceased to consult himself. He cannot bear to sit still among unexecuted decisions and unattempted projects. We wait to hear of his achievements, and are confident we shall not wait long. The possibility or the means may not be obvious to us, but we know that every thing will be attempted, and that a spirit of such determined will is like a river, which, in whatever manner it is obstructed, will make its way somewhere. It must have cost Cæsar many anxious hours of deliberation, before he decided to pass the Rubicon; but it is probable he suffered but few to elapse between the decision and the execution. And any one of his friends, who should have been apprised of his determination, and understood his character, would have smiled contemptuously to hear it insinuated that though Cæsar had resolved, Cæsar would not dare; or that though he might cross the Rubicon, whose opposite bank presented to him no hostile legions, he might come to other rivers, which he would not cross; or that either rivers, or any other obstacle, would deter him from prosecuting his determination from this ominous commencement to its very last consequence.

One signal advantage possessed by a mind of this character is, that its passions are not wasted. The whole measure of passion of which any one, with important transactions before him, is capable, is not more than enough to supply interest and energy for the required practical exertions; the therefore as little as possible of this costly flame should be expended in a way that does not augment the force of action. But nothing can less contribute or be more destructive to vigour of action, than protracted anxious fluctuation, through resolutions adopted, rejected, resumed, suspended; while yet nothing causes a greater expense of feeling. The heart is fretted and exhausted by being subjected to an alternation of contrary excitements, with the ultimate mortifying consciousness of their contributing to no end. The long-wavering deliberation, whether to perform some bold action of difficult virtue, has often cost more to feeling than the action itself, or a series of such actions, would have cost; with the great disadvantage too of not being relieved by any of that invigoration which the man in action finds in the activity itself, that spirit created to renovate the energy which the action is expending. When the passions are not consumed among dubious musings and abortive resolutions, their utmost value and use can be secured by throwing all their animating force into effective operation.

Another advantage of this character, is, that it exempts from a great deal of interference and obstructive annoyance, which an irresolute man may be almost sure to encounter. Weakness, in every form, tempts arrogance; and a man may be allowed to wish for a kind of character with which stupidity and impertinence may not make so free. When a firm decisive spirit is recognised, it is curious to see how the space clears around a man, and leaves him room and freedom. The disposition to interrogate, dictate, or banter, preserves a respectful and politic distance, judging it not unwise to keep the peace with a person of so much energy. A conviction that he understands and that he wills with extraordinary force, silences the conceit that intended to perplex or instruct him, and intimidates the malice that was disposed to attack him. There is a feeling, as in respect to Fate, that the decrees of so inflexible a spirit *must* be right, or that, at least, they *will* be accomplished.

But not only will he secure the freedom of acting for himself, he will obtain also by degrees the coincidence of those in whose company he is to transact the business of life. If the manners of such a man be free from arrogance, and he can qualify his firmness with a moderate degree of insinuation; and if his measures have partly lost the appearance of being the dictates of his will, under the wider and softer sanction of some experience that they are reasonable; both competition and fear will be laid to sleep, and his will may acquire an unresisted ascendency over many who will be pleased to fall into the mechanism of a system, which they find makes them more successful and happy than they could have been amidst the anxiety of adjusting plans and expedients of their own, and the consequences of often adjusting them ill. I have known several parents, both fathers and mothers, whose management of their families has answered this description; and has displayed a striking example of the facile complacency with which a number of persons, of different ages and dispositions, will yield to the decisions of a firm mind, acting on an equitable and enlightened system.

The last resource of this character, is, hard inflexible pertinacity, on which it may be allowed to rest its strength after finding it can be effectual in none of its milder forms. I remember admiring an instance of this kind, in a firm, sagacious and estimable old man, whom I well knew, and who has long been dead. Being

on a jury, in a trial of life and death, he was satisfied
of the innocence of the prisoner; the other eleven were
of the opposite opinion. But he was resolved the man
should not be condemned; and as the first effort for preventing it, very properly made application to the *minds*
of his associates, spending several hours in labouring to
convince them. But he found he made no impression,
while he was exhausting the strength which it was
necessary to reserve for another mode of operation. He
then calmly told them that it should now be a trial who
could endure confinement and famine the longest, and
that they might be quite assured he would sooner die
than release them at the expense of the prisoner's life.
In this situation they spent about twenty-four hours ;
when at length all acceded to his verdict of acquittal.

It is not necessary to amplify on the indispensable
importance of this quality, in order to the accomplishment of any thing eminently good. We instantly see,
that every path to signal excellence is so obstructed
and beset, that none but a spirit so qualified can pass.
But it is time to examine what are the elements of that
mental constitution which is displayed in the character
in question.

LETTER II.

Perhaps the best mode would be, to bring into our
thoughts, in succession, the most remarkable examples
of this character that we have known in real life, or
that we have read of in history or even in fiction ; and
attentively to observe, in their conversations, manners,
and actions, what principles appear to produce, or to
constitute, this commanding distinction. You will

easily pursue this investigation yourself. I lately made a partial attempt, and shall offer you a number of suggestions.

As a previous observation, it is beyond all doubt that very much depends on the constitution of the body. It would be for physiologists to explain, if it were explicable, the *manner* in which corporeal organization affects the mind; I only assume it as a fact, that there is in the material construction of some persons, much more than of others, some quality which augments, if it do not create, both the stability of their resolution, and the energy of their active tendencies. There is something that, like the ligatures which one class of the Olympic combatants bound on their hands and wrists, braces round, if I may so describe it, and compresses the powers of the mind, giving them a steady forcible spring and reaction, which they would presently lose if they could be transferred into a constitution of soft, yielding, treacherous debility. The action of strong character seems to demand something firm in its material basis, as massive engines require, for their weight and for their working, to be fixed on a solid foundation. Accordingly I believe it would be found, that a majority of the persons most remarkable for decisive character, have possessed great constitutional physical firmness. I do not mean an exemption from disease and pain, nor any certain measure of mechanical strength, but a tone of vigour, the opposite to lassitude, and adapted to great exertion and endurance. This is clearly evinced in respect to many of them, by the prodigious labours and deprivations which they have borne in prosecuting their designs. The physical nature has seemed a proud ally of the moral one, and with a hardness that would never shrink, nas sustained the energy that could never remit.

A view of the disparities between the different races of animals inferior to man, will show the effect of organization on disposition. Compare, for instance, a lion with the common beasts of our fields, many of them larger in bulk of animated substance. What a vast superiority of courage, and impetuous and determined action; which difference we attribute to some great dissimilarity of modification in the composition of the animated material. Now it is probable that a difference somewhat analogous subsists between some human beings and others in point of what we may call mere physical constitution; and that this is no small part of the cause of the striking inequalities in respect to decisive character. A man who excels in the power of decision has probably more of the physical quality of a *lion* in his composition than other men.

It is observable that women in general have less inflexibility of character than men; and though many moral influences contribute to this difference, the principal cause may probably be something less firm in the corporeal constitution. Now that physical quality, whatever it is, from the smaller measure of which in the constitution of the frame, women have less firmness than men, may be possessed by one man more than by men in general in a greater degree of difference than that by which men in general exceed women.

If there have been found some resolute spirits powerfully asserting themselves in feeble vehicles, it is so much the better; since this would authorize a hope, that if all the other grand requisites can be combined, they may form a strong character, in spite of an unadapted constitution. And on the other hand, no constitutional hardness will form the true character, without those superior properties; though it may produce that false and contemptible kind of decision which we term *obstinacy;* a stubbornness of temper, which can assign no reasons but mere will, for a constancy which acts in the nature of dead weight rather than of strength; resembling less the reaction of a powerful spring than the gravitation of a big stone.

The first prominent mental characteristic of the person whom I describe, is, a complete confidence in his own judgment. It will perhaps be said, that this is not so uncommon a qualification. I however think it is uncommon. It is indeed obvious enough, that almost all men have a flattering estimate of their own understanding, and that as long as this understanding has no harder task than to form opinions which are not to be tried in action, they have a most self-complacent assurance of being right. This assurance extends to the judgments which they pass on the proceedings of others. But let them be brought into the necessity of adopting actual measures in an untried situation, where, unassisted by any previous example or practice, they are reduced to depend on the bare resources of judgment alone, and you will see in many cases, this confidence of opinion vanish away. The mind seems all at once placed in a misty vacuity, where it reaches round on all sides, but can find nothing to take hold of. Or if not lost in vacuity, it is overwhelmed in confusion; and feels as if its faculties were annihilated in the attempt to think of schemes and calculations among the possibilities, chances, and hazards which overspread a wide untrodden field; and this conscious imbecility becomes severe distress, when it is believed that consequences, of serious or unknown good or evil, are depending on the decisions which are to be formed amidst so much uncertainty. The thought painfully recurs at each step and turn, I may by chance be right, but it is fully as probable I am wrong. It is like the case of a rustic walking in London, who, having no certain direction through the vast confusion of streets to the place where he wishes to be, advances, and hesitates, and turns, and inquires, and becomes, at each corner, still more inextricably perplexed.* A man in this situation feels he shall be very unfortunate if he cannot accomplish more than he can understand.—is not this frequently, when brought to the practical test, the state of a mind not disposed in general to undervalue its own judgment?

In cases where judgment is not so completely bewildered, you will yet perceive a great practical distrust of it. A man has perhaps advanced a considerable way towards a decision, but then lingers at a small distance from it, till necessity, with a stronger hand than conviction, impels him upon it. He cannot see the whole length of the question, and suspects the part beyond his sight to be the most important, for the most essential point and stress of it may be there. He fears that certain possible consequences, if they should follow, would cause him to reproach himself for his present determination. He wonders how this or the other person would have acted in the same circumstances; eagerly catches at any thing like a respectable precedent; would be perfectly willing to forego the pride of setting an example, for the safety of following one; and looks anxiously round to know what each person may think on the subject; while the various and opposite opinions to which he listens, perhaps only serve to confound his perception of the track of thought

---

* " Why does not the man call a hackney-coach ?" a gay reader, I am aware, will say of the person so bemazed in the great town. So he might, certainly; (that is. if he know where to find one ;) and the gay reader and I have only to deplore that there is no parallel convenience for the assistance of perplexed understandings.

by which he had hoped to reach his conclusion. Even when that conclusion is obtained, there are not many minds that might not be brought a few degrees back into dubious hesitation, by a man of respected understanding saying, in a confident tone, Your plan is injudicious; your selection is unfortunate; the event will disappoint you.

It cannot be supposed that I am maintaining such an absurdity as that a man's complete reliance on his own judgment is a proof of its strength and rectitude. Intense stupidity may be in this point the rival of clear-sighted wisdom. I had once some knowledge of a person whom no mortal could have surpassed, not Cromwell or Strafford, in confidence in his own judgment and consequent inflexibility of conduct; while at the same time his successive schemes were ill-judged to a degree that made his disappointments ridiculous still more than pitiable. He was not an example of that *simple* obstinacy which I have mentioned before; for he considered his measures, and did not want for reasons which seriously satisfied himself of their being most judicious. This confidence of opinion may be possessed by a person in whom it will be contemptible or mischievous; but its proper place is in a very different character, and without it there can be no dignified actors in human affairs.

If, after it is seen how foolish this confidence appears as a feature in a weak character, it be inquired what, in a rightfully decisive person's manner of thinking it is that authorizes him in this firm assurance that his view of the concerns before him is comprehensive and accurate; he may, in answer, justify his confidence on such grounds as these: that he is conscious that objects are presented to his mind with an exceedingly distinct and perspicuous aspect, not like the shapes of moon-light, or like Ossian's ghosts, dim forms of uncircumscribed shade; that he sees the different parts of the subject in an arranged order, not in unconnected fragments; that in each deliberation the main object keeps its clear pre-eminence, and he perceives the bearings which the subordinate and conducive ones have on it; that perhaps several trains of thought, drawn from different points, lead him to the same conclusion; and that he finds his judgment does not vary in servility to the moods of his feelings.

It may be presumed that a high degree of this character is not attained without a considerable measure of that kind of certainty, with respect to the relations of things, which can be acquired only from experience and observation. A very protracted course of time, however, may not be indispensable for this discipline. An extreme vigilance in the exercise of observation, and a strong and strongly exerted power of generalizing on experience, may have made a comparatively short time enough to supply a large share of the wisdom derivable from these sources; so that a man may long before he is old be rich in the benefits of experience, and therefore may have all the decision of judgment legitimately founded on that accomplishment. This knowledge from experience he will be able to apply in a direct and immediate manner, and without refining it into general principles, to some situations of affairs, so as to anticipate the consequences of certain actions in those situations by as plain a reason, and as confidently, as the kind of fruit to be produced by a given kind of tree. Thus far the facts of his experience will serve him as precedents; cases of such near resemblance to those in which he is now to act as to afford him a rule by the most immediate inference. At the next step, he will be able to apply this knowledge, now converted into general principles, to a multitude of cases bearing but a partial resemblance to any thing he has actually witnessed. And then, in looking forward to the possible occurrence of altogether new combinations of circumstances, he can trust to the resources which he is persuaded his intellect will open to him, or is humbly confident, if he be a devout man, that the Supreme Intelligence will not suffer to be wanting to him, when the occasion arrives. In proportion as his views include, at all events, more certainties than those of other men, he is with good reason less fearful of contingencies. And if, in the course of executing his design, unexpected disastrous events should befall, but which are not owing to any thing wrong in the plan and principles of that design, but to foreign causes; it will be characteristic of a strong mind to attribute these events discriminatively to their own causes, and not to the *plan*, which, therefore, instead of being disliked and relinquished, will be still as much approved as before, and the man will proceed calmly to the sequel of it without any change of arrangement;—unless indeed these sinister events should be of such consequence as to alter the whole state of things to which the plan was correctly adapted, and so create a necessity to form an entirely new one, adapted to that altered state.

Though he do not absolutely despise the understandings of other men, he will perceive their dimensions as compared with his own, which will preserve its independence through every communication and encounter. It is however a part of this very independence, that he will hold himself free to alter his opinion, if the information which may be communicated to him shall bring sufficient reason. And as no one is so sensible of the importance of a complete acquaintance with a subject as the man who is always endeavouring to think conclusively, he will listen with the utmost attention to the *information*, which may sometimes be received from persons for whose *judgment* he has no great respect. The information which they may afford him is not at all the less valuable for the circumstance, that his practical inferences from it may be quite different from theirs. If they will only give him an accurate account of facts, he does not care how indifferently they may reason on them. Counsel will in general have only so much weight with him as it supplies knowledge which may assist his judgment; he will yield nothing to it implicitly as authority, except when it comes from persons of approved and eminent wisdom; but he may hear it with more candour and good temper, from being conscious of this independence of his judgment, than the man who is afraid lest the first person that begins to persuade him, should baffle his determination. He feels it entirely a work of his own to deliberate and to resolve, amidst all the advice which may be attempting to control him. If, with an assurance of his intellect being of the highest order, he also holds a commanding station, he will feel it gratuitous to consult with any one, excepting merely to receive statements of facts. This appears to be exemplified in the man, who has lately shown the nations of Europe how large a portion of the world may, when Heaven permits, be at the mercy of the solitary workings of an individual mind.

The strongest trial of this determination of judgment is in those cases of urgency where something must immediately be done, and the alternative of right or wrong is of important consequence; as in the duty of a medical man, treating a patient whose situation at once requires a daring practice, and puts it in painful doubt what to dare. A still stronger illustration is the case of a general who is compelled, in the very instant, to make dispositions on which the event of a battle, the lives of thousands of his men, or perhaps almost the fate of a nation, may depend. He may even be placed in a dilemma which appears equally dreadful on both sides. Such a predicament is described in Denon's account of one of the sanguinary conflicts between the French and Mamelukes, as having for a while held in the most distressing hesitation General Desaix, though a prompt and intrepid commander.

LETTER III.

This indispensable basis, confidence of opinion, is however not enough to constitute the character in question. For many persons, who have been conscious and proud of a much stronger grasp of thought than ordinary men, and have held the most decided opinions on important things to be done, have yet exhibited, in the listlessness or inconstancy of their actions, a contrast and a disgrace to the operations of their understandings. For want of some cogent feeling impelling them to carry every internal decision into action, they have bee still left where they were; and a dignified judgment has been seen in the hapless plight of having no effective forces to execute its decrees.

It is evident then, (and I perceive I have partly anticipated this article in the first letter,) that another essential principle of the character is, a total incapability of surrendering to indifference or delay the serious determinations of the mind. A strenuous *will* must accompany the conclusions of thought, and constantly incite the utmost efforts to give them a practical result. The intellect must be invested, if I may so describe it, with a glowing atmosphere of passion, under the influence of which, the cold dictates of reason take fire, and spring into active powers.

Revert once more in your thoughts to the persons most remarkably distinguished by this quality. You will perceive, that instead of allowing themselves to sit down delighted after the labour of successful thinking, as if they had completed some great thing, they regard this labour but as a circumstance of preparation, and the conclusions resulting from it as of no more value, (till going into effect,) than the entombed lamps of the Rosicrucians. They are not disposed to be content in a region of mere ideas, while they ought to be advancing into the field of corresponding realities; they retire to that region sometimes, as ambitious adventurers anciently went to Delphi, to consult, but not to reside. You will therefore find them almost uniformly in determined pursuit of some object, on which they fix a keen and steady look, never losing sight of it while they follow it through the confused multitude of other things.

A person actuated by such a spirit, seems by his manner to say, Do you think that I would not disdain to adopt a purpose which I would not devote my utmost force to effect; or that having thus devoted my exertions, I will intermit or withdraw them, through indolence, debility, or caprice; or that I will surrender my object to any interference except the uncontrollable dispensations of Providence? No, I am linked to my determination with iron bands; it clings to me as if a part of my destiny; and if its frustration be, on the contrary, doomed a part of that destiny, it is doomed so only through calamity or death.

This display of systematic energy seems to indicate a constitution of mind in which the passions are commensurate with the intellectual part, and at the same time hold an inseparable correspondence with it, like the faithful sympathy of the tides with the phases of the moon. There is such an equality and connexion, that subjects of the decisions of judgment become proportionally and of course the objects of passion. When the judgment decides with a very strong preference, that same strength of preference, actuating also the passions, devotes them with energy to the object, as long as it is thus approved; and this will produce such a conduct as I have described. When therefore a firm, self-confiding, and unaltering judgment fails to make a decisive character, it is evident either that the passions in that mind are too languid to be capable of a strong and unremitting excitement, which defect makes an indolent or irresolute man; or that they perversely sometimes coincide with judgment and sometimes clash with it, which makes an inconsistent or versatile man.

There is no man so irresolute as not to act with determination in many single cases, where the motive is powerful and simple, and where there is no need of plan and perseverance; but this gives no claim to the term *character*, which expresses the habitual tenour of a man's active being. The character may be displayed in the successive unconnected undertakings, which are each of limited extent, and end with the attainment of their particular objects. But it is seen in its most commanding aspect in those grand schemes of action, which have no necessary point of conclusion, which continue on through successive years, and extend even to that dark period when the agent himself is withdrawn from human sight.

I have repeatedly, in conversation, remarked to you

the effect of what has been called a Ruling Passion. When its object is noble, and an enlightened understanding regulates its movements, it appears to me a great felicity; but whether its object be noble or not, it infallibly creates, where it exists in great force, that active ardent constancy, which I describe as a capital feature of the decisive character. The Subject of such a commanding passion wonders, if indeed he were at leisure to wonder, at the persons who pretend to attach importance to an object which they make none but the most languid efforts to secure. The utmost powers of the man are constrained into the service of the favourite Cause by this passion, which sweeps away, as it advances, all the trivial objections and little opposing motives, and seems almost to open a way through impossibilities. This spirit comes on him in the morning as soon as he recovers his consciousness, and commands and impels him through the day, with a power from which he could not emancipate himself if he would. When the force of habit is added, the determination becomes invincible, and seems to assume rank with the great laws of nature, making it nearly as certain that such a man will persist in his course as that in the morning the sun will rise.

A persisting untameable efficacy of soul gives a seductive and pernicious dignity even to a character which every moral principle forbids us to approve. Often in the narrations of history and fiction, an agent of the most dreadful designs compels a sentiment of deep respect for the unconquerable mind displayed in their execution. While we shudder at his activity, we say with regret, mingled with an admiration which borders on partiality, What a noble being this would have been, if goodness had been his destiny! The partiality is evinced in the very selection of terms, by which we show that we are tempted to refer his atrocity rather to his destiny than to his choice. I wonder whether an emotion like this, have not been experienced by each reader of Paradise Lost, relative to the Leader of the infernal spirits; a proof, if such were the fact, of some insinuation of evil into the magnificent creation of the poet. In some of the high examples of ambition (the ambition which is a vice), we almost revere the force of mind which impelled them forward through the longest series of action, superior to doubt and fluctuation, and disdainful of ease, of pleasures, of opposition, and of danger. We bend in homage before the ambitious spirit which reached the true sublime in the reply of Pompey to his friends, who dissuaded him from hazarding his life on a tempestuous sea in order to be at Rome on an important occasion: " It is necessary for me to go, it is not necessary for me to live."

Revenge has produced wonderful examples of this unremitting constancy to a purpose. Zanga is a well-supported illustration. And you may have read of a real instance of a Spaniard, who, being injured by another inhabitant of the same town, resolved to destroy him: the other was apprised of this, and removed with the utmost secresy, as he thought, to another town at a considerable distance, where however he had not been more than a day or two, before he found that his enemy also was there. He removed in the same manner to several parts of the kingdom, remote from each other; but in every place quickly perceived that his deadly pursuer was near him. At last he went to South America, where he had enjoyed his security but a very short time, before his relentless pursuer came up with him, and accomplished his purpose.

You may recollect the mention in one of our counversations, of a young man who wasted in two or three years a large patrimony, in profligate revels with a number of worthless associates calling themselves his friends, till his last means were exhausted, when they of course treated him with neglect or contempt. Reduced to absolute want, he one day went out of the house with an intention to put an end to his life; but wandering awhile almost unconsciously, he came to the brow of an eminence which overlooked what were lately his estates. Here he sat down, and remained fixed in thought a number of hours, at the end of which he sprang from the ground with a vehement exulting emotion. He had formed his resolution, which was that all these estates should be his again; he had formed his plan too, which he instantly began to execute. He walked hastily forward, determined to seize the very first opportunity, of however humble a kind, to gain any money, though it were ever so despicable a trifle, and resolved absolutely not to spend, if he could help it, a farthing of whatever he might obtain. The first thing that drew his attention was a heap of coals shot out of carts on the pavement before a house. He offered himself to shovel or wheel them into the place where they were to be laid, and was employed. He received a few pence for the labour; and then, in pursuance of the saving part o his plan, requested some small gratuity of meat and drink, which was given him. He then looked out for the next thing that might chance to offer; and went, with indefatigable industry, through a succession of servile employments, in different places, of longer and shorter duration, still scrupulously avoiding, as far as possible, the expense of a penny. He promptly seized *every* opportunity which could advance his design, without regarding the meanness of occupation or appearance.

By this method he had gained, after a considerable time, money enough to purchase, in order to sell again, a few cattle, of which he had taken pains to understand the value. He speedily but cautiously turned his first gains into second advantages; retained without a single deviation his extreme parsimony; and thus advanced by degrees into larger transactions and incipient wealth. I did not hear, or have forgotten the continued course of his life; but the final result was, that he more than recovered his lost possessions, and died an inveterate miser, worth 60,000*l*. I have always recollected this as a signal instance, though in an unfortunate and ignoble direction, of decisive character, and of the extraordinary *effect*, which, according to general laws, belongs to the strongest form of such a character.

But not less decision has been displayed by men of virtue. In this distinction no man ever exceeded, or ever will exceed, for instance, the late illustrious Howard.

The energy of his determination was so great, that if, instead of being habitual, it had been shown only for a short time on particular occasions, it would have appeared a vehement impetuosity; but by being unintermitted, it had an equability of manner which scarcely appeared to exceed the tone of a calm constancy, it was so totally the reverse of any thing like turbulence or agitation. It was the calmness of an intensity kept uniform by the nature of the human mind forbidding it to be more, and by the character of the individual forbidding it to be less. The habitual passion of his mind was a pitch of excitement and impulsion almost equal to the temporary extremes and paroxysms of common minds; as a great river, in its customary state, is equal to a small or moderate one when swollen to a torrent.

The moment of finishing his plans in deliberation, and commencing them in action, was the same. I wonder what must have been the amount of that bribe, in emolument or pleasure, that would have detained him a week inactive after their final adjustment. The law which carries water down a declivity was not more unconquerable and invariable than the determination of his feelings toward the main object. The importance of this object held his faculties in a state of determination which was too rigid to be affected by lighter interests, and on which therefore the beauties of nature and of art had no power. He had no leisure feeling which he could spare to be diverted among the innumerable varieties of the extensive scene which he traversed; his subordinate feelings nearly lost their separate existence and operation, by falling into the grand one. There have not been wanting trivial minds, to mark this as a fault in his character. But the mere men of taste ought to be silent respecting such a man as Howard; he is above their sphere of judgment. The invisible spirits, who fulfil their commission of philanthropy among mortals, do not care about pictures, statues, and sumptuous buildings; and no more did he, when the time in which he must have inspected and admired them, would have been taken from the work to which he had consecrated his life. The curiosity which he might feel, was reduced to wait till the hour should arrive, when its gratification should be presented by conscience, (which kept a scrupulous charge of all his time,) as the *duty* of that hour. If he was still at every hour, when it came, fated to feel the attractions of the fine arts but the second claim, they might be sure of their revenge; for no other man will ever visit Rome under such a despotic acknowledged rule of duty as to refuse himself time for surveying the magnificence of its ruins. Such a sin against taste is very far beyond the reach of common saintship to commit. It implied an inconceivable severity of conviction, that he had *one thing to do*, and that he who would do some great thing in this short life, must apply himself to the work with such a concentration of his forces, as, to idle spectators, who live only to amuse themselves, looks like insanity.

His attention was so strongly and tenaciously fixed on his object, that even at the greatest distance, as the Egyptian pyramids to travellers, it appeared to him with a luminous distinctness as if it had been nigh, and beguiled the toilsome length of labour and enterprise by which he was to reach it. So conspicuous was it before him, that not a step deviated from the direction, and every movement and every day was an approximation. As his method referred every thing he did and thought to the end, and as his exertion did not relax for a moment, he made the trial, so seldom made, what is the utmost effect which may be granted to the last possible efforts of a human agent: and therefore what he did not accomplish, he might conclude to be placed beyond the sphere of mortal activity, and calmly leave to the immediate disposal of Providence.

Unless the eternal happiness of mankind be an insignificant concern, and the passion to promote it an inglorious distinction, I may cite George Whitefield as a noble instance of this attribute of the decisive character, this intense necessity of action. The great cause which was so languid a thing in the hands of many of its advocates, assumed in his administrations an unmitigable urgency.

Many of the christian missionaries among the heathens, such as Brainerd, Elliot, and Schwartz, have displayed memorable examples of this dedication of their whole being to their office, this abjuration of all the quiescent feelings.

This would be the proper place for introducing (if I did not hesitate to introduce in any connexion with merely human instances) the example of him who said, "I must be about my Father's business. My meat and drink is to do the will of him that sent me, and to finish his work. I have a baptism to be baptized with and how am I straitened till it be accomplished!"

LETTER IV.

After the illustrations on the last article, it will seem but a very slight transition when I proceed to specify Courage, as an essential part of the decisive character. An intelligent man, adventurous only in thought, may sketch the most excellent scheme, and after duly admiring it, and himself as its author, may be reduced to say, What a noble spirit that would be which should dare to realize this! A noble spirit! is it I? And his heart may answer in the negative, while he glances a mortified thought of inquiry round to recollect persons who would venture what he dares not, and almost hopes not to find them. Or if by extreme effort he has brought himself to a resolution of braving the difficulty, he is compelled to execrate the timid lingerings that still keep him back from the trial. A man endowed with the complete character, might say, with a sober consciousness as remote from the spirit of bravado as it is from timidity, Thus, and thus, is my conviction and my determination; now for the phantoms of fear; let me look them in the face; their menacing glare and ominous tones will be lost on me: " I dare do all that may become a man." I trust I shall firm.y confront every thing that threatens me while prosecuting my purpose, and I am prepared to meet the conse· quences of it when it is accomplished. I should despise a being, though it were myself, whose agency could be held enslaved by the gloomy shapes of imagination, by the haunting recollections of a dream, by the whistling or the howling of winds, by the shriek of owls, by the shades of midnight, or by the threats or frowns of man. I should be indignant to feel that, in the commencement of an adventure, I could think of nothing but the deep pit by the side of the way where I must walk, into which I may slide, the mad animal which it is not impossible that I may meet, or the assassin who may lurk in a thicket of yonder wood. And I disdain to compromise the interests that rouse me to action, for the privilege of an ignoble security.

As the conduct of a man of decision is always individual, and often singular, he may expect some serious trials of courage. For one thing, he may be encountered by the strongest disapprobation of many of his connexions, and the censure of the greater part of the society where he is known. In this case, it is not a man of common spirit that can show himself just as at other times, and meet their anger in the same undisturbed manner as he would meet some ordinary inclemency of the weather; that can, without harshness or violence, continue to effect every moment some part of his design, coolly replying to each ungracious look and indignant voice, I am sorry to oppose you: I am not unfriendly to you, while thus persisting in what excites your displeasure; it would please me to have your approbation and concurrence, and I think I should have them if you would seriously consider my reasons; but meanwhile, I am superior to opinion, I am not to be intimidated by reproaches, nor would your favour and applause be any reward for the sacrifice of my object. As you can do without my approbation, I can certainly do without yours; it is enough that I can approve myself, it is enough that I appeal to the last authority in the creation. Amuse yourselves as you may, by continuing to censure or to rail; *I* must continue to act.

The attack of contempt and ridicule is perhaps a still greater trial of courage. It is felt by all to be an admirable thing, when it can in no degree be ascribed to the hardness of either stupidity or confirmed depravity, to sustain for a considerable time, or in numerous instances, the looks of scorn, or an unrestrained shower of taunts and jeers, with perfect composure, and proceed immediately after, or at the time, on the business that provokes all this ridicule. This invincibility of temper will often make even the scoffers themselves tired of the sport: they begin to feel that against such a man it is a poor sort of hostility to joke and sneer; and there is nothing that people are more mortified to spend in vain than their scorn. Till, however, a man shall become a veteran, he must reckon on sometimes meeting this trial in the course of virtuous enterprise. And if, at the suggestion of some meritorious but unprecedented proceeding, I hear him ask, with a look and tone of shrinking alarm, But will they not laugh at me?—I know that he is not the person whom this essay attempts to describe. A man of the right kind would say, They will smile, they will laugh, will they? Much good may it do them. I have something else to do than to trouble myself about their mirth. I do not care if the whole neighbourhood were to laugh in a chorus. I should indeed be sorry to see or hear such a number of fools, but pleased enough to find that they considered me as an outlaw to their tribe. The good to result from my project will not be less, because vain and shallow minds that cannot understand it, are diverted at it and at me. What should I think of my pursuits, if every trivial thoughtless being could comprehend or would applaud them; and of myself, if my courage needed levity and ignorance for their allies, or could be abashed at their sneers?

I remember, that on reading the account of the project for conquering Peru, formed by Almagro, Pizarro, and De Luques, while abhorring the actuating principle of the men, I could not help admiring the hardihood of mind which made them regardless of scorn. These three individuals, before they had obtained any associates, or arms, or soldiers, or more than a very imperfect knowledge of the power of the kingdom they were to conquer, celebrated a solemn mass in one or the great churches, as a pledge and a commencement of the enterprise, amidst the astonishment and contempt expressed by a multitude of people for what was deemed a monstrous project. They, however, proceeded through the service, and afterwards to their respective departments of preparation, with an apparently entire insensibility to all this triumphant contempt; and thus gave the first proof of possessing that invincible firmness with which they afterwards prosecuted their design, till they attained a success, the destructive process and many of the results of which humanity has ever deplored.

Milton's Abdiel is a noble illustration of the courage that rises invincible above the derision not only of the multitude, but of the proud and elevated.

But there may be situations where decision of character will be brought to trial against evils of a darker aspect than disapprobation or contempt. There may be the threatening of serious sufferings; and very often, to dare as far as conscience or a great cause required, has been to dare to die. In almost all plans of great enterprise, a man must systematically dismiss, at the entrance, every wish to stipulate with his destiny for safety. He voluntarily treads within the precincts of danger; and though it be possible he may escape, he ought to be prepared with the fortitude of a self-devoted victim. This is the inevitable condition on which heroes, travellers or missionaries among savage nations, and reformers on a grand scale, must commence their career. Either they must allay their fire of enterprise, or abide the liability to be exploded by it from the world.

The last decisive energy of a rational courage, which confides in the Supreme Power, is very sublime. It makes a man who intrepidly dares every thing that can oppose or attack him within the whole sphere of mortality; who will still press toward his object while death is impending over him; who would retain his purpose unshaken amidst the ruins of the world.

It was in the true elevation of this character that Luther, when cited to appear at the Diet of Worms, under a very questionable assurance of safety from high authority, said to his friends, who conjured him not to go, and warned him by the example of John Huss, whom, in a similar situation, the same pledge of protection had not saved from the fire, "I am called in the name of God to go, and I would go, though I were certain to meet as many devils in Worms as there are tiles on the houses."

A reader of the Bible will not forget Daniel, braving in calm devotion the decree which virtually consigned him to the den of lions: or Shadrach, Meshach, and Abed-nego, saying to the tyrant, "We are not careful to answer thee in this matter," when the "burning fiery" furnace was in sight.

The combination of these several essential principles constitutes that state of mind which is a grand requisite to decision of character, and perhaps its most striking distinction — the full agreement of the mind with itself, the consenting co-operation of all its powers and all its dispositions.

What an unfortunate task it would be for a charioteer, who had harnessed a set of horses, however strong, if he could not make them draw together; if while one of them would go forward, another was restiff, another struggled backward, another started aside. If even one of the four were unmanageably perverse, while the three were tractable, an aged beggar with his crutch might leave Phaëton behind. So in a human being, unless the chief forces act consentaneously, there can be no inflexible vigour, either of will or execution. *One* dissentient principle in the mind not only deducts so much from the strength and mass of its agency, but counteracts and embarrasses all the rest. If the judgment holds in low estimation that which yet the passions incline to pursue, the pursuit will be irregular and inconstant, though it may have occasional fits of animation, when those passions happen to be highly stimulated. If there is an opposition between judgment and habit, though the man will probably continue to act mainly under the sway of habit in spite of his opinions, yet sometimes the intrusion of those opinions will have for the moment an effect like that of Prospero's wand on the limbs of Ferdinand; and to be alternately impelled by habit, and checked by opinion, will be a state of vexatious debility. If two principal passions are opposed to each other, they will utterly distract any mind, whatever might be the force of its faculties if acting without embarrassment. The one passion may be somewhat stronger than the other, and therefore just prevail barely enough to give a feeble impulse to the conduct of the man; a feebleness which will continue till there be a greater disparity between these rivals, in consequence of a reinforcement to the slightly ascendent one, by new impressions, or the gradual strengthening of habit forming in its favour. The disparity must be no less than an absolute predominance of the one and subjection of the other, before the prevailing passion will have at liberty from the intestine conflict any large measure of its force to throw activity into the system of conduct. If, for instance, a man feels at once the love of fame which is to be gained only by arduous exertions, and an equal degree of the love of ease or pleasure which precludes those exertions; if he is eager to show off in splendour, and yet anxious to save money; if he has the curiosity of adventure, and yet that solicitude for safety, which forbids him to climb a precipice, descend into a cavern, or explore a dangerous wild; if he has the stern will of a tyrant, and yet the relentings of a man; if he has the ambition to domineer over his fellow-mortals, counteracted by a reluctance to inflict so much mischief as it might cost to subdue them; we may anticipate the irresolute contradictory tenour of his actions. Especially if conscience, that great troubler of the human breast, loudly declares against a man's wishes or projects, it will be a fatal enemy to decision, till it either reclaim the delinquent passions, or be debauched or laid dead by them.

Lady Macbeth may be cited as a harmonious character, though the epithet seem strangely applied. She had capacity, ambition, and courage; and she willed the death of the king. Macbeth had still more capacity, ambition, and courage; and he also willed the murder of the king. But he had, besides, humanity, generosity, conscience, and some measure of what forms the *power* of conscience, the fear of a Superior Being. Consequently, when the dreadful moment approached, he felt an insupportable conflict between these opposite principles, and when it was arrived his utmost courage began to fail. The worst part of his nature fell prostrate under the power of the better; the angel of goodness arrested the demon that grasped the dagger; and would have taken that dagger away, if the pure demoniac firmness of his wife, who had none of these counteracting principles, had not shamed and hardened him to the deed.

The poet's delineation of Richard III. offers a dreadful specimen of this indivisibility of mental impulse. After his determination was fixed, the whole mind with the compactest fidelity supported him in prosecuting it. Securely privileged from all interference of doubt that could linger, or humanity that could soften, or timidity that could shrink, he advanced with a concentrated constancy through scene after scene of atrocity, still fulfilling his vow to "cut his way through with a bloody axe." He did not waver while he pursued his object, nor relent when he seized it.

Cromwell (whom I mention as a parallel, of course not to Richard's wickedness, but to his inflexible vigour,) lost his mental consistency in the latter end of a career which had displayed a superlative example of decision. It appears that the wish to be a king, at last arose in a mind which had contemned royalty, and battled it from the land. As far as he really had any republican principles and partialities, this new desire must have been a very untoward associate for them, and must have produced a schism in the breast where-all the strong forces of thought and passion had acted till then in concord. The new form of ambition became just predominant enough to carry him, by slow degrees, through the embarrassment and the shame of this incongruity, into an irresolute determination to assume the crown; so irresolute, that he was reduced again to a mortifying indecision by the remonstrances of some of his friends, which he could have slighted, and by an apprehension of the public disapprobation, which he could have braved, if some of the principles of his own mind had not shrunk or revolted from the design. When at last the motives for relinquishing this design prevailed, it was by so small a degree of preponderance, that his reluctant refusal of the offered crown was the voice of only half his soul.

Not only two distinct counteracting passions, but one passion interested for two objects, both equally desirable, but of which the one must be sacrificed, may annihilate in that instance the possibility of a resolute promptitude of conduct. I recollect reading in an old divine, a story from some historian, applicable to this remark. A father went to the agents of a tyrant, to endeavour to redeem his two sons, military men, who, with some other captives of war, were condemned to die. He offered, as a ransom, a sum of money, and to surrender his own life. The tyrant's agents who had them in charge, informed him that this equivalent would be accepted for one of his sons, and for one only, because they should be accountable for the execution of two persons; he might therefore choose which he would redeem. Anxious to save even one of them thus at the expense of his own life, he yet was unable to decide which should die, by choosing the other to live, and remained in the agony of this dilemma so long that they were both irreversibly ordered for execution.

LETTER V.

It were absurd to suppose that any human being can attain a state of mind capable of acting in all instances invariably with the full power of determination; but it is obvious that many have possessed a habitual and very commanding measure of it; and I think the preceding remarks have taken account of its chief characteristics and constituent principles. A number of additional observations remains.

The slightest view of human affairs shows what fatal and wide-spread mischief may be caused by men of this character, when misled or wicked. You have but to recollect the conquerors, despots, bigots, unjust conspirators, and signal villains of every class, who have blasted society by the relentless vigour which could act consistently and heroically wrong. Till therefore the virtue of mankind be greater, there is reason to be pleased that so few of them are endowed with extraordinary decision.

Even when dignified by wisdom and principle, this quality requires great care in the possessors of it to prevent its becoming unamiable. As it involves much practical assertion of superiority over other human beings, it should be as temperate and conciliating as possible in manner; else pride will feel provoked, affection hurt, and weakness oppressed. But this is not the manner which will be most natural to such a man; rather it will be high-toned, laconic, and careless of pleasing. He will have the appearance of keeping himself always at a distance from social equality; and his friends will feel as if their friendship were continually sliding into subserviency; while his intimate connexions will think he does not attach the due importance either to their opinions or to their regard. His manner, when they differ from him, or complain, will be too much like the expression of slight estimation, and sometimes of disdain.

When he can accomplish a design by his own personal means alone, he may be disposed to separate himself to the work with the cold self-enclosed individuality on which no one has any hold, which seems to recognise no kindred being in the world, which takes little account of good wishes and kind concern, any more than it cares for opposition; which seeks neither aid nor sympathy, and seems to say, I do not want any of you, and I am glad that I do not; leave me alone to succeed or die. This has a very repellent effect on the friends who wished to feel themselves of some importance, in some way or other, to a person whom they are constrained to respect. When assistance is indispensable to his undertakings, his mode of signifying it will seem to command, rather than invite, the co-operation.

In consultation, his manner will indicate that when he is equally with the rest in possession of the circumstances of the case, he does not at all expect to hear any opinions that shall correct his own; but is satisfied that either his present conception of the subject is the just one, or that his own mind must originate that which shall be so. This difference will be apparent between him and his associates, that *their* manner of receiving *his* opinions is that of agreement or dissent; *his* manner of receiving *theirs* is judicial—that of sanction or rejection. He has the tone of authoritatively deciding on what they say, but never of submitting to decision what himself says. Their coincidence with his views does not give him a firmer assurance of his being right, nor their dissent any other impression than that of their incapacity to judge. If his feeling took the distinct form of a reflection, it would be, Mine is the business of comprehending and devising, and I am here to rule this company, and not to consult them; I want their docility, and not their arguments; I am come, not to seek their assistance in thinking, but to determine their concurrence in executing what is already thought for them. Of course, many suggestions and reasons which appear important to those they come from will be disposed of by him with a transient attention, or a light facility, that will seem very disrespectful to persons who possibly hesitate to admit that he is a demi-god, and that they are but idiots. Lord Chatham, in going out of the House of Commons, just as one of the speakers against him concluded his speech by emphatically urging what he perhaps rightly thought the unanswerable question, "*Where* can we find means to support such a war?" turned round a moment, and gaily chanted, "Gentle shepherd tell me where?"

Even the assenting convictions, and practical compliances, yielded by degrees to this decisive man, may be somewhat undervalued; as they will appear to him no more than simply coming, and that very slowly, to a right apprehension; whereas *he* understood and decided justly from the first, and has been right all this while.

He will be in danger of rejecting the just claims of charity for a little tolerance to the prejudices, hesitation, and timidity, of those with whom he has to act. He will say to himself, I wish there were any thing like manhood among the beings called men; and that they could have the sense and spirit not to let themselves be hampered by so many silly notions and childish fears! Why cannot they either determine with some promptitude, or let me, that can, do it for them? Am I to wait till debility become strong, and folly wise?—If full scope be allowed to these tendencies, they may give too much of the character of a tyrant to even a man of elevated virtue, since, in the consciousness of the right intention, and the assurance of the wise contrivance, of his designs, he will hold himself justified in being regardless of every thing but the accomplishment of them. He will forget all respect for the feelings and liberties of beings who are accounted but a subordinate machinery, to be actuated, or to be thrown aside when not actuated, by the spring of his commanding spirit.

I have before asserted that this strong character *may* be exhibited with a mildness, or at least temperance, of manner; and that, generally, it will thus best secure its efficacy. But this mildness must often be at the cost of great effort; and how much considerate policy or benevolent forbearance it will require, for a man to exert his utmost vigour in the very task, as it will appear to him at the time, of cramping that vigour! — Lycurgus appears to have been a high example of conciliating patience in the resolute prosecution of designs to be effected among a perverse multitude.

It is probable that the men most distinguished for decision, have not in general possessed a large share of tenderness; and it is easy to imagine, that the laws of our nature will, with great difficulty, allow the combination of the refined sensibilities with a hard, never-shrinking, never-yielding firmness. Is it not almost of the essence of this temperament to be free from even the *perception* of such impressions as cause a mind, weak through susceptibility, to relax or waver; just as the skin of the elephant, or the armour of the rhinoceros, would be but indistinctly sensible to the application of a force by which a small animal, with a skin of thin and delicate texture, would be pierced or lacerated to death ? No doubt, this firmness consists partly in a commanding and repressive power over feelings, but it may consist fully as much in not having them. To be exquisitely alive to gentle impressions, and yet to be able to preserve, when the prosecution of a design requires it, an immovable heart amidst the most imperious causes of subduing emotion, is perhaps not an impossible constitution of mind, but it must be the rarest endowment of humanity.

If you take a view of the first rank of decisive men, you will observe that their faculties have been too much bent to arduous effort, their souls have been kept in too military an attitude, they have been begirt with too much iron, for the melting movements of the heart. Their whole being appears too much arrogated and occupied by the spirit of severe design, urging them toward some defined end, to be sufficiently at ease for the indolent complacency, the soft lassitude of gentle affections, which love to surrender themselves to the present felicities, forgetful of all " enterprises of great pith and moment." The man seems rigorously intent still on his own affairs, as he walks, or regales, or mingles with domestic society; and appears to despise all the feelings that will not take rank with the grave labours and decisions of intellect, or coalesce with the unremitting passion which is his spring of action; he values not feelings which he cannot employ either as weapons or as engines. He loves to be actuated by a passion so strong as to compel into exercise the utmost force of his being, and fix him in tone, compared with which, the gentle affections, if he had felt them, would be accounted tameness, and their exciting causes insipidity.

Yet we cannot willingly admit that those gentle affections are totally incompatible with the most impregnable resolution and vigour; nor can we help believing that such men as Timoleon, Alfred, and Gustavus Adolphus, must have been very fascinating associates in private and domestic life, whenever the urgency of their affairs would allow them to withdraw from the interests of statesmen and warriors, to indulge the affections of men : most fascinating, for, with relations or friends who had any right perceptions, an effect of the strong character would be recognised in a peculiar charm imparted by it to the gentle moods and seasons. The firmness and energy of the man whom nothing could subdue, would exalt the quality of the tenderness which softened him to recline.

But it were much easier to enumerate a long train of ancient and modern examples of the vigour unmitigated by the sensibility. Perhaps indeed these indomitable spirits have yielded sometimes to some species of love, as a mode of amusing their passions for an interval, till greater engagements have summoned them into their proper element; when they have shown how little the sentiment was an element of the heart, by the ease with which they could relinquish the temporary favourite. In other cases, where there have not been the selfish inducements, which this passion supplies, to the exhibition of something like softness, and where they have been left to the trial of what they might feel of the sympathies of humanity in their simplicity, no rock on earth could be harder.

The celebrated King of Prussia occurs to me, as a capital instance of the decisive character ; and there occurs to me, at the same time, one of the anecdotes related of him.* Intending to make, in the night, an important movement in his camp, which was in sight of the enemy, he gave orders that by eight o'clock all the lights in the camp should be put out, on pain of death. The moment that the time was passed, he walked out himself to see whether all were dark. He found a light in the tent of a Captain Zietern, which he entered just as the officer was folding up a letter. Zietern knew him, and instantly fell on his knees to entreat his mercy. The king asked to whom he had been writing; he said it was a letter to his wife, which he had retained the candle these few minutes beyond the time in order to finish. The king coolly ordered him to rise, and write one line more, which he should dictate. This line was to inform his wife, without any explanation, that by such an hour the next day, he should be a dead man. The letter was then sealed, and despatched as it had been intended; and, the next day, the captain was executed. I say nothing of the justice of the punishment itself; but this cool barbarity to the affection both of the officer and his wife, proved how little the decisive hero and reputed philosopher was capable of the tender affections, or of sympathizing with their pains.

At the same time, it is proper to observe, that the case may easily occur, in which a man, sustaining a

* The authenticity of this anecdote, which I read in some trifling fugitive publication many years since, has been questioned. Possibly enough it might be one of the many stories only half true which could not fail to go abroad concerning a man who made, in his day, so great a figure. But as it does not at all misrepresent the general character of his mind, since there are many incontrovertible facts proving against him as great a degree of cruelty as this anecdote would charge on him, the want of means to prove this one fact does not seem to impose any necessity for omitting the illustration.

high responsibility, *must* be resolute to act in a manner which may make him appear to want the finer feelings. He may be placed under the necessity of doing what he knows will cause pain to persons of a character to feel it severely. He may be obliged to resist affectionate wishes, expostulations, entreaties, and tears. Take this same instance. Suppose the wife of Zietern had come to supplicate for him, not only the remission of the punishment of death, but an exemption from any other severe punishment, which was perhaps justly due to the violation of such an order issued no doubt for important reasons; it had then probably been the duty and the virtue of the commander to deny the most interesting suppliant, and to resist the most pathetic appeals which could have been made to his feelings.

LETTER VI.

Various circumstances might be specified as adapted to confirm such a character as I have attempted to describe. I shall notice two or three.

And first, *opposition*. The passions which inspirit men to resistance, and sustain them in it, such as anger, indignation, and resentment, are evidently far stronger than those which have reference to friendly objects; and if any of these strong passions are frequently excited by opposition, they infuse a certain quality into the general temperament of the mind, which remains after the immediate excitement is past. They continually strengthen the principle of re-action; they put the mind in the habitual array of defence and self-assertion, and often give it the aspect and the posture of a gladiator, when there appears no confronting combatant. When these passions are provoked in such a person as I describe, it is probable that each excitement is followed by a greater increase of this principle of re-action than in other men, because this result is so congenial with his naturally resolute disposition. Let him be opposed then, throughout the prosecution of one of his designs, or in the general tenour of his actions, and this constant opposition would render him the service of an ally, by augmenting the resisting and defying power of his mind. An irresolute spirit indeed might be quelled and subjugated by a formidable and persisting opposition; but the strong wind which blows out a taper, exasperates a powerful fire (if there be fuel enough) to an indefinite intensity. It would be found, in fact, on a recollection of instances, that many of the persons most conspicuous for decision, have been exercised and forced to this high tone of spirit in having to make their way through opposition and contest; a discipline under which they were wrought to both a prompt acuteness of faculty, and an inflexibility of temper, hardly attainable even by minds of great natural strength, if brought forward into the affairs of life under indulgent auspices, and in habits of easy and friendly coincidence with those around them. Often, however, it is granted, the firmness matured by such discipline is, in a man of virtue, accompanied with a Catonic severity, and in a mere man of the world is an unhumanized repulsive hardness.

Desertion may be another cause conducive to the consolidation of this character. A kind mutually reclining dependence, is certainly for the happiness of human beings; but this necessarily prevents the development of some great individual powers which would be forced into action by a state of abandonment.

I lately happened to notice, with some surprise, an ivy, which, finding nothing to cling to beyond a certain point, had shot off into a bold elastic stem, with an air of as much independence as any branch of oak in the vicinity. So a human being thrown, whether by cruelty, justice, or accident, from all social support and kindness, if he have any vigour of spirit, and be not in the bodily debility of either childhood or age, will begin to act for himself with a resolution which will appear like a new faculty. And the most absolute inflexibility is likely to characterize the resolution of an individual who is obliged to deliberate without consultation, and execute without assistance. He will disdain to yield to beings who have rejected him, or to forego a particle of his designs or advantages in concession to the opinions or the will of all the world. Himself, his pursuits, and his interests, are emphatically his own. " The world is not his friend, nor the world's law;" and therefore he becomes regardless of every thing but its power, of which his policy carefully takes the measure, in order to ascertain his own means of action and impunity, as set against the world's means of annoyance, prevention. and retaliation.

If this person have but little humanity or principle, he will become a misanthrope, or perhaps a villain, who will resemble a solitary wild beast of the night, which makes prey of every thing it can overpower, and cares for nothing but fire. If he be capable of grand conception and enterprise, he may, like Spartacus, make a daring attempt against the whole social order of the state where he has been oppressed. If he be of great humanity and principle, he may become one of the noblest of mankind, and display a generous virtue to which society had no claim, and which it is not worthy to reward, if it should at last become inclined. No, he will say, give your rewards to another; as it has been no part of my object to gain them, they are not necessary to my satisfaction. I have done good, without expecting your gratitude, and without caring for your approbation. If conscience and my Creator had not been more auspicious than you, none of these virtues would ever have opened to the day. When I ought to have been an object of your compassion, I might have perished; now, when you find I can serve your interests, you will affect to acknowledge me and reward me; but I will abide by my destiny to verify the principle that virtue is its own reward.—In either case, virtuous or wicked, the man who has been compelled to do without assistance, will spurn interference.

Common life would supply illustrations of the effect of desertion, in examples of some of the most resolute men having become such partly from being left friendless in early life. The case has also sometimes happened, that a wife and mother, remarkable perhaps for gentleness and acquiescence before, has been compelled, after the death of her husband on whom she depended, and when she has met with nothing but neglect or unkindness from relations and those who had been accounted friends, to adopt a plan of her own, and has executed it with a resolution which has astonished even herself.

One regrets that the signal examples, real or fictitious, that most readily present themselves, are still of the depraved order. I fancy myself to see Marius sitting on the ruins of Carthage, where no arch or column, that remained unshaken amidst the desolation, could present a stronger image of a firmness beyond the power of disaster to subdue. The rigid constancy which had before distinguished his character, would be aggravated by his finding himself thus an outcast from all human society; and he would proudly shake off every sentiment that had ever for an instant checked his designs in the way of reminding him of social obligations. The lonely individual was placed in the alternative of becoming the victim or the antagonist of the power of the empire. While, with a spirit capable of confronting that power, he resolved, amidst those ruins, on a great experiment, he would enjoy a kind of sullen luxury in surveying the dreary situation into which he was driven, and recollecting the circumstances of his expulsion; since they would seem to him to sanction an unlimited vengeance; to present what had been his country as the pure legitimate prize for desperate achievement; and to give him a proud consequence in being reduced to maintain singly a mortal quarrel against the bulk of mankind. He would exult that the very desolation of his condition rendered but the more complete the proof of his possessing a mind which no misfortunes could repress or intimidate, and that it kindled an animosity intense enough to force that mind from firm endurance into impetuous action. He would feel that he became stronger for enterprise, in proportion as his exile and destitution rendered him more inexorable; and the sentiment with which he quitted his solitude would be,—Rome expelled her patriot, let her receive her evil genius.

The decision of Satan, in Paradise Lost, is represented as consolidated by his reflections on his hopeless banishment from heaven, which oppress him with sadness for some moments, but he soon resumes his invincible spirit, and utters the impious but sublime sentiment,

" What matter where, if *I* be still the same."

You remember how this effect of desertion is represented in Charles de Moor.* His father's supposed cruel rejection consigned him irretrievably to the career of atrocious enterprise, in which, notwithstanding the most interesting emotions of humanity and tenderness, he persisted with heroic determination till he considered his destiny as accomplished.

Success tends considerably to reinforce this commanding quality. It is true that a man possessing it in a high degree will not lose it by occasional failure; for if the failure was caused by something entirely beyond the reach of human knowledge and ability, he will remember that fortitude is the virtue required in meeting unfavourable events which in no sense depended on him; if by something which *might* have been known and prevented, he will feel that even the experience of failure completes his competence, by admonishing his prudence, and enlarging his understanding. But as schemes and measures of action rightly adjusted to their proposed ends will generally attain them, continual failure would show something essentially wrong in a man's system, and destroy his confidence, or else expose it as mere absurdity or obstinacy. On the contrary, when a man has ascertained by experiment the justness of his calculations and the extent of his powers, when he has measured his force with various persons, when he has braved and vanquished difficulty, and partly seized the prize, he will carry forward the result of all this in an intrepid self-sufficiency for whatever may yet await him.

In some men, whose lives have been spent in constant perils, continued success has produced a confidence beyond its rational effect, by inspiring a presumption

* A wildly extravagant, certainly, but most imposing and gigantic character in Schiller's tragedy, *The Robbers*.

that the common laws of human affairs were, in their case, superseded by the decrees of a peculiar destiny, securing them from almost the possibility of disaster; and this superstitious feeling, though it has displaced the unconquerable resolution from its rational basis, has often produced the most wonderful effects. This dictated Cæsar's expression to the mariner who was terrified at the storm and billows, "What art thou afraid of?—thy vessel carries Cæsar." The brave men in the times of the English Commonwealth were, some of them, indebted in a degree for their magnanimity to this idea of a special destination, entertained as a religious sentiment.

The wilfulness of an obstinate person is sometimes fortified by some single instance of remarkable success in his undertakings, which is promptly recalled in every case where his decisions are questioned or opposed, as a proof, or ground of just presumption, that he must in this instance too be right; especially if that one success happened contrary to your predictions.

I shall only add, and without illustration, that the habit of associating with *inferiors*, among whom a man can always, and therefore does always, take the precedence and give the law, is conducive to a subordinate coarse kind of decision of character. You may see this exemplified any day in an ignorant country 'squire among his vassals; especially if he wear the lordly uperaddition of Justice of the Peace.

In viewing the characters and actions of the men who have possessed in imperial eminence the quality which I have attempted to describe, one cannot but wish it were possible to know how much of this mighty superiority was created by the circumstances in which they were placed; but it is inevitable to believe that there was some vast intrinsic difference from ordinary men in the original constitutional structure of the mind. In observing lately a man who appeared too vacant almost to think of a purpose, too indifferent to resolve upon it, and too sluggish to execute it if he had resolved, I was distinctly struck with the idea of the distance between him and Marius, of whom I happened to have been reading; and it was infinitely beyond my power to believe that any circumstances on earth, though ever so perfectly combined and adapted, would have produced in this man, if placed under their fullest influence from his childhood, any resemblance (unless perhaps the courage to enact a diminutive imitation in revenge and cruelty) of the formidable Roman.

It is needless to discuss whether a person who is practically evinced, at the age of maturity, to want the stamina of this character, can, by any process, acquire it. Indeed such a person cannot have sufficient force of *will* to make the complete experiment. If there were the unconquerable *will* that would persist to seize all possible means, and apply them in order to attain, if I may so express it, this stronger mode of active existence, it would prove the possession already of a high degree of the character sought; and if there is not this *will*, how then is the supposed attainment possible?

Yet though it is improbable that a very irresolute man can ever become a habitually decisive one, it should be observed, that since there are *degrees* of this powerful quality, and since the essential principles of it, when partially existing in those degrees, cannot be supposed subject to definite and ultimate limitation, like the dimension of the bodily stature, it might be possible to apply a discipline which should advance a man from the lowest degree to the next, from that to the third, and how much further—it will be worth his trying, if his first successful experiments have not cost more in the efforts for making the attainment, than he judges likely to be repaid by any good he shall gain from its exercise. I have but a very imperfect conception of the discipline; but will suggest a hint or two.

In the first place, the indispensable necessity of a clear and comprehensive knowledge of the concerns before us, seems too obvious for remark; and yet no man has been sufficiently sensible of it, till he has been placed in circumstances which forced him to act before he had time, or after he had made ineffectual efforts, to obtain the needful information and understanding. The pain of having brought things to an unfortunate issue, is hardly greater than that of proceeding in the conscious ignorance which continually threatens such an issue. While thus proceeding at hazard, under some compulsion which makes it impossible for him to remain in inaction, a man looks round for information as eagerly as a benighted wanderer would for the light of a human dwelling. He perhaps labours to recall what he thinks he once heard or read as relating to a similar situation, without dreaming at that time that such instruction could ever come to be of importance to him; and is distressed to find his best recollection so indistinct as to be useless. He would give a considerable sum, if some particular book could be brought to him at the instant; or a certain document which he believes to be in existence; or the detail of a process, the terms of a prescription, or the model of an implement. He thinks how many people know, without its being of any present use to them, exactly what could be of such important service to him, if he could know it. In some cases, a line, sentence, a monosyllable of affirming or denying, or a momentary sight of an object, would be inexpressibly valuable and welcome. And he resolves that if he can once happily escape from the present difficulty, he will apply himself day and night to obtain knowledge, not concerning one particular matter only, but divers others, in provision against possible emergencies, rather than be so involved and harassed again. It might really be of service to have been occasionally forced to act under the disadvantage of conscious ignorance (if the affair was not so important as to allow the consequence to be very injurious), as an effectual lesson on the necessity of knowledge in order to decision either of plan or execution. It must indeed be an extreme case that will compel a considerate man to act in the absence of knowledge; yet he may sometimes be necessitated to proceed to action, when he is sensible his information is far from extending to the whole of the concern in which he is going to commit himself. And in this case, he will feel no little uneasiness, while transacting that part of it in which his knowledge is competent, when he looks forward to the point where that knowledge terminates; unless he be conscious of possessing an exceedingly prompt faculty of catching information at the moment that he wants it for use; as Indians set out on a long journey with but a trifling stock of provision, because they are sure that their bows or guns will procure it by the way. It is one of the nicest points of wisdom to decide how much less than complete knowledge, in any question of practical interest, will warrant a man to venture on an undertaking, in the presumption that the deficiency will be supplied in time to prevent either perplexity or disaster.

A thousand familiar instances show the effect of

complete knowledge on determination. An artisan may be said to be decisive as to the mode of working a piece of iron or wood, because he is certain of the proper process and the effect. A man perfectly acquainted with the intricate paths of a woodland district, takes the right one without a moment's hesitation; while a stranger, who has only some very vague information, is lost in perplexity. It is easy to imagine what a number of circumstances may occur in the course of a life, or even of a year, in which a man cannot thus readily determine, and thus confidently proceed without a compass and an exactness of knowledge which few persons have application enough to acquire. And it would be frightful to know to what extent human interests are committed to the direction of ignorance. What a consolatory doctrine is that of a particular Providence!

In connexion with the necessity of knowledge, I would suggest the importance of cultivating, with the utmost industry, a conclusive manner of thinking. In the first place, let the general course of thinking partake of the nature of *reasoning;* and let it be remembered that this name does not belong to a series of thoughts and fancies which follow one another without deduction or dependence, and which can therefore no more bring a subject to a proper issue, than a number of separate links will answer the mechanical purpose of a chain. The conclusion which terminates such a series, does not deserve the name of *result* or *conclusion*, since it has little more than a casual connexion with what went before; the conclusion might as properly have taken place at an earlier point of the train, or have been deferred till that train had been extended much further. Instead of having been busily employed in this kind of thinking, for perhaps many hours, a man might possibly as well have been sleeping all the time; since the single thought which is now to determine his conduct, might have happened to be the first thought that occurred to him on awaking. It only *happens* to occur to him now; it does not follow from what he has been thinking these hours; at least, he cannot prove that some other thought might not just as appropriately have come in its place at the end, and to make an end, of this long series. It is easy to see how feeble that determination is likely to be, which is formed on so narrow a ground as the last accidental idea that comes into the mind, or on so loose a ground as this crude uncombined assemblage of ideas. Indeed it is difficult to form a determination at all on such slight ground. A man delays, and waits for some more satisfactory thought to occur to him; and perhaps he has not waited long, before an idea arises in his mind of a quite contrary tendency to the last. As this additional idea is not, more than that which preceded it, the result of any process of reasoning, nor brings with it any arguments, it may be expected to give place soon to another, and still another; and they are all in succession of equal authority, that is properly of none. If at last an idea occurs to him which seems of considerable authority, he may here make a stand, and adopt his resolution, with firmness, as he thinks, and commence the execution. But still, if he cannot see *whence* the principle which has determined him derives its authority—on what it holds for that authority—his resolution is likely to prove treacherous and evanescent in any serious trial. A principle so little verified by sound reasoning, is not terra firma for a man to trust himself upon; it is only as a slight incrustation on a yielding element; it is like the sand compacted into a thin surface on the lake Serbonis, which broke away under the unfortunate army which had begun to advance on it, mistaking it for solid ground.—These remarks may seem to refer only to a *single instance* of deliberation; but they are equally applicable to all the deliberations and undertakings of a man's life; the same connected manner of thinking, which is so necessary to give firmness of determination and of conduct in a particular instance, will, if habitual, greatly contribute to form a decisive character.

Not only should thinking be thus reduced, by a strong and patient discipline, to a train or process, in which all the parts at once depend upon and support one another, but also this train should be followed on to a full conclusion. It should be held as a law generally in force, that the question must be disposed of before it is let alone. The mind may carry on this accurate process to some length, and then stop through indolence, or start away through levity; but it can never possess that rational confidence in its opinions which is requisite to the character in question, till it is conscious of acquiring them from an exercise of thought continued on to its result. The habit of thinking thus completely is indispensable to the general character of decision; and in any particular instance, it is found that short pieces of courses of reasoning, though correct as far as they go, are inadequate to make a man master of the immediate concern. They are besides of little value for aid to future thinking; because from being left thus incomplete they are but slightly retained by the mind, and soon sink away; in the same manner as the walls of a structure left unfinished speedily moulder.

After these remarks, I should take occasion to observe, that a vigorous exercise of thought may sometimes for a while seem to increase the difficulty of decision, by discovering a great number of unthought-of reasons for a measure and against it, so that the most discriminating mind may, during a short space, find itself in the state of the magnetic needle under the equator. But no case in the world can really have a perfect equality of opposite reasons; nor will it long appear to have it, in the estimate of a clear and well-disciplined intellect, which after some time will ascertain, though the difference is small, which side of the question has ten, and which has but nine. At any rate this is the mind to come nearest in the approximation.

Another thing that would powerfully assist toward complete decision, both in the particular instance, and in the general spirit of the character, is for a man to place himself in a situation analogous to that in which Cæsar placed his soldiers, when he burnt the ships which brought them to land. If his judgment is *really* decided, let him commit himself irretrievably, by doing something which shall oblige him to do more, which shall lay on him the necessity of doing all. If a man resolves as a general intention to be a philanthropist, I would say to him, Form some actual plan of philanthropy, and begin the execution of it to-morrow, (if I may not say *to-day*,) so explicitly that you cannot relinquish it without becoming degraded even in your own estimation. If a man would be a hero, let him, if it be possible to find a good cause in arms, go presently to the camp. If a man is desirous of a travelling adventure through distant countries, and deliberately approves both his purpose and his scheme, let him actually prepare to set off. Let him not still dwell, in imagination, on mountains, rivers, and temples; but give directions about his remittances, his personal equipments, or the carriage, or the vessel, in which he is to go. Ledyard surprised the official person who asked him how soon he could be ready to set off for the interior of Africa, by replying promptly and firmly, "To-morrow."

Again, it is highly conducive to a manly firmness, that the interests in which it is exerted should be of a dignified order, so as to give the passions an ample scope, and a noble object. The degradation they suffer in being devoted to mean and trivial pursuits, often perceived to be such in spite of every fallacy of the imagination, would in general, I should think, also debilitate their energy, and therefore preclude strength of character, to which nothing can be more adverse, than to have the fire of the passions damped by the mortification of feeling contempt for the object, as often as its meanness is betrayed by failure of the delusion which invests it.

And finally, I would repeat that one should think a man's own conscientious approbation of his conduct must be of vast importance to his decision in the outset, and his persevering constancy; and I would attribute it to defect of memory that a greater proportion of the examples, introduced for illustration in this essay, do not exhibit goodness in union with the moral and intellectual power so conspicuous in the quality described. Certainly a bright constellation of such examples might be displayed; yet it is the mortifying truth that much the greater number of men pre-eminent for decision, have been such as could not have their own serious approbation, except through an utter perversion of judgment or abolition of conscience. And it is melancholy to contemplate beings represented in our imagination as of adequate power, (when they possessed great external means to give effect to the force of their minds,) for the grandest utility, for vindicating each good cause which has languished in a world adverse to all goodness, and for intimidating the collective vices of a nation or an age—to contemplate such beings as becoming them--selves the mighty exemplars, giants, and champions of those vices; and it is fearful to follow them in thought, from this region, of which not all the powers and difficulties and inhabitants together could have subdued their adamantine resolution, to the Supreme Tribunal where that resolution must tremble and melt away.

ESSAY III.

ON THE APPLICATION OF THE EPITHET ROMANTIC.

LETTER I.

MY DEAR FRIEND,

A THOUGHTFUL judge of sentiments, books, and men, will often find reason to regret that the language of censure is so easy and so undefined. It costs no labour, and needs no intellect, to pronounce the words, foolish, stupid, dull, odious, absurd, ridiculous. The weakest or most uncultivated mind may therefore gratify its vanity, laziness, and malice, all at once, by a prompt application of vague condemnatory words, where a wise and liberal man would not feel himself warranted to pronounce without the most deliberate consideration, and where such consideration might perhaps result in applause. Thus excellent performances, in the department of thinking or of action, might be consigned to contempt, if there were no better judges, on the authority of those who could not so much as understand them. A man who wishes some decency and sense to prevail in the circulation of opinions, will do well, when he hears these decisions of ignorant arrogance, to call for a precise explication of the manner in which the terms of the verdict apply to the subject.

There is a competent number of words for this use of cheap censure; but though a man doubts not he is giving a tolerable proof of sagacity in the confident readiness to condemn, even with this impotence of language, he may however have an irksome consciousness that there is wanting to him a certain dexterity of biting expression that would do more mischief than the words dull, stupid, and ridiculous, which he is repeating many times to compensate for the incapacity of hitting off the right thing at once. These vague epithets describe nothing, discriminate nothing; they express no species, are as applicable to ten thousand things as to this one, and he has before employed them on a numberless diversity of subjects. He has a fretted feeling of this their inefficiency; and can perceive that censure or contempt has the smartest effect, when its expressions have a special cast which fits them more peculiarly to the present subject than to another; and he is therefore secretly dissatisfied in uttering the expressions which say "about it and about it," but do not say the thing itself; which showing his good will betray his deficient power. He wants words and phrases which would make the edge of his clumsy meaning fall just where it ought. Yes, he wants words; for his meaning is sharp, he knows, if only the words would come.

Discriminative censure must be conveyed, either by a marked expression of thought in a sentence, or by an epithet or other term so specifically appropriate, that the single word is sufficient to fix the condemnation by the mere precision with which it describes. But as the censurer perhaps cannot succeed in either of these ways, he is willing to seek some other resource. And he may often find it in cant terms, which have a more spiteful force, and seem to have more particularity of meaning, than plain common words, while yet needing no shrewdness for their application. Each of these is supposed to denominate some one class or character of scorned or reprobated things, but so little defines it, that dull malice may venture to assign to the class any thing which it would desire to throw under the odium of the denomination. Such words serve for a mode of collective execution, somewhat like the vessels which, in a season of outrage in a neighbouring country, received a promiscuous crowd of reputed criminals, of unexamined and dubious similarity, and were then sunk in the flood. You cannot wonder that such compendious words of decision, which can give quick vent to crude impatient censure, emit plenty of antipathy in a few syllables, and save the condemner the difficulty of telling exactly what he wants to mean, should have had an extensive circulation.

Puritan was, doubtless, welcomed as a term most luckily invented or revived, when it began to be applied in contempt to a class of men of whom the world was not worthy. Its odd peculiarity gave it almost such an advantage as that of a proper name among the lumber of common words by which they were described and reviled; while yet it meant any thing, every thing, which the vain world disliked in the devout and conscientious character. To the more sluggish it saved, and to the more loquacious it relieved, the labour of endlessly repeating " demure rogues," " sanctimonious pretenders," " formal hypocrites."

The abusive faculty of this word has long been extinct, and left it to become a grave and almost venerable term in history; but some word of a similar cast was indispensably necessary to the vulgar of both kinds. The vain and malignant spirit which had decried the elevated piety of the Puritans, sought about (as Milton describes the wicked one in Paradise) for some convenient form in which it might again come forth to hiss at zealous Christianity; and in another lucky moment fell on the term *Methodist.* If there is no *sense* in the word, as now applied, there seems however to be a great deal of aptitude and execution. It has the advantage of being comprehensive as a general denomination, and yet opprobrious as a special badge, for every thing that ignorance and folly may mistake for fanaticism, or that malice may wilfully assign to it. Whenever a formalist feels it his duty to sneer at those operations of religion on the passions, by which he has never been disturbed, he has only to call them *methodistical;* and though the word be both so trite and so vague, he feels as if he had uttered a good pungent thing. There is a satiric smartness in the word, though there be none in the man. In default of keen faculty in the mind, it is delightful thus to find something that will do as well, ready bottled up in odd terms. It is not less convenient to a profligate, or a coxcomb, whose propriety of character is to be supported by laughing indiscriminately at religion in every form; the one, to evince that his courage is not sapped by conscience, the other, to make the best advantage of his instinct of catching at impiety as a compensative substitute for sense. The word *Methodism* so readily sets aside all religion as superstitious folly, that they pronounce it with an air as if no more needed to be said. Such terms have a pleasant facility of throwing away the matter in question to scorn, without any trouble of making a definite intelligible charge of extravagance or delusion, and attempting to prove it.

In politics, *Jacobinism* has, of late years, been the brand by which all sentiments referring to the principles of liberty, in a way to censure the measures of the ascendent party in the State, have been sentenced to execration. What a quantity of noisy zeal would have been quashed in dead silence, if it had been possible to enforce the substitution of statements and definitions for this vulgar, senseless, but most efficacious term of reproach! What a number of persons have vented the superabundance of their loyalty, or their rancour, by means of this and two or three similar words, who, if by some sudden lapse of memory they had lost these two or three words, and a few names of persons, would have looked round with an idiotic vacancy, totally at a loss what was the *subject* of their anger or their approbation. One may here catch a glimpse of the policy of men of a superior class, in employing these terms as much as the vulgar, in order to keep them in active currency. If a rude populace, whose understandings they despise, and do not wish to improve, could not be excited and kept up to loyal animosity, but by means of a clear comprehension of what they were to oppose, and of the reasons why, a political party would have but feeble hold on popular zeal, and might vociferate, and intrigue, and fret itself to nothing. But if a single word, devised in hatred and defamation of political liberty, can be made the symbol of all that is absurd and execrable, so that the very sound of it shall irritate the passions of this ignorant and scorned multitude, as dogs have been taught to bark at the name of a neighbouring tyrant, it is a commodious expedient for rendering these passions available and subservient to the interests of those who despise, while they cajole, their duped auxiliaries. The popular passions are the imps and demons of the political conjuror, and he can raise them, as other conjurors affect to do theirs, by terms of gibberish.*

* It is curious that, within no long time after this was first printed, the terms *jacobin* and *jacobinism* became completely worn out and

The epithet *romantic* has obviously no similarity to these words in its coinage, but it is considerably like them in the mode and effect of its application. For having partly quitted the rank of plain epithets, it has become a convenient exploding word, of more special deriding significance than the other words of its order, such as wild, extravagant, visionary. It is a standard expression of contemptuous despatch, which you have often heard pronounced with a very self-complacent air, that said, "How much wiser I am than some people," by the indolent and inanimate on what they would not acknowledge practicable, by the apes of prudence on what they accounted foolishly adventurous, and by the slaves of custom on what startled them as singular. The class of absurdities which it denominates is left so undefined, that all the views and sentiments which a narrow cold mind could not like or understand in an ample and fervid one, might be referred thither; and yet the word *seems*, or assumes, to discriminate their character so conclusively as to put them out of argument. With this cast of sapience and vacancy of sense, it is allowed to depreciate without being acountable; it has the license of a parrot, to call names without being taxed with insolence. And when any sentiments are decisively stigmatized with this denomination, it would require considerable courage to attempt their rescue and defence; since the imputation which the epithet fixes on them will pass upon the advocate; and he may expect to be himself enrolled among the heroes of whom Don Quixote is from time immemorial the commander-in-chief. At least he may be assigned to that class which occupies a dubious frontier space between the rational and the insane.

---

obsolete. It is not worth a guess how long the term *radical*, to which the duty of the defunct ones was transferred, may continue of any service against the doctrines and persons of reformists.

If, however, the suggestions and sketches which I had endeavoured to exhibit as interesting and practicable, were attempted to be turned into vanity and "thin air" by the enunciation of this epithet, I would say, Pray now what do you mean by *romantic?* Have you, as you pronounce it, any precise conception in your mind, which you can give in some other words, and then distinctly fix the charge? Or is this a word, which because it is often used in some such way as you now use it, may be left to tell its own meaning better than the speaker knows how to explain it? Or perhaps you mean, that the notions which I am expressing recall to your mind, as kindred ideas, the fantastic images of Romance; and that you cannot help thinking of enchanted castles, encounters with giants, solemn exorcisms, fortunate surprises, knights and wizards. You cannot exactly distinguish what the absurdity in my notions *is*, but you fancy what it is *like*. You therefore condemn it, not by defining its nature and exposing its irrationality, but by applying an epithet which arbitrarily assigns it to a class of things of which the absurdity stands notorious and unquestioned: for evidently the epithet should signify a resemblance to what is the prominent folly in the works of romance. Well then, take advantage of this resemblance, to bring your censure into something of a definite form. Delineate precisely the chief features of the absurdity of the works of romance, and then show how the same characteristics are flagrant on my notions or schemes. I will then renounce at once all my visionary follies, and be henceforward at least a very sober, if I cannot be a very rational man.

The great general characteristic of those works has been the ascendency of imagination over judgment. And the description is correct as applied to the books however well endowed with intellect the authors or them might be. If they chose, for their own and others' amusement, to dismiss a sound judgment awhile from its office, to stimulate their imagination to the wildest extravagances, and to depicture the fantastic career in writing, the book might be partly the same thing as if produced by a mind in which sound judgment had no place; it would exhibit imagination *actually* ascendent by the writer's voluntary indulgence. though not *necessarily* so by the constitution of his mind. It was a different case, if a writer kept his judgment active amidst these very extravagances, with the intention of shaping and directing them to some particular end, of satire or sober truth. But however, the romances of the ages of chivalry and the preceding times were composed under neither of these intellectual conditions. They were not the productions either of men who, possessing a sound judgment, chose formally to suspend its exercise, in order to riot awhile in scenes of extravagant fancy, only keeping that judgment so far awake as to retain a continual consciousness in what degree they *were* extravagant; or of men designing to give effect to truth or malice under the disguise of a fantastic exhibition. It is evident that the authors were under the real ascendency of imagination; so that, though they must at times have been conscious of committing great excesses, yet they were on the whole wonderfully little sensible of the enormous extravagance of their fictions. They could drive on their career through monstrous absurdities of description and narration, without, apparently, any check from a sense of inconsistency, improbability, or impossibility; and with an air as if they really reckoned on being taken for the veritable describers of something that could exist or happen within the mundane system And the general state of intellect of the age in which they lived seems to have been well fitted to allow them the utmost license. The irrationality of the romancers, and of the age, provoked the observing and powerful mind of Cervantes to expose it by means of a parallel and still more extravagant representation of the prevalence of imagination over reason, drawn in a ludicrous form, by which he rendered the folly palpable even to the sense of that age. From that time the delirium abated; the works which inspirited its ravings have been blown away beyond the knowledge and curiosity of any but bibliomaniacs; and the fabrication of such is gone among the lost branches of manufacturing art.

Yet romance was in some form to be retained, as indispensable to the craving of the human mind for something more vivid, more elated, more wonderful, than the plain realities of life; as a kind of mental balloon, for mounting into the air from the ground of ordinary experience. To afford this extra-rational kind of luxury, it was requisite that the fictions should still partake, in a *limited degree*, of the quality of the earlier romance. The writers were not to be the *dupes* of wild fancy; they were not to feign marvels in such a manner as if they knew no better; they were not wholly to lose sight of the actual system of things, but to keep within *some* measures of relation and proportion to it; and yet they were required to disregard the strict laws of verisimilitude in shaping their inventions, and to magnify and diversify them with an indulgence of fancy very considerably beyond the bounds of probability. Without this their fictions would have lost what was regarded as the essential quality of romance.

If, therefore, the epithet Romantic, as now employed for description and censure of character, sentiments, and schemes, is to be understood as expressive of the quality which is characteristic of that class of fictions it imputes, in substance, a great excess of imagination in proportion to judgment; and it imputes, in particulars, such errors as naturally result from that excess. —It may be worth while to look for some of the practical exemplifications of this unfortunate disproportion between these two powers of the mind.

It should first be noted that a defective judgment is not necessarily accompanied by any thing in the least romantic in disposition, since the imagination may be as inert as the judgment is weak; and this double and equal deficiency produces mere dulness. But it is obvious that a weak judgment may be associated with an active strength of that faculty which is of such lively power even in childhood, in dreams, and in the state of insanity.

Again, there may be an intellect not *positively* feeble (supposing it estimated separately from the other power) yet practically reduced to debility by a disproportionate imagination, which continually invades its sphere, and takes every thing out of its hands. And then the case is made worse by the unfortunate circumstance, that the exercise of the faculty which should be repressed, is incomparably more easy and delightful, than of that which should be promoted. Indeed the term *exercise* is hardly applicable to the activity of a faculty which can be active without effort, which is so far from needing to be stimulated to its works of magic, that it often scorns the most serious injunctions to forbear. It is not exercise, but indulgence; and even minds possessing much of the power of understanding, may be little disposed to undergo the labour of it, when amidst the ease of the deepest indolence they can revel in the activity of a more animating employment. Imagination may be indulged till it usurp an entire ascendency over the mind, and then every subject presented to that mind will be taken under the action of imagination, instead of understanding; imagination will throw its colours where the intellectual faculty ought to draw its lines; will accumulate metaphors where reason ought to deduce arguments; images will take the place of thoughts, and scenes of disquisitions. The whole mind may become at length something like a hemisphere of cloud-scenery, filled with an ever-moving train of changing melting forms, of every colour, mingled with rainbows, meteors, and an occasional gleam of pure sunlight, all vanishing away, the mental like this natural imagery, when its hour is up, without leaving any thing behind but the wish to recover the vision. And yet, the while, this series of visions may be mistaken for operations of thought, and each cloudy image be admitted in the place of a proposition or a reason; or it may even be mistaken for something sublimer than thinking. The influence of this habit of dwelling on the beautiful fallacious forms of imagination, will accompany the mind into the most serious speculations, or rather musings, on the real world, and what is to be done in it, and expected; as the image from looking at any dazzling object still appears before the eye wherever it turns. The vulgar materials that constitute the actual economy of the world, will rise up to sight in fictitious forms, which the mind cannot disenchant into plain reality; which indeed it may hardly suspect of being illusory; and would not be very desirous to reduce to the proof if it did. For such a mind is not disposed to examine, with any severity of inspection, the real condition of things. It is content with ignorance, because environed with something far more delicious than such knowledge, in the paradise which imagination creates. In that paradise it walks delighted, till some imperious circumstance of real life call it thence, and gladly escapes thither again as soon as the cause of the avocation can be got rid of. There, every thing is beautiful and noble as could be desired to form the residence of angels. If a tenth part of the felicities that have been enjoyed, the great actions that have been performed, the beneficent institutions that have been established, and the beautiful objects that have been seen, in that happy region, could have been imported into this terrestrial place—what a delightful thing, my dear friend, it would have been each morning to awake and look on such a world once more.

It is not strange that a faculty, of which the exercise is so easy and bewitching, and the scope infinite, should obtain a predominance over judgment, especially in young persons, and in such as may have been brought up, like Rasselas and his companions, in great seclusion from the sight and experience of the world. Indeed, a considerable vigour of imagination, though it be at the expense of a frequent predominance over juvenile understanding, seems necessary, in early life, to cause a generous expansion of the passions, by giving the most lively aspect to the objects which must attract them in order to draw forth into activity the faculties of our nature. It may also contribute to prepare the mind for the exercise of that faith which converses with things unseen, but converses with them through the medium of those ideal forms in which imagination presents them, and in which only a strong imagination can present them impressively.* And I should deem it the indication of a character not destined to excel in

---

* The Divine Being is the only one of these objects which a Christian would wish it possible to contemplate without the aid of imagination; and every reflective man has felt how difficult it is to apprehend even this Object without the intervention of an image. In

the liberal, the energetic, or the devout qualities, if I observed in the youthful age a close confinement of thought to bare truth and minute accuracy, with an entire aversion to the splendours, amplifications, and excursions of fancy. The opinion is warranted by instances of persons so distinguished in youth, who have become subsequently very intelligent indeed, in a certain way, but dry, cold, precise, devoted to detail, and incapable of being carried away one moment by any inspiration of the beautiful or the sublime. They seem to have only the bare intellectual mechanism of the human mind, without the addition of what is to give it life and sentiment. They give one an impression analogous to that of the leafless trees observed in winter, admirable for the distinct exhibition of their branches and minute ramifications so clearly defined on the sky, but destitute of all the green soft luxury of foliage which is requisite to make a perfect tree. And the affections which may exist in such minds seem to have a bleak abode, somewhat like those bare deserted nests which you have often seen in such trees.

If, indeed, the signs of this exclusive understanding indicated also such an extraordinary vigour of the faculty, as to promise a very great mathematician or metaphysician, one would perhaps be content to forego some of the properties which form a complete mind, for the sake of this pre-eminence of one of its endowments; even though the person were to be so defective in sentiment and fancy, that, as the story goes of an eminent mathematician, he could read through a most animated and splendid epic poem, and on being asked

thinking of the transactions and personages of history, the final events of time foretold by prophecy, the state of good men in another world, the superior ranks of intelligent agents, &c. he has often had occasion to wish his imagination much more vivid.

what he thought of it, gravely reply, "What does it prove?" But the want of imagination is never an evidence, and perhaps but rarely a concomitant, of superior understanding.

Imagination may be allowed the ascendency in early youth; the case should be reversed in mature life; and if it is not, a man may consider his mind either as not the most happily constructed, or as unwisely disciplined. The latter indeed is probably true in every such instance

LETTER II.

The ascendency of imagination operates in various modes; I will endeavour to distinguish those which may justly be called romantic.

The extravagance of imagination in romance has very much consisted in the display of a destiny and course of life totally unlike the common condition of mankind. And you may have observed in living individuals, that one of the effects sometimes produced by the predominance of this faculty is, a persuasion in a person's own mind that he is born to some peculiar and extraordinary destiny, while yet there are no extraordinary indications in the person or his circumstances. There was something rational in the early presentiment which some distinguished men have entertained of their future career. When a celebrated general of the present times exclaimed, after performing the common military exercise, as one of a company of juvenile volunteers, "I shall be a commander-in-chief,"* a sagacious observer of the signs of talents yet but partially developed, might have thought it indeed a

* Related of Moreau.

rather sanguine but probably not a quite absurd anticipation. An elder and intelligent associate of Milton's youth might without much difficulty have believed himself listening to an oracle, when a spirit which was shaping in such gigantic proportions avowed to him a confidence, of being destined to produce a work which should distinguish the nation and the age. The opening of uncommon faculties may be sometimes inspirited by such anticipations; which the young genius may be allowed to express, perhaps as a stimulus encouraged to indulge. But in most instances these magnificent presumptions form, in the observer's eye, a ludicrous contrast with the situation and apparent abilities of the person who entertains them. And in the event, how few such anticipations have been proved the genuine promptings of an extraordinary mind.

The visionary presumption of a peculiar destiny is entertained in more forms than that which implies a confidence of possessing uncommon talent. It is often the flattering self-assurance simply of a life of singular felicity. The captive of fancy fondly imagines his prospect of life as a delicious vale, where from each side every stream of pleasure is to flow down to his feet; and while it cannot but be seen that innumerable evils do harass other human beings, some mighty spell is to protect him against them all. He takes no deliberate account of what is inevitable in the lot of humanity, of the sober probabilities of his own situation, or of any principles in the constitution of his mind which are perhaps very exactly calculated to frustrate the anticipation and the scheme of happiness.

If this excessive imagination is combined with tendencies to affection, it makes a person *sentimentally* romantic. With a great, and what might, in a mind of finer elements, be a just contempt of the ordinary rate of attachments, both in friendship and love, he indulges a most assured confidence that his peculiar lot is to realize all the wonders of generous, virtuous, noble, unalienable friendship, or of enraptured, uninterrupted, and unextinguishable love, that the inebriation of fiction and poetry ever sung; while perhaps a shrewd indifferent observer can descry nothing in the horoscope, or the character, or the actual circumstances of the man, or in the qualities of the human creatures that he adores, or in the nature of his devotion, to promise an elevation or permanence of felicity beyond the destiny of common mortals.

If a passion for variety and novelty accompanies this extravagant imagination, it will exclude from its bold sketches of future life every thing like confined regularity, and common plodding occupations. It will suggest that *I* was born for an adventurer, whose story will one day be a wonder of the world. Perhaps I am to be an universal traveller; and there is not on the globe a grand city, or ruin, or volcano, or cataract, but I must see it. Debility of constitution, deficiency of means, innumerable perils, unknown languages, oppressive toils, extinguished curiosity, worn out fortitude, failing health, and the shortness of life, are very possibly all left out of the account.

If there is in the disposition a love of what is called glory, and an idolatry of those capacious and intrepid spirits one of which has often, in a portentous crisis, decided, by an admirable series of exertions, or by one grand exploit of intelligence and valour, the destiny of armies and of empires, a predominant imagination may be led to revel amidst the splendours of military achievement, and to flatter the man that he too is to be a hero, a great commander.

When a mind under this influence recurs to precedents as a foundation and a warrant of its expectations, they are never the usual, but always the extraordinary examples, that are contemplated. An observer of the ordinary instances of friendship is perhaps heard to assert that the sentiment is sufficiently languid in general to admit of an almost unqualified self-interest, of absence without pain, and of ultimate indifference. Well, so let it be; Damon and Pythias were friends of a different order, and *our* friendship is to be like theirs. Or if the subject of musing and hope is the union in which love commonly results, it may be true and obvious enough that the generality of instances would not seem to tell of more than a mediocrity of happiness in this relation ; but a visionary person does not live within the same world with these examples. The few instances which have been recorded of tender and never-dying enthusiasm, together with the numerous ones which romance and poetry have created, form the class to which he belongs, and from whose enchanting history, excepting their misfortunes, he reasons to his own future experience. So too the man, whose fancy anticipates political or martial distinction, allows his thoughts to revert continually to those names which a rare conjunction of talents and circumstances has elevated into fame; forgetting that many thousands of men of great ability have died in at least comparative obscurity, for want of situations in which to display themselves; and never suspecting it possible that his own abilities are not competent to any thing great, if some extraordinary event were just now to place him in the most opportune concurrence of circumstances. That there has been one very signal man to a million, more avails to the presumption that he shall be a signal man, than there having been a million to one signal man, infers a probability of his remaining one of the multitude.

You will generally observe, that persons thus self-appointed, of either sex, to be exceptions to the usual lot of humanity, endeavour at a kind of consistency of character, by a great aversion to the common modes of action and language, and a habitual affectation of something extraordinary. They will perhaps disdain regular hours, punctuality to engagements, usual dresses, a homely diction, and common forms of transacting business; this you are to regard as the impulse of a spirit whose high vocation authorizes it to renounce all signs of relation to vulgar minds.

The epithet romantic then may be justly applied to those presumptions (if entertained after the childish or very youthful age) of a peculiarly happy or important destiny in life, which are not clearly founded on certain palpable distinctions of character or situation, or which greatly exceed the sober prognostics afforded by those distinctions.—It should be observed here that *wishes* merely do not constitute a character romantic. A person may sometimes let his mind wander into vain wishes for all the fine things on earth, and yet be too sober to expect any of them. In this case however he will often check and reproach himself for the folly of indulging in such mental dissoluteness.

The absurdity of such anticipations consists simply in the improbability of their being realized, and not in their objects being uncongenial with the human mind; but another effect of the predominance of imagination may be a disposition to form schemes or indulge expectations essentially incongruous with the nature of man. Perhaps however you will say, What is that nature? Is it not a mere passive thing, variable almost to infinity, according to climate, to institutions, and to the different ages of time? Even taking it in a civilized state, what relation is there between such a four of human nature as that displayed at Sparta, and, for instance, the modern society denominated Quakers, or the Moravian Fraternity? And how can we ascertain what is congenial with it or not, unless itself were first ascertained? Allow me to say, that I speak of human nature in its most general principles only, as social, self-interested, inclined to the wrong, slow to improve, passing through several states of capacity and feeling in the successive periods of life, and the few other such permanent distinctions. Any of these distinctions may vanish from the sight of a visionary mind, while forming, for itself, or for others, such schemes as could have sprung only from an imagination become wayward through its uncontrolled power, and its victory over sober reason. I remember, for example, a person, very young I confess, who was so enchanted with the stories of Gregory Lopez, and one or two more pious hermits, as almost to form the resolution to betake himself to some wilderness and live as Gregory did. At any time, the very word *hermit* was enough to transport him, like the witch's broomstick, to the solitary hut, which was delightfully surrounded by shady solemn groves, mossy rocks, crystal streams, and gardens of radishes. While this fancy lasted, he forgot the most obvious of all facts, that man is not made for habitual solitude, nor can endure it without misery, except when transformed into a genuine superstitious ascetic;—questionable whether even then.*

Contrary to human nature, is the proper description

* Lopez indeed was often visited by pious persons who sought his instructions; this was a great modification of the loneliness, and of the trial involved in enduring it; but my hermit was fond of the idea of an uninhabited island, or of a wilderness so deep that these good people would not have been able to come at him, without a more formidable pilgrimage than was ever yet made for the sake of obtaining instruction.

of these theories of education, and those flatteries of parental hope, which presume that young people in general may be matured to eminent wisdom, and adorned with the universality of noble attainments, by the period at which in fact the intellectual faculty is but beginning to operate with any thing like clearness and sustained force. Because some individuals, remarkable exceptions to the natural character of youth, have in their very childhood advanced beyond the youthful giddiness, and debility of reason, and have displayed, at the age perhaps of twenty, a wonderful assemblage of all the strong and all the graceful endowments, it therefore only needs a proper system of education to make other young people, (at least those of *my* family, the parent thinks,) be no longer what nature has always made youth to be. Let this be adopted, and we shall see multitudes at that age possessing the judgment of sages, or the diversified acquirements and graces of all-accomplished gentlemen and ladies. And what, pray, are the beings which are to become, by the discipline of ten or a dozen years, such finished examples of various excellence? Not, surely, these boys here, that love nothing so much as tops, marbles and petty mischief— and those girls, that have yet attained but few ideas beyond the dressing of dolls? Yes, even these!

The same charge of being unadapted to man, falls on the speculations of those philosophers and philanthropists, who have eloquently displayed the happiness, and asserted the practicability, of something near an equality of property and modes of life throughout society. Those who really anticipated or projected the practical trial of the system, must have forgotten on what planet those apartments were built, or those arbours were growing, in which they were favoured with such visions. For in these visions they beheld the ambition of one part of the inhabitants, the craft or audacity of another, the avarice of another, the stupidity or indolence of another, and the selfishness of almost all, as mere adventitious faults, super-induced on the character of the species, and instantly flying off at the approach of better institutions, which shall prove, to the confusion of all the calumniators of human nature, that nothing is so congenial to it as industry, moderation, and disinterestedness. It is at the same time but just to acknowledge, that many of them have admitted the necessity of such a grand transformation as to make man another being *previously* to the adoption of the system. This is all very well: when the proper race of *men* shall come from Utopia, the system and polity may very properly come along with them; or these sketches of it, prepared for them by us, may be carefully preserved here, in volumes more precious than those of the Sibyls, against their arrival. Till then, the sober observers of the human character will read these beautiful theories as romances, offering the fairest game for sarcasm in their splenetic hours, when they are disgusted with human nature, and infusing melancholy in their benevolent ones, when they look on it with a commiserating and almost desponding sentiment.

The character of the age of chivalry presents itself conspicuously among this class of illustrations. One of its most prominent distinctions was, an immense incongruity with the simplest principles of human nature. For instance, in the concern of love: a generous young man became attached to an interesting young woman—interesting as he believed, from having once seen her: for probably he never heard her speak. His heart would naturally prompt him to seek access to the object whose society, it told him, would make him happy; and if in a great measure debarred from that society, he would surrender himself to the melting mood of his passion, in the musings of pensive retirement. But this was not the way. He must exile himself for successive years from her society and vicinity, and every soft indulgence of feeling, and rush boldly into all sorts of hardships and perils, deeming no misfortune so great as not to find constant occasions of hazarding his life among the roughest foes, or, if he could find or fancy them, the strangest monsters; and all this, not as the alleviation of despair, but as the courtship of hope. And when he was at length betrayed to flatter himself that such a probation, through every kind of patience and danger, might entitle him to throw his trophies and himself at her imperial feet, it was very possible she might be affronted at his having presumed to be still alive. It is unnecessary to refer to the other parts of the institution of chivalry, the whole system of which would seem more adapted to any race of beings exhibited in the Arabian Nights, or to any still wilder creation of fancy, than to a community of creatures appointed to live by cultivating the soil, anxious to avoid pain and trouble, seeking the reciprocation of affection on the easiest terms, and nearest to happiness in regular pursuits and quiet domestic life.

One cannot help reflecting here, how amazingly accommodating this human nature has been to all institutions but wise and good ones; insomuch that an order of life and manners conceived in the wildest deviation from all plain sense and native instinct, could be practically adopted, by some of those who had rank and courage enough, and adored and envied by the rest of mankind. Still, the genuine tendencies of nature have survived the strange but transient sophistications of time, and remain the same after the age of chivalry is gone far toward that oblivion, to which you will not fail to wish that many other institutions might speedily follow it. Forgive the prolixity of these illustrations intended to show, that schemes and speculations respecting the interests either of an individual or of society, which are inconsistent with the natural constitution of man, may, except where it should be reasonable to expect some supernatural intervention, be denominated romantic.

The tendency to this species of romance, may be caused, or very greatly promoted, by an exclusive taste for what is *grand*, a disease with which some few minds are affected. They have no pleasure in contemplating the system of things as the Créator has ordered it, a combination of great and little, in which the great is much more dependent on the little, than the little on the great. They cut out the grand objects, to dispose them into a world of their own. All the images in their intellectual scene must be colossal and mountainous. They are constantly seeking what is animated into heroics, what is expanded into immensity, what is elevated above the stars. But for great empires, great battles, great enterprises, great convulsions, great geniuses, great temples, great rivers, there would be nothing worth naming in this part of the creation.* All that belongs to connexion, gradation, harmony, regularity, and utility, is thrown out of sight behind these forms of vastness. The influence of this exclusive taste will reach into the system of projects and expectations. The man will wish to summon the world to throw aside its tame accustomed pursuits, and adopt at once more magnificent views and objects, and will be indignant at mankind that they

---

* Just as, to employ a humble comparison, a votary of fashion, after visiting a crowded public place which happened at that time not to be graced by the presence of many people of consequence, tells you, with an affected tone, " There was not a creature there."

cannot or will not be sublime. Impatient of little mean and slow processes, he will wish for violent transitions and entirely new institutions. He will perhaps determine to set men the example of performing something great. in some ill-judged sanguine project in which he will fail; and, after being ridiculed by society, both for the scheme and its catastrophe, may probably abandon all the activities of life, and become a misanthrope the rest of his days. At any rate, he will disdain all labour to perform well in little or moderate things, when fate has frowned on his higher ambition.

LETTER III.

One of the most obvious distinctions of the works of romance is, an utter violation of all the relations between ends and means. Sometimes such ends are proposed as seem quite dissevered from means, inasmuch as there are scarcely any supposable means on earth to accomplish them: but no matter; if we cannot ride we must swim, if we cannot swim we must fly; the object is effected by a mere poetical omnipotence that wills it. And very often practicable objects are attained by means the most fantastic, improbable, or inadequate; so that there is scarcely any resemblance between the method in which they are accomplished by the dexterity of fiction, and that which we are condemned to follow if we will attempt the same things in the actual economy of the world. Now, when you see this absurdity of imagination prevailing in the calculations of real life, you may justly apply the epithet —romantic.

Indeed a strong and habitually indulged imagination may be absorbed in the end, if it be not a concern of absolute immediate urgency, as for a while quite to forget the process of attainment. That power has incantations to dissolve the rigid laws of time and distance, and place a man in something so like the presence of his object, as to create the temporary hallucination of an ideal possession; and it is hard, when occupying the verge of Paradise, to be flung far back in order to find or make a path to it, with the slow and toilsome steps of reality. In the luxury of promising himself that what he wishes will by some means take place at some time, he forgets that he is advancing no nearer to it—except on the wise and patient calculation that he must, by the simple fact of growing older, be coming somewhat nearer to every event that is yet to happen to him. He is like a traveller, who, amidst his indolent musings in some soft bower, where he has sat down to be shaded a little while from the rays of noon, falls asleep, and dreams he is in the midst of all the endearments of home, insensible that there are many hills and dales for him yet to traverse. But the traveller will awake; so too will our other dreamer; and if he has the smallest capacity of just reflection he will regret to have wasted in reveries the time which ought to have been devoted to practical exertions.

But even though reminded of the necessity of intervening means, the man of imagination will often be tempted to violate their relation with ends, by permitting himself to dwell on those happy *casualties*, which the prolific sorcery of his mind will promptly figure to him as the very things, if they would but occur, to accomplish his wishes at once, without the toil of a sober process. If they would occur—and things as strange might and do happen: he reads in the newspapers that an estate of ten thousand per annum was lately adjudged to a man who was working on the road. He has even heard of people dreaming that in such a place something valuable was concealed; and that, on searching or digging that place, they found an old earthen pot, full of gold and silver pieces of the times of good King Charles the Martyr. Mr. B. was travelling by the mail-coach, in which he met with a most interesting young lady whom he had never seen before; they were mutually delighted, and were married in a few weeks. Mr. C., a man of great merit in obscurity, was walking across a field when Lord D., in chase of a fox, leaped over the hedge and fell off his horse into a ditch. Mr C. with the utmost alacrity and kind solicitude helped his lordship out of the ditch, and recovered for him his escaped horse. The consequence was inevitable; his lordship, superior to the pride of being mortified to have been seen in a condition so unlucky for giving the impression of nobility, commenced a friendship with Mr. C., and introduced him into honourable society and the road to fortune. A very ancient maiden lady of a large fortune happening to be embarrassed in a crowd, a young clergyman offered her his arm and politely attended her home; this attention so captivated her, that she bequeathed and soon after left him her whole estate —though she had many poor relations.

That class of fictitious works called *novels*, though much more like real life than the romances which preceded, is yet full of these lucky incidents and adventures, which are introduced as the chief means toward the ultimate success. A young man, without fortune, for instance, is precluded from making his addresses to a young female in a superior situation, whom he believes not indifferent to him, until he can approach her with such worldly advantages as it might not be imprudent or degrading for her to cast a look upon. Now how is this to be accomplished?—Why,

I suppose, by the exertion of his talents in some practicable and respectable department; and perhaps the lady, besides, will generously and spontaneously condescend to abdicate from partiality to him, some of the trappings and luxuries of rank. You really suppose this is the plan? I am sorry you have so much less genius than a novel-writer. This young man has an uncle, who has been absent many years, nobody knew where, except the young man's lucky stars. During his absence, the old uncle has made a large fortune, with which he returns to his native land, at a time most opportune for every one but a highwayman, who, attacking him in a road through a wood, is frightened away by the young hero, who happens to come there at the instant, to rescue and recognize his uncle, and to be in return recognized and made the heir to as many thousands as the lady or her family could wish. Now what is the intended impression of all this on the reader's mind? What if he certainly *have* no uncle in any foreign fortune-making country? But there are rich old gentlemen who are uncles to nobody. Is our novel-reader to reckon on it as a *likely* and a *desirable* chance, that one of these, just after returning from the Indies with a ship-load of wealth, shall be set upon by a highwayman; and to take it for certain that in that case he, the novel-reader, shall have the luck to come to the very spot in the nick of time, to send the dastard robber galloping off, to make an instant and entire seizure of the old gentleman's affections, find himself constrained to go and take a present share of the opulence, and the heirship of the whole, and have his patron to join his pleading that Amelia, or Alicia, or Cecilia, (as the case may be,) may now be willing and be permitted to favour his addresses? One's indignation is excited at the immoral tendency of such lessons to young readers, who are thus taught to undervalue and reject all sober regular plans for compassing an object, and to muse on improbabilities till they become foolish enough to expect them; thus betrayed, as an inevitable consequence, into one folly more, that of being melancholy when they find they may expect them in vain. It is unpardonable that these pretended instructors by example should thus explode the calculations and exertions of manly resolution, destroy the connexion between ends and means, and make the rewards of virtue so dependent on chance, that if the reader does not either regard the whole fable with contempt, or promise himself he shall receive the favours of fortune in some similar way, he must close the book with the conviction that he may hang or drown himself as soon as he pleases; that is to say, unless he has learnt from some other source a better morality and religion than these books will ever teach him.

Another deception in respect to means, is the facility with which fancy passes along the train of them, and reckons to their ultimate effect at a glance, without resting at the successive stages, and considering the labours and hazards of the protracted slow process from each point to the next. If a given number of years are allowed requisite for the accomplishment of an object, the romantic mind vaults from one last day of December to another, and seizes at once the whole product of all the intermediate days, without condescending to recollect that the sun never shone yet on three hundred and sixty-five days at once, and that they must be slowly told and laboured one by one. If a favourite plan is to be accomplished by means of a certain large amount of property, which is to be produced from what is at present a very small one, the calculations of a sanguine mind can change shillings into guineas, and guineas into hundreds of pounds, a thousand times faster than, in the actual experiment, those lazy shillings and guineas can be compelled to mount to these higher denominations of value. You remember the noble calculation of Alnaschar on his basket of earthenware, which was so soon to obtain him the Sultan's daughter.

Where imagination is not delusive enough to embody future casualties as effective means, it may yet represent very inadequate means as competent. In a well-balanced mind, no conception will grow into a favourite purpose, unaccompanied by a process of the judgment, deciding its practicability by an estimate of the means; in a mind under the ascendency of imagination this is a subordinate after-task. By the time that this comes to be considered, the projector is too much enamoured of an end that is deemed to be great, to abandon it because the means are suspected to be little. But then they must cease to *appear* little; for there must be an apparent proportion between the means and the end. Well, trust the whole concern to the plastic faculty, and presently every insignificant particle of instrumentality, and every petty contrivance for its management, will swell into magnitude; pigmies and Lilliputians with their tiny arrows will soon grow up into giants wielding spears; and the diffident consciousness which was at first somewhat afraid to measure the plan, as to its means of execution, against the object, will give place to a generous scorn of the timidity of doubting. The mind will most ingeniously place the apparatus between its eye and the object at a distance, and be deluded by the false position which makes the one look as large as the other.

The consideration of the deceptive calculations on the effect of insufficient means, would lead to a wide variety

of particulars; I will only touch slightly on a few
various projects of a *benevolent* order would come under
this charge. Did you ever listen to the discussion of
plans for the civilization of barbarous nations without
the intervention of conquest? I have, with the most
sceptical kind of interest.* That very many millions
of the species should form only a brutal adjunct to
civilized and enlightened man is a disasterous thing,
notwithstanding the whimsical attempts of some ingenious men to represent the state of roving savages as preferable to every other condition of life; a state for which,
no doubt, they would have been willing, if they could
have the requisite physical seasoning for it, to abandon
their fame and proud refinements. But where are the
means to reclaim these wretched beings into the civilized family of man? A few examples indeed are found
in history, of barbarous tribes being formed into well-
ordered and considerably enlightened states by one man,
who began the attempt without any power but that of
persuasion, and perhaps delusion. There are other instances, of the success obtained by a small combination
of men employing the same means; as in the great
undertaking of the Jesuits in South America. But
have not these moral phenomena been far too few to be
made a standard for the speculations of sober men? And
have they not also come to us with too little explanation
to illustrate any general principles? To me it appears
extremely difficult to comprehend how the means, recorded by historians to have been employed by some of
the unarmed civilizers, could have produced so great
an effect. In observing the half-civilized condition of
a large part of the population of these more improved
countries, and in reading what travellers describe of the

* I here place out of view that religion by which Omnipotence will
at length transform the world.

state and dispositions of the various orders of savages, it would seem a presumption unwarranted by any thing we ever saw of the powers of the human mind to suppose that any man, or any ten men now on earth, if landed and left on a savage coast, would be able to transform a number of stupid or ferocious tribes into a community of mild intelligence and regular industry. We are therefore led to believe that the few unaccountable instances conspicuous in the history of the world, of the success of one or a few men in this work, must have been the result of such a combination of favourable circumstances, cooperating with their genius and perseverance, as no other man can hope to experience. Such events seem like Joshua's arresting the sun and moon, things that have been done, but can be done no more. Pray, which of you, I should say, could expect to imitate with success, if indeed he could think it right to try, the deception of Manco Capac, and awe a wild multitude into order by something analogous to a pretended commission from the sun? What would be your first expedient in the attempt to substitute that regularity and constraint which they hate, for that lawless liberty which they love? How could you reduce them to be conscious, or incite them to be proud, of those wants, for being subject to which they would regard you as their inferiors; wants of which, unless they could comprehend the refinement, they must necessarily despise the debility? By what magic are you to render visible and palpable any part of the world of science or of abstraction, to beings who have hardly words to denominate even their sensations? And by what concentrated force of all kinds of magic together, that Egypt or Chaldea ever pretended, are you to introduce humanity and refinement among such creatures as the Northern Indians, described by Mr. Hearne?

If an animated young philanthropist still zealously maintained that it might be done, I should be amused to think how that warm iamgination would be quelled, if he were obliged to make the experiment. It is easy for him to be romantic while enlivened by the intercourse of cultivated society, while reading of the contrivances and the patience of ancient legislators, or while infected with the enthusiasm of poetry. He feels as if he could be the moral conqueror of a continent. He becomes a Hercules amidst imaginary labours; he traverses untired, while in his room, wide tracts of the wilderness; he surrounds himself with savage men, without either trembling or revolting at their aspects or fierce exclamations, or the proudly exhibited and vaunted trophies of their sanguinary exploits; he makes eloquent speeches to them, not knowing a word of their language, which language, if he did know it, he would find a wretched vehicle for the humblest of his meanings; they listen with the deepest attention, are convinced of the necessity of adopting new habits of life, and speedily soften into humanity and brighten into wisdom. Bu. he would become sober enough, if compelled to travel half a thousand miles through the desert, or over the snow, with some of these subjects of his lectures and legislation; to accompany them in a hunting excursion; to choose in a stormy night between exposure in the open air and the smoke and grossness of their cabins; to observe the intellectual faculty narrowed almost to a point, limited to a scanty number of the meanest class of ideas; to find by repeated experiments that *his* kind of ideas could neither reach their understanding nor excite their curiosity; to see the ravenous appetite of wolves succeeded for a season by a stupefaction insensible even to the few interests which kindle the ardour of a savage; to witness loathsome habits occasionally diversified by abominable ceremonies; or to be for once the spectator of some of the circumstances attendant on the wars of savages.

But there are many more familiar illustrations of the extravagant estimate of means. One is, the expectation of far too much from mere direct instruction. This is indeed so general, that it will hardly be denominated romantic, except in the most excessive instances. Observe it, however, a moment in the concern of education. Nothing seems more evident than the influence of external circumstances, distinct from the regular discipline of the parent or tutor, in forming the character of youth. Nothing again seems more evident than that direct instruction, though an useful cooperator with the influence of these circumstances when they are auspicious, is a feeble counteractor if they be malignant. And yet this mere instruction is enough, in the account of thousands of parents, to lead the youth to wisdom and happiness; even that very youth whom the united influence of almost all things else which he is exposed to see, and hear, and participate, is drawing, with the unrelaxing grasp of a fiend, to destruction.

A too sanguine opinion of the efficacy of instruction, has sometimes possessed those who teach from the pulpit. Till the dispensations of a better age shall be opened on the world, the measure of effect which may reasonably be expected from preaching, is to be determined by a view of the visible effects which are actually produced on congregations from week to week; and this view is far from flattering. One might appeal to preachers in general—What striking improvements are apparent in your societies? When you inculcate charity on the Sunday, do the misers in your congregations liberally open their chests and purses to the distressed on Monday? Might I not ask as well, whether the stones and trees really *did* move at the voice of Orpheus? After you have unveiled even the scenes of eternity to the gay and frivolous, do you find in more than some rare instances a dignified seriousness take place of their follies? What is the effect, on the splendid, sumptuous, and fashionable professors of christianity, of your inculcation (if indeed you venture it) of that solemn interdiction of their habits, " Be not conformed to this world?" Yet, notwithstanding this melancholy state of facts, some preachers, from the persuasion of a mysterious apostolic sacredness in the office, or from a vain estimate of their talents, or from mistaking the applause with which the preacher has been flattered, for the proof of a salutary effect on the minds of the hearers, or, in some instances, from a much worthier cause, the affecting influence of sacred truth on their own minds, have been inclined to anticipate striking effects from their public ministrations. Melancthon was a romantic youth when he began to preach. He expected that all must be inevitably and immediately persuaded, when they should hear what he had to tell them. But he soon discovered, as he said, that old Adam was too hard for young Melancthon. In addition to the grand fact of the depravity of the human heart, there are so many causes operating injuriously through the week on the characters of those who form a congregation, that a thoughtful man often feels an invading melancholy amidst his religious addresses, from the reflection that he is making a feeble effort against a powerful evil, a single effort against a combination of evils, a temporary and transient effort against evils of almost continual operation, and a purely intellectual effort against evils, many of which act on the senses. When the preacher considers the effect naturally resulting from the sight of so many bad examples, the communications of so many injurious acquaintance, the hearing and talking of what would be, if written, so many volumes of vanity and nonsense, the predominance of fashionable dissipation in a higher class, and of a coarser corruption in a lower; he must indeed imagine himself endowed with a super-human power of eloquence, if the instructions expressed in an hour or two on the sabbath, and soon, as he might know, forgotten by most of his hearers, are to leave in the mind something which shall be, through the week, the efficacious repellant to the contact and contamination of all these forces of mischief. But how soon he would cease to imagine such an efficacy in his exhortations, if the greater number of his hearers could sincerely and accurately tell him, toward the end of the week, in what degree these admonitions had affected and governed them, in opposition to their corrupt tendencies, their habits, and their temptations! What would be, in the five or six days, the number of the moments and the instances in which these instructions would be proved to have been effectual, compared with the whole number of moments and circumstances to which they were applicable by appropriateness of instruction and warning? How often, while hearing such a week's detail of the lives of a considerable proportion of a congregation, a man would have occasion to say, By whose instructions were these persons influenced *then*, in that neglect of devout exercises, that excess of levity, that waste of time, that avowed contempt of religion, that language of profaneness and imprecation, those contrivances of selfishness, those paroxysms of passion, that study of sensuality, or that habitual general obduracy in evil?

But the preacher to whose sanguine temperament I am reluctantly applying these cooling suggestions, may tell me, that it is not by means of any force which *he* can throw into his religious instructions, that he expects them to be efficacious; but that he believes a *divine* energy will accompany what is undoubtedly a message from heaven. I am pleased with the piety, and the sound judgment, (as I esteem it,) with which he expects the conversion of careless or hardened men from nothing *less* than an operation strictly considered as of divine power. But I would remind him, that the probability, at any given season, that such a power will intervene, must be in proportion to the frequency or infrequency with which its intervention is actually manifested in the general course of experience; that is, in proportion to the number of happy transformations of character which we see taking place under the efficacy of religious truth. He must admit this to be substantially the rule: if he require that it be modified by the consideration of promises and signs from the Supreme Power of the *near approach* of an augmented divine interference for the efficacy of religion I shall willingly admit what I can of such a reason for conceding such a modification.

Reformers in general are very apt to overrate the power of the means by which their theories are to be realized. They are for ever introducing the story of Archimedes, who was to have moved the world if he could have found any second place on which to plant his engines; and imagination discloses to moral and political projectors a cloud-built and truly extra-mundane position, which they deem to be exactly such a convenience in their department, as the mathematician, whose converse with demonstrations had saved *part* of his reason from being run away with by his fancy, confessed to be a desideratum in his. This terra firma is named the Omnipotence of Truth.

It is presumed, that truth must at length, through the indefatigable exertions of intellect, become generally victorious; and that all vice, being the result of a mistaken judgment of the nature or the means of happiness, must therefore accompany the exit of error. By the same rule it is presumed of the present times also, or at least of those immediately approaching, that in every society and every mind where truth is clearly admitted, the reforms which it dictates must substantially follow. I have the most confident faith that the prevalence of truth, making its progress by a far mightier agency than mere philosophic inquiry, is appointed to irradiate the latter ages of a dark and troubled world; and, on the strength of prophetic intimations, I anticipate its coming sooner, by at least a thousand ages, than a disciple of that philosophy which rejects revelation, as the first proud step toward the improvement of the world, is warranted, by a view of the past and present state of mankind, to predict. The assurance from the same oracle is the authority for believing that when truth shall have acquired the universal dominion over the understanding, it will evince a still nobler power in the general effect of conforming the heart and the life to its laws. But in the present state of the moral system, our expectations of the effect of truth on the far greater number of the persons who shall assent to its dictates, have no right to exceed such measures of probability as have been given by experience. It would be gratifying no doubt to believe, that the several powers in the human constitution are in such faithful combination, that to gain the judgment would be to secure the whole man. And if all history, and the memory of our own observation and experience, could be merged in Lethe, it might be believed—perhaps for two or three hours.

How could an attentive observer or reflector believe
t longer? How long would it be that a keenly self-
inspecting mind could detect no schism, none at all,
between its convictions and inclinations? And as to
others, is it not flagrantly evident that very many
persons, with a most absolute conviction, by their own
ingenuous avowal, that one certain course of action is
virtue and happiness, and another, vice and misery, do
yet habitually choose the latter? It is not improbable
that several millions of human beings are at this very
hour thus acting in violation of the laws of rectitude,
while those laws are acknowledged by them, not only
as impositions of moral authority, but as vital principles of their own true self-interest.* And do not
even the best men confess a fierce discord between the
tendencies of their imperfectly renovated nature, and
the dictates of that truth which they revere? They say
with St. Paul, " That which I do, I allow not; for what
I would, that I do not; but what I hate, that I do; to
will is present with me, but how to perform that which
is good, I find not; the good that I would, that I do

* The criminal himself has the clearest consciousness that he
violates the dictates of his judgment. How trifling is the subtilty
which affects to show that he does *not* violate them, by alleging,
that every act of choice must be preceded by a determination of the
judgment, and that therefore in choosing an evil, a man does at the
time judge it to be on some account preferable, though he may
know it to be wrong. It is not to be denied that the choice does
imply such a conclusion of the judgment. But this conclusion is
made according to a narrow and subordinate scale of estimating
good and evil, while the mind is conscious that, judging according to
a larger scale, that is, the rightfully authoritative one, the opposite
conclusion is true. It judges a thing better for immediate pleasure,
which it knows to be worse for ultimate advantage. The criminal
therefore may be correctly said to act *according* to his judgment, in
choosing it for present pleasure. But since it is the great office of
the judgment to decide what is wisest and best *on the whole*, the
man may truly be said to act *against* his judgment, who acts in
opposition to the conclusion which it forms on this greater sin.

not, and the evil which I would not, that I do." The serious self-observer recollects instances, (what a singularity of happiness if he cannot!) in which a temptation, exactly addressed to his passions or his habits, has prevailed in spite of the sternest interdict of his judgment, pronounced at the very crisis. Perhaps the most awful sanctions by which the judgment can ever enforce its authority, were distinctly brought to his view at the same moment with its dictates. In the subsequent hour he had to reflect, that the ideas of God, a future account, a world of retribution, could not prevent him from violating his conscience. That he did not at the critical moment dwell deliberately on these remonstrant ideas, in order to give them effect on his will, is nothing against my argument. It is of the very essence of the fatal disorder, that the passions will not *let* the mind strongly fix on the preventive considerations. And what greater power than this could they need to defeat the power of truth? If the passions *can* thus prevent the mind from strongly fixing on the most awful considerations when distinctly presented by truth in counteraction to temptation, they can destroy the efficacy of the truth which presents them. Truth can do no more than discriminate the good from the evil before us, enforce the inducements to choose right, and declare the consequences of our choice. When this is inefficacious, its power has failed. And no fact can be more evident than that perceptive truth, apprehended and acknowledged, often thus fails. Let even its teacher and advocate confess honestly whether he have not had to deplore numberless times the deficient efficacy of his own clearest convictions. And if we survey mankind as under an experiment relative to this point, it will be found, in instances innumerable, that to have informed and convinced a man may be but little toward emancipating him from the habits which he sincerely acknowledges to be wrong. There is then no such inviolable connexion as some men have supposed between the admission of truth, and consequent action. And therefore, most important though it is that truth be exhibited and admitted, the expectations that presume its omnipotence, without extraordinary intervention, are romantic delusion.

You will observe that in this case of trying the efficacy of the truth on others, I have supposed the great previous difficulty, of presenting it to the understanding so luminously as to impress irresistible conviction, to be already overcome; though the experimental reformer will find this introductory work such an arduous undertaking that he will be often tempted to abandon it as hopeless.

LETTER IV.

When the gloomy estimate of means and of plans for the amendment of mankind does not make an exception of the actual human administration of the religion of Christ, I am anxious not to seem to fail in justice to that religion, by which I believe that every improvement of a sublime order yet awaiting our race must be effected. I trust I do not fail; since I keep in my mind a clear distinction between christianity itself as a thing of divine origin and nature, and the administration of it by a system of merely human powers and means. These means are indeed of divine appointment, and to a certain extent are accompanied by a special divine agency. But how far this agency accompanies them is seen in the measure and limit of their success. Where *that* stands arrested, the fact itself is the proof that further than so the superior operation does not attend the human agents and means. There it stops, and leaves them to accomplish, if they can, what remains. What is it that remains? If the general transformation of mankind into such persons as could be justly deemed true disciples of Christ, were regarded as the object of his religion, how mysteriously small a part of that object has the divine agency ever yet been exerted to accomplish! And then, the awful and immense remainder evinces the inexpressible imbecility of the means, when left to be applied as a mere human administration. The manifestation of its incompetency is fearfully conspicuous in the vast majority, the numerous millions of Christendom, and the millions of even our own country, on whom this religion has no direct influence. I need not observe what numbers of these latter have heard or read the evangelic declaration thousands of times, nor how very many of them are fortified in an insensibility, on which its most momentous announcements strike as harmless as the slenderest arrows on the shield of Ajax. Probably each religious teacher can recollect, besides his general experience, very particular instances, in which he has set himself to exert the utmost force of his mind, in reasoning, illustration, and serious appeal, to impress some one important idea, on some one class of persons to whom it was most specifically applicable and needful; and has perceived the plainest indications, both at the instant and immediately after, that it was an attempt of the same kind as that of demolishing a tower by assaulting it with pebbles. Nor do I need to observe how generally, if a momentary impression be made, it is forgotten the following hour.

A man convinced of the truth and excellence of christianity, yet entertaining a more flattering notion of the reason and moral dispositions of man than any doctrine of that religion agrees to, may be very reluctant to admit that there is such a fatal disproportion between the apparatus, if I may call it so, of the christian means as left to be actuated by mere human energy, and the object which is to be attempted. But how is he to help himself? Will he reject the method of conclusion from facts, in an affair where they so peculiarly constitute the evidence? He cannot look at the world of facts and contradict the representation in the preceding paragraph, unless his imagination is so illusive as to interpose an absolute phantasm between his eyes and the obvious reality. He cannot affirm that there is *not* an immense number of persons, even educated persons, receiving the christian declarations with indifference, or rejecting them with a carelessness partaking of contempt. The right means are applied, and with all the force that human effort can give them, out with a suspension, in these instances, of the divine agency,—and *this* is the effect! While the fact stands out so palpably to view, I listen with something of wonder, and something of curiosity, when some professed believers and advocates of the gospel are avowing high anticipations of its progressive efficacy, chiefly or solely by means of the intrinsic force which it carries as a rational address to rational creatures. I cannot help inquiring what length of time is to be allowed for the experiment, which is to prove the adequacy of the means independently of special divine intervention. Nor can it be impertinent to ask what is, thus far, the state of the experiment and the success, among those who scout the idea of such a divine agency, as a dream of fanaticism. Might it not be prudent, to moderate the expressions of contempt for the persuasion which excites an importunity for extraordinary influence from the Almighty, till the success without it shall be greater? The utmost arrogance of this contempt will venture no comparison between the respective success, in the conversion of vain and wicked men, of the christian means as administered by those who implore and rely upon this special agency of heaven, and by those who deny any such operation on the mind; deny it in sense and substance, whatever accommodating phrases they may sometimes employ. Has there indeed been any success at all, in that great business of conversion, to vindicate the calculations of this latter class from the imputation of all the vainest folly that should be meant by the word Romantic?

But, when I introduced the mention of reformers and their projects, I was not intending any reference to delusive presumptions of the operations of christianity, but to those speculations and schemes for the amendment of mankind which anticipate their effect independently of its assistance; some of them perhaps silently coinciding with several of its principles, while others expressly disclaim them. Unless these schemes bring with them, like spirits from heaven, an intrinsic competence to the great operation, without requiring to be met or aided by forwardness in the nature of the Subject, it may be predicted they will turn to the mortification of their fond projectors. There is no avoiding the ungracious perception, in surveying the general character of the race, that, after some allowance for what is called natural affection, and for compassionate sympathy, (an excellent principle, but extremely limited and often capricious in its operation,) the main strength of human feelings consists in the love of sensual gratification, of trifling amusement, of distinction, of power, and of money. And by what suicidal inconsistency are these principles to lend their force to accomplish the schemes of pure reason and virtue, which, they will not fail to perceive, are plotting against them? * And if *they* have far too perfect an instinct to be trepanned into such an employment of their force, and yet are the preponderating agents in the human heart, what *other* active principles of it can the renovator of human character call to his effectual aid, against the evils which are accumulated and defended by what is at once the baser and the stronger part? Whatever principles of a better kind there may be in the nature, they can hold but a feeble and inert existence under this predominance of the worse, and could make but a faint insurrection in favour of the invading virtue. The very worst of them may indeed seem to become its allies when it happens, as it occasionally will, that the course of action which reforming virtue enforces, falls in the same line in which some of these meaner principles can attain their own ends. Then, and so far, an unsound coincidence may take place, and the external effect of those principles may be clad in specious appearances of virtue; but the moment that the reforming projector summons their co-operation to a service in which they must desert their own object and their corrupt character, they will desert *him*. As long as he is condemned to depend, for the efficacy of his schemes, on the aid of so much pure propensity as he shall find in the corrupted subject, he will be nearly in the case of a man attempting to climb a tree by laying hold, first on this side, and then on that, of some rotten twig, which still breaks off in his hand, and lets him fall among the nettles.

* I am here reminded of the Spanish story, of a village where the devil, having made the people excessively wicked, was punished by being compelled to assume the appearance and habit of a friar, and to preach so eloquently, in spite of his internal repugnance and rage, that the inhabitants were completely reformed.

Look again to the state of facts. Collective man *is* human nature; and the conduct of this assemblage, under the diversified experiments continually made on it, expresses its true character, and indicates what may be expected from it. Now then, to what principle in human nature, as thus illustrated by trial, could you with confidence appeal in favour of any of the great objects which a benevolent man desires to see accomplished? If there were in it any one grand principle of goodness which an earnest call, and a great occasion, would raise into action, to assert or redeem the character of the species, one should think it would be what we call, incorrectly enough, Humanity. Consider then, in this nation for instance, which extols its own generous virtues to the sky, what lively and rational appeals have been made to the whole community, respecting the slave trade,* the condition of the poor, the immensity of cruelty perpetrated on brute animals, and the general, national, desperate complacency manifested for what is named honourable war, during a whole half century of lofty christian pretension,—appeals substantially in vain. And why in vain? If humanity *were* a powerful principle in the nature of the community, they would not, in contempt of knowledge, expostulation, and spectacles of misery, persist in the most enormous violations of it. Why in vain? but plainly because

* Happily this topic of accusation is in a measure now set aside; but it would have remained as immovable as the continent of Africa, if the legislature had not been forced into a conviction that, on the whole, the slave trade was not advantageous in point of pecuniary interest. At least the guilt would so have remained upon the nation acting in its capacity of a *state*.—This note is added subsequently to the first edition.—It may be subjoined, in qualification of the reproach relative to the next article,—the condition of the poor,—that during a later period there has been an increase of the attention and exertion directed to that condition; which has, nevertheless, become worse and worse.

there is not enough of that virtue of humanity, even in what is deemed a highly cultivated state of the human nature, to answer to the importunate call. Or if this be not the cause, let the idolaters of human divinity call, like the worshippers of Baal, in a louder voice. Their success is likely to be the same; they will obtain no extraordinary exertion of power, though they cry from morning till the setting sun. And meanwhile the observer, who foresees their disappointment, would think himself warranted, but for the melancholy feeling that the nature in question is his own, to deride their expectations.—You know that a multitude of exemplifications might be added. And the thought of so many great and interesting objects, concerning the welfare of the human economy, as a sober appreciation of means, seems to place beyond the reach of the moral revolutionist,* will often, if he has a genuine benevolence, make him sad. He will repeat to himself, "How easy it is to conceive these inestimable improvements, and how nobly they would exalt my species; but how to work them into the actual condition of man!—Are there somewhere in possibility," he will ask, "intellectual and moral engines mighty enough to perform the great process? Where in darkness is the sacred repository in which they lie? What Marraton† shall explore the unknown way to it? The man who would not as part of the price of

---

* It is obvious that I am not supposing this moral revolutionist to be armed with any power but that of persuasion. If he were a monarch, and possessed virtue and talents equal to his power, the case would be materially different. Even then, he would accomplish but little compared with what he could imagine, and would desire; yet, to all human appearance, he might be the instrument of wonderfully changing the condition of society within his empire. If the soul of Alfred could return to the earth!—

† Spectator, No. 56.

the discovery, be glad to close up all the transatlantic mines, would deserve to be immured as the last victim of those deadly caverns."

But each projecting visionary thinks the discovery is made; and while surveying his own great magazine of expedients, consisting of Fortunatus's cap, the philosopher's stone, Aladdin's lamp, and other equally efficient articles, he is confident that the work may speedily be done. These powerful instruments of melioration perhaps lose their individual names under the general denomination of Philosophy, a term that would be venerable, if it could be rescued from the misfortune of being hackneyed into cant, and from serving the impiety which substitutes human ability to divine power. But it is of little consequence what denomination the projectors assume to themselves or their schemes: it is by their fruits that we shall know them. Their work is before them; the scene of moral disorder presents to them the plagues which they are to stop, the mountain which they are to remove, the torrent which they are to divert, the desert which they are to clothe in verdure and bloom. Let them make their experiment, and add each his page to the humiliating records in which experience contemns the folly of elated imagination.*

* In reading lately some part of a tolerably well-written book published a few years since, I came to the following passage, which though in connexion indeed with the subject of *elections*, expresses the author's general opinion of the state of society, and of the means of exalting it to wisdom and virtue. "The bulk of the community begin to examine, to feel, to understand, their rights and duties. *They only require the fostering care of the Philosopher to ripen them into complete rationality,* and furnish them with the requisites of political and moral action." Here I paused in wondering mood. The fostering care of the Philosopher! Why then is not the Philosopher about his business? Why does he not go and indoctrinate a company of peasants in the intervals of a ploughing or a harvest

All the speculations and schemes of the sanguine projectors of all ages, have left the world still a prey to infinite legions of vices and miseries, an immortal band, which has trampled in scorn on the monuments and the dust of the self-idolizing men, who dreamed, each in his day, that they were born to chase these evils out of the earth. If these vain demigods of an hour, who trusted to change the world, and who perhaps wished to change it only to make it a temple to their fame, could be awaked from the unmarked graves into which they sunk, to look a little while round on the scene for some traces of the success of their projects, would they not be eager to retire again into the chambers of death, to hide the shame of their re-

day, when he will find them far more eager for his instructions than for drink? Why does he not introduce himself among a circle of farmers, who cannot fail, as he enters, to be very judiciously discussing, with the aid of their punch and their pipes, the most refined questions respecting their rights and duties, and wanting but exactly *his* aid, instead of *more* punch and tobacco, to possess themselves completely of the requisites of political and moral action? The populace of a manufactory, is another most promising seminary, where all the moral and intellectual endowments are so nearly "ripe," that he will seem less to have the task of cultivating than the pleasure of reaping. Even among the company in the ale-house, though the Philosopher might at first be sorry, and might wonder, to perceive a slight merge of the moral part of the man in the sensual, and to find in so vociferous a mood that inquiring reason which, he had supposed, would be waiting for him with the silent anxious docility of a pupil of Pythagoras, yet he would find a most powerful predisposition to truth and virtue, and there would be every thing to hope from the accuracy of his logic, the comprehensiveness of his views, and the beauty of his moral sentiments. But perhaps it will be explained, that the Philosopher does not mean to visit all these people in person; but that having first secured the *source* of influence, having taken entire possession of princes, nobility, gentry, and clergy, which he expects to do in a very short time, he will manage *them* like an electrical machine, to operate on the bulk of the community. Either way the achievement will be great and admirable; the *latter* event seems to have been predicted in that sibylline sentence, " When the sky falls we shall catch larks " membered presumption? The wars and tyranny, the rancour, cruelty and revenge, together with all the other unnumbered vices and crimes with which the earth is still infested, are enough, if the whole mass could be brought within one section of the inhabited world, of the extent of a considerable kingdom, to constitute its whole population literally infernal, all but their being incarnate; which last they would soon, through mutual destruction, cease to be. Hitherto the power of the radical cause of these many forms of evil, the corruption of the human heart, has sported with the weakness, or seduced the strength, of all human contrivances to subdue them. Nor are there as yet more than glimmering signs that we are commencing a better era, in which the means that have failed before, or the expedients of a new and more fortunate invention, are appointed to victory and triumph. The nature of man still "casts ominous conjecture on the whole success." While *that* is corrupt, it will pervert even the very schemes and operations by which the world should be improved, though their first principles were pure as heaven. The innate principle of evil, instead of indifferently letting them alone, to work what good they can, will put forth a stupendous force to compel them into subserviency; so that revolutions, great discoveries, augmented science, and new forms of polity, shall become in *effect* what may be denominated the sublime mechanics of depravity.

LETTER V

This view of moral and philosophical projects, added to that of the limited exertion of energy which the Almighty has made to attend, as yet, the dispensation of true religion, and accompanied with the consideration of the impotence of human efforts to make that dispensation efficacious where his will does not, forms a melancholy and awful contemplation. In the hours when it casts its gloom over the mind of the thoughtful observer, unless he can fully resign the condition of man to the infinite wisdom and goodness of his Creator, he will feel an emotion of horror, as if standing on the verge of a hideous gulf, into which almost all the possibilities, and speculations, and efforts, and hopes, relating to the best improvements of mankind, are brought down by the torrent of ages, in a long abortive series, to be lost in final despair.

To an atheist of enlarged sensibility, if there could be such a man, how dark and hideous, beyond all power of description, must be the long review and the undefinable prospect of this triumph of evil, unaccompanied, as it must be presented to his thoughts, by any sublime process of intelligent power, converting, in some manner unknown to mortals, this evil into good, either during the course or in the result. A devout theist, when he becomes sad amidst his contemplations, recovers a submissive tranquillity, by reverting to his assurance of such a wise and omnipotent sovereignty and agency. As a believer in revelation, he is consoled by the confidence both that this dark train of evils will ultimately issue in transcendent brightness, and that the evil itself in this world will at a future period almost cease. He is persuaded that the Great Spirit, who presides over this mysterious scene, has an energy of influence yet in reserve to beam forth on the earth, such as its inhabitants have never, except in a few momentary glimpses, beheld; and that when the predestined period is completed for his kingdom to come, he will command this chaos of turbulent and malignant elements to become transformed into a fair and happy moral world.

And is it not strange, my dear friend, to observe how carefully some philosophers, who deplore the condition of the world, and profess to expect its melioration, keep their speculations clear of every idea of divine interposition? No builders of houses or cities were ever more attentive to guard against the access of flood or fire. If *He* should but touch their prospective theories of improvement, they would renounce them, as defiled and fit only for vulgar fanaticism. Their system of Providence would be profaned by the intrusion of the Almighty. Man is to effect an apotheosis for himself, by the hopeful process of exhausting his corruptions. And should it take a long series of ages, vices, and woes, to reach this glorious attainment, patience may sustain itself the while by the thought that when it is realized, it will be burdened with no duty of religious gratitude. No time is too long to wait, no cost too deep to incur, for the triumph of proving that we have no need of a Divinity, regarded as possessing that one attribute which makes it delightful to acknowledge such a Being, the benevolence that would make us happy. But even if this noble self-sufficiency cannot be realized, the independence of spirit which has laboured for it must not sink at last into piety. This afflicted world, "this poor terrestrial citadel of man," is to lock its gates, and keep its miseries, rather than admit the degradation of receiving help from God.

I wish it were not true that even men who firmly believe in the general doctrine of the divine government of the world, are often betrayed into the impiety of attaching an excessive importance to human agency in its events. How easily a creature of thei own species is transformed by a sympathetic pride into a God before them! If what they deem the cause of truth and justice, advances with a splendid front of distinguished names of legislators, or patriots, or martial heroes, it must then and must therefore triumph; nothing can withstand such talents, accompanied by the zeal of so many faithful adherents. If these shining insects of fame are crushed, or sink into the despicable reptiles of corruption, alas, then, for the cause of truth and justice! All this while, there is no due reference to the "Blessed and only Potentate." If, however, the foundations of their religious faith have not been shaken, and they possess any docility to the lessons of time, they will after awhile be taught to withdraw their dependence and confidence from all subordinate agents, and habitually regard the Supreme Being as the sole possessor of real and absolute power.

Perhaps it is not improbable, that the grand moral improvements of a future age may be accomplished in a manner that shall leave nothing to man but humility and grateful adoration. His pride so obstinately ascribes to himself whatever good is effected on the globe, that perhaps the Deity will evince his own interposition, by events as evidently independent of the might of man as the rising of the sun. It may be that some of them may take place in a manner but little connected even with human operation. Or if the activity of men shall be employed as the means of producing all of them, there will probably be as palpable a disproportion between the instruments and the events, as there was between the rod of Moses and the amazing phænomena which followed when it was stretched forth. No Israelite was foolish enough to ascribe to the rod the power that divided the sea; nor will the witnesses of the moral wonders to come attribute them to man. "Not by might, nor by power, but by my Spirit, saith the Lord of hosts."

I hope these extended observations will not appear like an attempt to exhibit the whole stock of means, as destitute of all value, and the industrious application of them as a labour without reward. It is not to depreciate a thing, if, in the attempt to ascertain its real magnitude, it is proved to be little. It is no injustice to mechanical powers, to say that slender machines will not move rocks and massive timbers: nor to chemical ones, to assert that though an earthquake may fling a promontory from its basis, the explosion of a canister of gunpowder will not.—Between moral forces also, and the objects to which they are to be applied, there are constituted measures of proportion; and it would seem an obvious principle of good sense, that an estimate moderately correct of the value of each of our means according to those measures, as far as they can be ascertained, should precede every application of them. Such an estimate has no place in a mind under the ascendency of imagination, which, therefore, by extravagantly magnifying the virtue of its means, inflates its projects with hopes which may justly be called romantic. The best corrective of such irrational expectation is an appeal to experience. There is an immense record of experiments, which will assign the force of almost all the engines, as worked by human hands, in the whole moral magazine. And if a man expects any one of them to produce a greater effect than ever before, it must be because the talents of him that repeats the trial are believed to transcend those of all former experimenters, or else because the season appears more auspicious.

The estimate of the power of means, which comes in answer to the appeal to experience, is indeed most humiliating; but what then? It is a humble thing to be a man. The feebleness of means is, in fact, the feebleness of him that employs them; for instruments to all human apprehension the most inconsiderable, can produce the most prodigious effects when wielded by celestial powers. Till, then, the time shall arrive for us to attain a nobler rank of existence, we must be content to work on the present level of our nature, and effect that little which we can effect; unless it be greater magnanimity and piety to resolve that because our powers are limited to do only little things, they shall therefore, as if in revenge for such an economy, do nothing. Our means will do something; that something is what they were meant to be adequate to in our hands, and not some indefinitely greater effect, which we may all be tempted to wish, and which a sanguine visionary confidently expects.

This disproportion between the powers and means with which mortals are confined to work, and the great objects which good men would desire to accomplish, is a part of the appointments of Him who determined all the relations in the universe; and he will see to the consequences. For the present, he seems to say to his servants, " Forbear to inquire why so small a part of those objects to which I have summoned your activity, is placed within the reach of your powers. Your feeble ability for action is not accompanied by such a capacity of understanding, as would be requisite to comprehend why that ability was made no greater. Though it had been made incomparably greater, would there not still have been objects before it too vast for its operation? Must not the highest of created beings still have something in view, which they feel they can but partially accomplish till the sphere of their active force be enlarged? Must there not be an end of improvement in my creation, if the powers of my creatures had become perfectly equal to the magnitude of their designs? How mean must be the spirit of that being that would not make an effort now, toward the accomplishment of something higher than he will be able to accompl sh till hereafter. Because mightier labourers would have been requisite to effect all that you wish, will you murmur that I have honoured you, the inferior ones, with the appointment of making a noble exertion with however limited success? If there is but little power in *your* hands, is it not because I retain the power in *mine?* Are you afraid lest that power should fail to do all things right, only because *you* are so little made its instruments? Be grateful that *all* the work is not to be done without you, and that God employs you in that in which he also is employed. But remember, that while the employment is yours, the success is altogether his; and that your diligence therefore, and not the measure of effect which it produces, will be the test of your characters. Good men have been employed in all ages under the same economy of inadequate means, and what appeared to them inconsiderable success. Go to your labours: every sincere effort will infallibly be one step more in your own progress to a perfect state; and as to the Cause, when *I* see it necessary for a God to interpose in his own manner, I will come."

I might deem a train of observations of the melancholy hue which shades some of the latter pages of this essay of too depressive a tendency, were I not convinced that a serious exhibition of the feebleness of human agency in relation to all great objects, may aggravate the impression, often so insufficient, of the absolute supremacy of God, of the total dependence of all mortal strength and effort on him, and of the necessity of maintaining habitually a devout respect to his intervention. It might promote that last attainment of a zealously good man, the resignation to be as diminutive and as imperfectly successful an agent as God pleases. I am assured also that, in a pious mind, the humiliating estimate of means and human sufficiency, and the consequent sinking down of all lofty expectations founded on them, will leave one single mean, and that far the best of all, to be held not only of undiminished but of more eminent value than ever was ascribed to it before. The most excellent of all human means must be that of which the effect is to obtain the exertion of divine power. The means which are to be employed in a direct immediate instrumentality toward the end, seem to bear such a measured proportion to their objects, as to assign and limit the probable effect. This regulated proportion exists no longer, and therefore the possible effects become too great for calculation, when *that* expedient is solemnly employed which is appointed as the mean of engaging the divine energy to act on the object. If the only means by which Jehoshaphat sought to overcome his superior enemy, had been his troops, horses, and arms, there would have been nearly an assignable proportion between these means and the end, and the probable result of the conflict would have been a matter of ordinary calculation. But when he said, "Neither know we what to do, but our eyes are up unto thee," he moved (if I may reverently express it so) another and an infinite force to invade the host of Moab and Ammon; and the consequence displayed in their camp, the difference between an irreligious leader, who could fight only with arms and on the level of the plain, and a pious one who could thus assault from Heaven. It may not, I own, be perfectly correct to cite, in illustration of the efficacy of prayer, the most memorable ancient examples. Nor is it needful, since the experience of devout and eminently rational men, in latter times, has supplied numerous striking instances of important advantages so connected in time and circumstance with prayer, that with good reason they regarded them as the evident result of it.* This experience, taken in confirmation of the assurances of the Bible, warrants ample expectations of the efficacy of an earnest and habitual devotion; provided still, as I need not remind you, that this mean be employed as the grand auxiliary of the other means, and not alone, till all the rest are exhausted or impracticable. And no doubt any man who should, amidst his serious projects, become sensible, with any thing approaching to an adequate apprehension, of his dependence on God, would far more earnestly and constantly press on this great resource than is common even among good men. He would as little, without it, promise himself any distinguished success, as a mariner would expect to reach a distant coast by means of his sails spread in a stagnation of the air.—I have intimated my fear that it is visionary to expect an unusual success in the human administration of religion, unless there were unusual omens; now an emphatical spirit of prayer would be such an omen; and the individual who should solemnly resolve to make proof of its last possible efficacy, might probably find himself becoming a much more prevailing agent of good in his little sphere. And if the whole, or the greater number, of the disciples of Christianity, were, with an earnest unfailing resolution of each, to combine that Heaven should not withhold one single influence which the very utmost effort of conspiring and persevering supplication would obtain, it would be the sign of a revolution of the world being at hand.

* Here I shall not be misunderstood to believe the multitude of stories which have been told by deluded fancy, or detestable imposture.

My dear friend, it is quite time to dismiss this whole subject; though it will probably appear to you that I have entirely lost and forgotten the very purpose for which I took it up, which certainly was to examine the correctness of some not unusual applications of the epithet Romantic. It seemed necessary, first, to describe, with some exemplifications, the characteristics of that extravagance which ought to be given up to the charge. The attempt to do this, has led me into a length of detail far beyond all expectation. The intention was, next, to display and to vindicate, in an extended illustration, several schemes of life, and models of character; but I will not prolong the subject. I shall only just specify, in concluding, two or three of those modes of feeling and action on which the censure of being romantic has improperly fallen.

One is, a disposition to take high examples for imitation. I have condemned the extravagance which presumes on rivalling the career of action and success that has been the appointment of some individuals, so extraordinary as to be the most conspicuous phenomena of history. But this delirium of ambitious presumption is distinguishable enough from the more temperate, yet warm aspiration to attain some resemblance to examples, which it will require the most strenuous and sustained exertion to resemble. Away with any such sobriety and rationality as would repress the disposition to contemplate with a generous emulation the class of men who have been illustrious for their excellence and their wisdom; to observe with interested self-reference the principles that animated them and the process of their attainments; and to fix the standard of character high by keeping these exemplars in view. A man may, without a presumptuous estimate of his talents, or the expectation of passing through any course of unexampled events, indulge the ambition to resemble and follow, in the essential determination of their characters, those sublime spirits who are now removed to the kingdom where they are to "shine as the stars for ever and ever," and those yet on earth who are evidently on their way to the same illustrious end.

A striking departure from the order of custom in the rank to which a man belongs, exhibited in his devoting the privileges of that rank to a mode of excellence which the generality of the people who compose it never dreamed to be a duty, will by them be denominated and scouted as romantic. They will wonder why a man who ought to be like themselves, should affect quite a different style of life, a deserter and alien from the reign of fashion, should attempt unusual plans of doing good, and should put himself under some extraordinary discipline of virtue—while yet every point in his system may be a dictate of reason and conscience, speaking in a voice heard by him alone.

The irreligious will apply this epithet to the determination to make, and the zeal to inculcate, great exertions and sacrifices for a purely moral ideal reward. Some gross and palpable prize is requisite to excite their energies; and therefore self-denial repaid by conscience, beneficence without fame, and the delight of resembling the Divinity, appear visionary felicities.

The epithet will be in readiness for application to a man who feels it an imperious duty to realize, as far as possible, and as soon as possible, every thing which he approves and applauds in theory. You will often hear a circle of perhaps respectable persons agreeing entirely that this one thing spoken of is a worthy principle of action, and that other an estimable quality, and a third a sublime excellence, who would be amazed at your fanaticism, if you were to adjure them thus: "My friends, from this moment you are bound, from this moment we are all bound, on peril of the displeasure of God, to realize in ourselves, to the last possible extent, all that we have thus in good faith deliberately applauded." Through some fatal defect of conscience, there is a very general feeling, regarding the high order of moral and religious attainments, that though it is a happy exaltation to possess them, yet it is perfectly safe to stop contented where we are, on a far lower ground. One is confounded to hear irritable persons praising a character of self-command; persons who trifle away their days professing to admire the instances of a strenuous improvement of time; rich persons lavishing fine words on examples of beneficence which they know to be far surpassing themselves, though perhaps with no larger means; and all expressing deep respect for the men who have been most eminent in piety;—and yet all this apparently with the ease of a perfect freedom from any admonition of conscience, that they are themselves standing in the very serious predicament of having to choose, whether they will henceforward earnestly and practically aim at these higher attainments, or resign themselves to be found wanting in the day of final account.

Finally, in the application of this epithet, but little allowance is generally made for the great difference between a man's entertaining high designs and hopes for himself alone, and his entertaining them relative to other persons. It might be very romantic for a man to reckon on effecting such designs with respect to others, as it may be reasonable to meditate for himself. If he feels the powerful habitual impulse of conviction, urging and animating him to the highest attainments of wisdom and excellence, he may perhaps justly hope to approach them himself, though it would be most extravagant to extend the same hope to all the persons to whom he may wish and try to impart the impulse. I specify the strictly personal attainments, *wisdom* and *excellence*, for the reason that, besides the difference, in probability of realization, between large schemes and hopes as indulged by a man for himself or entertained for others, there is a distinction to be made in respect to such as he might entertain only for himself. His extraordinary plans and expectations for himself might be of such a nature as to depend on other persons for their accomplishment, and might therefore be as extravagant as if other persons alone, persons in no degree at his command, had been their object. Or, on the contrary, they may be of a kind which shall not need the co-operation of other persons, and may be realized independently of their will. The design of acquiring immense riches, or becoming the commander of an army, or a person of high official importance in national affairs, must in its progress be dependent on other men in incalculably too many points and ways for a considerate man to presume that he shall be fortunate in them all. But the schemes of eminent personal improvement, depending comparatively little on the will, capacity, or conduct of other persons, are romantic only when there is some fatal intellectual or moral defect in the individual himself who has adopted them.

ESSAY IV.

ON SOME OF THE CAUSES BY WHICH EVANGELICAL RELIGION HAS BEEN RENDERED UNACCEPTABLE TO PERSONS OF CULTIVATED TASTE.

LETTER I.

MY DEAR FRIEND,

It is striking to observe, under what various forms of character men are passing through this introductory season of their being, to enter on its future greater stage. Some one of these, it may be presumed, is more eligible than all the rest for proceeding to that greater stage; and to ascertain which it is, must be felt by a wise man the most important of his inquiries. We, my friend, are persuaded that the inquiry, if made in good faith, will soon terminate, and that the christian character will be selected as the only one, in which it is wise to advance to the entrance on the endless futurity. Indeed the assurance of our permanent existence itself rests but on that authority which dictates also the right introduction to it.

The christian character is simply a conformity to the whole religion of Christ. This implies a cordial admission of that whole religion; but it meets, on the contrary, in many minds not denying it to be a communication from God, a disposition to shrink from some of its peculiar properties and distinctions, or an effort to displace or neutralize them. I am not now to learn that the substantial cause of this is that repugnance in human nature to what is purely divine, which revelation affirms, and all history proves, and which perhaps some of the humiliating points of the christian system are more adapted to provoke, than any other thing that bears the divine impress. Nor do I need to be told how much this chief cause has aided and aggravated the power of those subordinate ones, which may have conspired to prevent the success of evangelical religion among a class of persons that I have in view, I mean those of refined taste, whose feelings, concerning what is great and excellent, have been disciplined to accord to a literary or philosophical standard. But even had there been less of this natural aversion in such minds, or had there been none, some of the causes which have acted on them would have tended, necessarily, to produce an effect injurious to the claims of pure christianity.—I wish to illustrate several of these causes, after briefly describing the antichristian feelings in which I have observed that effect.

It is true that many persons of taste have, without any formal disbelief of the christian truth, so little concern about religion in any shape, that the unthinking dislike to the evangelical principles, occasionally rising and passing among their transient moods of feeling with no distinctness of apprehension, hardly deserves to be described. These are to be assigned, whatever may be their faculties or improvements, to the multitude of triflers relatively to the gravest concerns, on whom we can pronounce only the general condemnation of irreligion, their feelings not being sufficiently marked for a more discriminative censure. But the aversion is of a more defined character, as it exists in a mind too serious for the follies of the world and the neglect of all religion, and in which the very sentiment itself becomes, at times, the subject of painful and apprehensive reflection, from an internal monition that it is an unhappy symptom, if the truth should be that the religious system which excites the displacency, has really the sanction of divine revelation. If a person in this condition of mind disclosed himself to you, he would describe how the elevated sentiment, inspired by the contemplation of other sublime subjects, is confounded, and sinks mortified into the heart, when this new subject is presented to his view. It seems to cquire almost a total change of his mental habits to admit this as the most interesting subject of all, while yet he dares not reject the authority which supports its claim. The dignity of religion, as a general and refined speculation, he may have long acknowledged; but it appears to him as if it lost that aspect of dignity, in taking the specific form of the evangelical system; just as if an ethereal being were reduced to combine his radiance and subtility with an earthly conformation. He is aware that religion in the abstract, or in other words, the principles which constitute the obligatory relation of all intelligent creatures to the Supreme Being, must receive a special modification, by means of the addition of some other principles, in order to become a peculiar religious economy for a particular race of those creatures, especially for a race low in rank and corrupted in nature. And the christian revelation assigns the principles by which this religion in the abstract, the religion of the universe, is thus modified into the peculiar form required for the nature and condition of man. But when he contemplates some of these principles, framed on an assumption, and conveying a plain declaration of an ignominious and deplorable condition of our nature, he can hardly help regretting that, even if our condition *be* so degraded, the system of our relations' with the Divinity, though constituted according and in adaptation to that degraded state, is not an economy of a brighter character. The gospel indeed appears to him like the image in Nebuchadnezzar's dream; it is refulgent with a head of gold; the sublime truths or facts of religious theory, which stand antecedent and superior to every peculiarity of the special dispensations of religion, are luminously exhibited; but the doctrines which are added as distinctive of the peculiar circumstances of the christian economy, appear less splendid, and as if descending towards the qualities of iron and clay. If he must admit this portion of the system as a part of the truth, his feelings amount to the wish that a different theory *had been true.* 't is therefore with a degree of shrinking reluctance that he sometimes adverts to the ideas peculiar to the gospel. He would willingly lose this specific scheme of doctrines in a more general theory of religion, instead of resigning every wider speculation for this scheme, in which God has comprised, and distinguished by a very peculiar character, all the religion which he wills to be known, or to be useful, to our world. It is not a welcome conviction, that the gospel, instead of being a modification of religion exhibited in competition with others, and subject to choice or rejection according to his taste, is peremptorily and exclusively *the* religion for our lapsed race; insomuch that he who has not a religion conformed to the model in the New Testament does not stand in the only right and safe relation to the Supreme Being. He suffers himself to pass the year in a dissatisfied uncertainty, and a criminal neglect of deciding, whether his cold reception of the specific views of christianity will render unavailing his regard for those more general truths, respecting the Deity, moral rectitude, and a future state, which are necessarily at the basis of the system. He is afraid to examine and determine the question, whether he may with impunity rest in a scheme composed of the general principles of wisdom and virtue, selected from the christian oracles and the speculations of philosophy, harmonized by reason, and embellished by taste. If it were safe, he would much rather be the dignified professor of such a philosophic refinement on christianity, than yield himself a submissive and wholly conformed disciple of Jesus Christ. This refined system would be clear of the undesirable peculiarities of christian doctrine, and it would also allow some different ideas of the nature of moral excellence. He would not be so explicitly condemned for indulging a disposition to admire and imitate some of those models of character which, however opposite to pure christian excellence, the world has always idolized.

I wish I could display, in the most forcible manner, the considerations which show how far such a state of mind is wrong. But my object is, to remark on a few of the causes which may have contributed to it.

I do not, for a moment, place among these causes that continual dishonour which the religion of Christ has suffered through the corrupted institutions, and the depraved character of individuals or communities, of what is called the christian world. Such a man as I have supposed, understands what the dictates and tendency of that religion really are, so far at least, that in contemplating the bigotry, persecution, hypocrisy, and worldly ambition, which have been forced as an opprobrious adjunct on christianity during all ages of its occupancy on earth, his mind dissevers, by a decisive glance of thought, all these evils, and the pretended christians who are accountable for them, from the religion which is as distinct from them as the Spirit that pervades all things is pure from matter and from sin. In his view, these odious things and these wicked men, that have arrogated and defiled the christian name, sink out of sight through a chasm like Korah, Dathan, and Abiram, and leave the camp and the cause holy, though they leave the numbers small. It needs so very moderate a share of discernment, in a protestant country at least, where a well-known volume exhibits the religion itself, genuine and entire as it came from heaven, to perceive the essential disunion and antipathy between it and all these abominations, that to take them as congenial and inseparable, betrays, in every instance, a detestable want of principle, or a most wretched want of sense. The defect of cordiality toward the religion of Christ, in the persons that I am accusing, does not arise from this debility or this injustice. They would not be less equitable to christianity than they would to some estimable man, whom they would not esteem the less because villains that hated him, knew, however, so well the excellence of his name and character, as gladly to avail themselves of them in any way they could to aid their schemes, or to shelter their crimes.—But indeed these remarks are not strictly to the purpose; since the prejudice which a weak or corrupt mind receives from such a view of the christian history, operates, as we see by facts, not discriminately against particular characteristics of christianity, but against the whole system, and leads toward a denial of its divine origin. On the contrary, the class of persons now in question fully admit its divine authority, but feel a repugnance to some of its most peculiar distinctions. These peculiarities they may wish, as I have said, to refine away; but in moments of impartial seriousness, are constrained to admit something very near at least to the conviction, of their being inseparable from the sacred economy. This however fails to subdue or conciliate the heart; and the dislike to some of the parts has often an influence on the affections in regard to the whole. That portion of the system which they think they *could* admire, is admitted with the coldness of a mere speculative assent, from the effect of the intruding recollection of its being combined with something else which they cannot admire. Those distinctions from which they recoil, are chiefly comprised in that view of christianity which, among a large proportion of the professors of it, is denominated in a somewhat specific sense, Evangelical; and therefore I have adopted this denomination in the title of this letter. Christianity taken in this view contains—a humiliating estimate of the moral condition of man, as a being radically corrupt —the doctrine of redemption from that condition by the merit and sufferings of Christ—the doctrine of a divine influence being necessary to transform the character of the human mind, in order to prepare it for a higher station in the universe—and a grand moral peculiarity by which it insists on humility, penitence, and a separation from the spirit and habits of the world.—I do not see any necessity for a more formal and amplified description of that mode of understanding christianity which has acquired the distinctive epithet Evangelical; and which is not. to say the least, more discriminatively designated among the scoffing part of the wits, critics, and theologians of the day, by the terms Fanatical, Calvinistical, Methodistical.

I may here notice that, though the greater share of the injurious influences on which I may remark operates more pointedly against the peculiar *doctrines* of christianity, yet some of them are perniciously effectual against its *moral* sentiments and laws, which are of a tenour corresponding to the principles it prescribes to our faith. I would observe also, that though I have specified the more refined and intellectual class of minds, as indisposed to the religion of Christ by the causes on which I may comment, and though I keep them chiefly in view, yet the influence of some of these causes extends in a degree to many persons of subordinate mental rank.

LETTER II.

In the view of an intelligent and honest mind the religion of Christ stands as clear of all connexion with the corruption of men, and churches, and ages, as when it was first revealed. It retains its purity like Moses in Egypt, or Daniel in Babylon, or the Saviour of the world himself while he mingled with scribes and pharisees, or publicans and sinners. But though it thus instantly and totally separates itself from all appearance of relation to the vices of bad men, a degree of effort may be required in order to display it, or to view it in an equally perfect separation from the weakness of good ones. It is in reality no more identified with the one than with the other; its essential sublimity is as incapable of being reduced to littleness, as its purity is of uniting with vice. But it may have a vital connexion with a weak mind, while it necessarily disowns a wicked one; and the qualities of that mind with which it confessedly unites itself, will much more seem to adhere to it, than of that with which all its principles are plainly in antipathy. It will be more natural to take those persons who are acknowledged the real subjects of its influence, as illustrations of its nature, than those on whom it is the heaviest reproach that they pretend to be its friends. The perception of its nature and dignity must be clear and absolute, in the man who can observe it under the appearance it acquires in intimate combination with the thoughts, feelings, and language of its disciples, without ever losing sight of its own essential qualities and lustre. No possible associations indeed can diminish the grandeur of some arts of the christian system. The doctrine of immortality, for instance, cannot be reduced to take even a transient appearance of littleness, by the meanest or most uncouth words and images that shall ever be employed to represent it. But some other things in the system have not the same obvious philosophic dignity; and these are capable of acquiring, from the mental defects of their believers, such associations as will give a character much at variance with our ideas of magnificence, to so much as they constitute of the evangelical economy. One of the causes therefore which I meant to notice, as having excited in persons of taste a sentiment unfavourable to the reception of evangelical religion, is, that this is the religion of many weak and uncultivated minds.

The schools of philosophy have been composed of men of superior faculties and extensive accomplishments, who could sustain, by eloquence and capacious thought, the dignity of the favourite themes; so that the proud distinctions of the disciples and advocates appeared as the attributes of the doctrines. The adepts could attract refined and aspiring spirits by proclaiming, that the temple of *their* goddess was not profaned by being a rendezvous for vulgar men. On the contrary, it is the beneficent distinction of the gospel, that though it is of a magnitude to interest and to surpass angelic investigation, (and therefore assuredly to pour contempt on the pride of human intelligence rejecting it for its *meanness*,) it is yet most expressly sent to the class which philosophers have always despised. And a good man feels it a cause of grateful joy, that a communication has come from heaven, adapted to effect the happiness of multitudes in spite of natural debility or neglected education. While he observes that confined capacities do not preclude the entrance, and the permanent residence, of that sacred combination of truth and power, which finds no place in the minds of many philosophers, and wits, and statesmen, he is grateful to him who has "hidden these things from the wise and prudent, and revealed them to babes."

But it is not to be denied that the natural consequence follows. Contracted and obscured in its abode, the inhabitant will appear, as the sun through a misty sky, with but little of its magnificence, to a man who can be content to receive his impression of the intellectual character of the religion from the form of its manifestation made from the minds of its disciples; and, in doing so, can indolently and perversely allow himself to regard its weakest display as its truest image. In taking such a dwelling, the religion seems to imitate what was prophesied of its Author, that, when he should be seen, there would be no beauty that he should be desired. This humiliation is inevitable; for unless miracles were wrought, to impart to the less intellectual disciples an enlarged power of thinking, the evangelic truth must accommodate itself to the dimensions and habitudes of their minds. And perhaps the exhibitions of it will come forth with more of the character of those minds, than of its own celestial distinctions: insomuch that if there were no declaration of the sacred system, but in the forms of conception and language in which they give it forth, even a candid man might hesitate to admit it as the most glorious gift of heaven. Happily, he finds its quality declared by other oracles; but while from them he receives it in its own character, he is tempted to wish he could detach it from all the associations which he feels it has acquired from the humbler exhibition. And he does not greatly wonder that other men of the same intellectual habits, and with a less candid solicitude to receive with simplicity every thing that really comes from God, should have admitted a prejudice from these associations.

They would not make this impression on a man already devoted to the religion of Jesus Christ. No passion that has become predominant is ever cooled by any thing which can be associated with its object, while that object itself continues unaltered. The passion is even willing to verify its power, and the merit of that which interests it, by sometimes letting the unpleasing associations surround and touch the object for an instant, and then chasing them away; and it welcomes with augmented attachment that object coming forth from them unstained; as happy spirits at the last day will receive with joy their bodies recovered from the dust in a state of purity that will leave every thing belonging to the dust behind. A zealous christian exults to feel in contempt of how many counteracting circumstances he can still love his religion; and that this counteraction, by exciting his understanding to make a more defined estimate of its excellence, has resulted in his loving it the more. It has now in some degree even pre-occupied those avenues of taste and imagination, by which alone the ungracious effect of associations could have been admitted. The thing itself is close to his mind, and therefore the causes which would have misrepresented it by coming between have lost their power. As he hears the sentiments of sincere christianity from the weak and illiterate, he says to himself—All this is indeed little, but I am happy to feel that the subject itself is great, and that this humble display of it cannot make it appear to me different from what I absolutely know it to be; any more than a clouded atmosphere can diminish my idea of the grandeur of the heavens, after I have so often beheld the pure azure, and the host of stars. I am glad that it has in this man all the consolatory and all the purifying efficacy, which I wish that my more elevated views of it may not fail to have in me. This is the chief end for which a divine communication can have been granted to the world. If this religion, instead of being designed to make its disciples pure and happy amidst their littleness, had required to receive lustre from their mental dignity, it would have been sent to none of us. At least, not to me; for though I would be grateful for my intellectual advantage over my uncultivated fellow-christian, I am conscious that the noblest forms of thought in which I apprehend, or could represent, the subject, do but contract its amplitude, do but depress its sublimity. Those superior spirits who are said to rejoice over the first proof of the efficacy of divine truth, have rejoiced over its introduction, even in so humble a form, into the mind of this man, and probably see in fact but little difference, in point of speculative greatness, between his manner of viewing and illustrating it and mine. If Jesus Christ could be on earth as before, he would receive this disciple, and benignantly approve, for its operation on the heart, that faith in his doctrines, which men of taste might be tempted to despise for its want of intellectual refinement. And since all his true disciples are destined to attain greatness at length, the time is coming, when each pious, though now contracted mind, will do justice to this high subject. Meanwhile, such as this subject will appear to the intelligence of immortals, and such as it will be expressed in their eloquence, such it really is now; and I should deplore the perversity of my mind, if I felt more disposed to take the character of the religion from that style of its exhibition in which it appears humiliated, than from that in which I am assured it will be sublime. If, while we are all advancing to meet the revelations of eternity, I have a more vivid and comprehensive idea than these less privileged christians, of the glory of our religion, as displayed in the New Testament, and if I can much more delightfully participate the sentiments which devout genius has uttered in the contemplation of it, I am therefore called upon to excel them as much in devotedness to this religion, as I have a more luminous view of its excellence.

Let the spirit of the evangelical system once have the ascendency, and it may thus defy the threatening mischief of disagreeable associations with its principles; as the angels in the house of Lot repelled the base assailants. But it requires a most extraordinary cogency of conviction, and indeed more than simple intellectual conviction, to obtain a cordial reception for these principles, if such associations are in prepossession of the mind. And that they should be so in the man of taste is not wonderful, if you consider how early, how often, and by what diversities of the same general cause, they may have been made on him. As the gospel comprises an ample assemblage of intellectual views, and as the greater number of christians are inevitably incapable of presenting them in a dignified character of conception and language from the same causes which disqualify them to do such justice to other intellectual subjects, it is not improbable that far the greater number of expressions which he has heard in his whole life, have been utterly below the subject. Obviously this is a very serious circumstance; for if he had heard a much spoken on any other subject of high intellectual rank, as moral philosophy, or poetry, or rhetoric, in which perhaps he now takes great interest, and if a similar proportion of what he had heard had been as much below the subject, it is probable that he and the subject would have remained strangers. And it is a melancholy deposition against the human heart, that fewer unfavourable associations will cause it to recoil from the gospel, than from any other subject which comes with high claims.

The prejudicial influence of mental deficiency or meanness associated with evangelical doctrine, may have beset him in many ways. For instance, he has met with some zealous christians, who not only were very slightly acquainted with the evidences of the truth, and the illustrations of the reasonableness, of their religion, but who actually felt no interest in the inquiry. Perhaps more than one individual attempted to deter him from pursuing it, by suggesting that inquiry either implies doubt, which was pronounced a criminal state of mind, or will probably lead to it, as a judgment on the profane inquisitiveness which, on such a subject, is not satisfied with implicitly believing. An attempt to examine the foundation would be likely to end in a wish to demolish the structure.

He may sometimes have heard the discourse o sincere christians, whose religion involved no intellectual exercise, and, strictly speaking, no *subject* of intellect. Separately from their feelings, it had no definition, no topics, no distinct succession of views. And if he or some other person attempted to talk on some part of the religion *itself,* as a thing definable and important, independently of the feelings of any individual, and as consisting in a vast congeries of ideas, concerning the divine government of the world, the relations of rational creatures with the Creator, the general nature of the economy disclosed by the Messiah, the system of moral principles and rules, and the greatness of the future prospects of man, they seemed to have no concern in *that* religion, and impatiently interrupted such discourse with the observation —That is not experience.

Others he has heard continually recurring to two or three points of opinion, adopted perhaps in servile addiction to a system, or perhaps by some chance seizure of the individual's preference, and asserted to be the life and essence of christianity. These opinions he has heard zealously though not argumentatively defended, even when they were not attacked or questioned. If they *were* called in question, it was an evidence not less of depraved principle than of perverted judgment. All other religious truths were represented as deriving their authority and importance purely from these, and as being so wholly included and subordinate, that it is needless and almost impertinent to give them a distinct attention. The neglect of constantly repeating and enforcing these opinions was said to be the chief cause of the comparative failure of the efforts to promote christianity in the world, and of the decay of particular religious societies. Though he perhaps could not perceive how these points were essential to christianity, even admitting them to be true, they were made the sole and decisive standard for distinguishing between a genuine and a false profession of it. And perhaps they were applied in eager haste to any sentiment which *he* happened to express concerning religion, as a test of its quality, and a proof of its corruptness.

Instances may have occurred in which he has observed some one idea or doctrine, that was not the distinctive peculiarity of any system, to have so monopolized the mind, that every conversation, from whatever point of the compass it started, was certain to find its way to the favourite topic, while he was sometimes fretted, sometimes amused, never much improved, by observing its instinctive progress to the appointed place. If his situation and connexions rendered it unavoidable for him often to hear this unfortunate manner of discoursing on religion, his mind probably fell into a fault very similar to that of his well-meaning acquaintance. As this worthy man could never speak on the subject without soon bringing the whole of it down to one particular point, so the indocile and recusant auditor became unable to think on the subject without adverting immediately to the narrow illustration of it exhibited by this one man; insomuch that this image of combined penury and conceit became established in his mind as representative of the subject. In consequence of this connexion of ideas, he perhaps became disinclined to think on the subject at all; or, if he was disposed or constrained to think of it, he was so averse to let his views of christianity thus converge to th littleness of a point, that he laboured to expand them till they lost all specifically evangelical distinctions in the wideness of generality and abstraction.

Again, the majority of christians are precluded, by their condition in life, from any considerable acquirement of general knowledge. It would be unpardonable in the more cultivated man not to make the large allowance for the natural effect of this on the extent of their religious ideas. But it shall have happened, that he has met with numbers who had no inconsiderable means, both in the way of money, judging by their unnecessary expenses, and of leisure, judging by the quantity of time consumed in trivial talk, or in needless sleep, to furnish their minds with various information, but who were quite on a level, in this respect, with those of the humblest rank. They never even suspected that knowledge could have any connexion with religion; or that they could not be as clearly and comprehensively in possession of the great subject as a man whose faculties had been exercised, and whose extended acquaintance with things would supply an ample diversity of ideas illustrative of religion. He has perhaps even heard them make a kind of merit of their indifference to knowledge, as if it were the proof or the result of a higher value for religion. If there was ventured a hint of reprehensive wonder at their reading so little, and within so very confined a scope, it would be replied, that they thought it enough to read the Bible; as if it were possible for a person whose mind fixes with inquisitive attention on what is before him, to read through the Bible without thousands of such questions being started in his thoughts, as can be answered only from sources of information extraneous to the Bible. But he perceived that this reading the Bible was no work of inquiring thought; and indeed he has commonly found, that those who have no wish for any thing like a general improvement in knowledge, have no disposition for the real business of thinking even in religion, and that their discourse on that subject is the exposure of intellectual poverty. He has seen them live on for a number of years content with the same confined views, the same meagre list of topics, and the same uncouth religious language. In so considerable a space of time, the habitual inquisitiveness after various truth would have given much more clearness to their faculties, and much more precision to the articles of their belief. They might have ramified the few leading articles, into a rich variety of subordinate principles and important inferences. They might have learned to place the christian truth in all those combinations with the other parts of our knowledge, by which it is enabled to present new and striking aspects, and to multiply its arguments to the understanding, and its appeals to the heart. They might have enriched themselves by rendering nature, history, and the present views of the moral world, tributary to the illustration and the effect of their religion. But they neglected, and even despised, all these means of enlarging their ideas of a subject which they professed to hold of infinite importance. Yet perhaps, if this man of more intellectual habits showed but little interest in conversing with them on that subject, or seemed intentionally to avoid it, this was considered as pure aversion to religion; and what had been uninteresting to him as doctrine, then became revolting as reproof.*

He may not unfrequently have heard worthy but illiterate persons expressing their utmost admiration of sayings, passages in books, or public discourses, which he could not help perceiving to be hardly sense, or to be the dictates of conceit, or to be common-place inflated to fustian. While on the other hand, if *he* has introduced a favourite passage, or an admired book, they have perhaps acknowledged no perception of its beauty, or expressed a doubt of its tendency, from its not being in canonical diction. Or perhaps they have directly avowed that they could not understand it, in a manner plainly implying that *therefore* it could be of no value. Possibly when he has expressed his high

---

* I own that what I said of Jesus Christ's gladly receiving one of the humbler intellectual order for his disciple, would be but little applicable to some of the characters that I describe.

admiration of some of the views of the gospel, not ordinarily recognised or exhibited, and bearing what I may perhaps call a philosophical aspect, (such, for instance, as struck the mind of Rousseau,) he has been mortified to find, that some peculiar and even sublime distinctions of the religion of Christ are lost to many of his disciples, from being of too abstract a kind for the apprehension of any but improved and intellectual men.

If he had generally found in those professed christians whose mental powers and attainments were small, a candid humility, instructing them, while expressing their animated gratitude for what acquaintance with religion they had been able to attain, and for the immortal hopes springing from it, to feel that they had but a confined view of a subject which is of immense variety and magnitude, he might have been too much pleased by this amiable temper to be much repelled by the defective character of their conceptions and expressions. But often, on the contrary, they may have shown such a complacent assurance of sufficiency in the little sphere, as if it self-evidently comprised every thing which it is possible, or which it is of consequence, for any mind to see in the christian religion. They were like persons who should doubt the information that myriads more of stars can be seen through a telescope than they ever beheld, and who should have no curiosity to try.

Many christians may have appeared to him to attach an extremely disproportionate importance to the precise *modes* of religious observances, not only in the hour of controversy respecting them, when they are always extravagantly magnified, but in the habitual course of their religious references. These modes may be either such as are adhered to by communities and sects of christians, perhaps as their respective marks of distinction from one another; or any smaller ceremonial peculiarities, devised and pleaded for by particular individuals or families.

Certain things in the religious habits of some christians may have disgusted him excessively. Every thing which could even distantly remind him of grimace, would inevitably do this; as, for instance, a solemn lifting up of the eyes, artificial impulses of the breath, grotesque and regulated gestures and postures in religious exercises, an affected faltering of the voice, and, I might add, abrupt religious exclamations in common discourse, though they were even benedictions to the Almighty, which he has often heard so ill-timed as to have an irreverent and almost a ludicrous effect. In a man of correct and refined taste, the happiest improvement in point of veneration for genuine religion will produce no tolerance for such habits. Nor will the dislike to them be lessened by ever so perfect a conviction of the sincere piety of any of the persons who have fallen into them. I shall be justified in laying great stress on this particular; for I have known instances of extreme mischief done to the feelings relative to religion, in young persons especially, through the continued irritation of disgust caused by such displeasing habits deforming personal piety.

In the conversation of illiterate christians the supposed man of taste has perhaps frequently heard the most unfortunate metaphors and similes, employed to explain or enforce evangelical sentiments; and probably, if he twenty times recollected one of those sentiments, the repulsive figure was sure to recur to his imagination. If he has heard so many of these, that each christian topic has acquired its appropriate offensive images, you can easily conceive what a lively perception of the importance of the subject itself must be requisite to overcome the disgust of the associations. The feeling accompanying these topics, as connected with these distasteful ideas, will be somewhat like that which spoils the pleasure of reading a noble poet, Virgil for instance, when each admired passage recalls the phrases and images into which it has been degraded in that kind of imitation denominated *travesty*. It may be added, that the reluctance to think of the subject because it is connected with these ideas, strengthens that connexion. For often the striving not to dwell on he disagreeable images, produces a mischievous reaction by which they press in more forcibly. The tenacity with which ideas adhere to the mind, is in proportion to the degree of interest, whether pleasing or unpleasing, with which they affect it; and an idea cannot well excite a stronger kind of interest than the earnest wish to escape from it. If we could cease to dislike it, it would soon cease to haunt us. It may also be observed, that the infrequency of thinking on the evangelical subjects, will confirm the injurious associations. The same mental law prevails in regard to subjects as to persons. If any unfortunate incident, or any circumstance of expression or conduct, displeased us in our first meeting with a person, it will be strongly recalled each time that we see him again, if we meet him but seldom; on the contrary, if our intercourse become frequent or habitual, such a first unpleasing circumstance, and others subsequent to it, may be forgotten. This observation might be of some use to a man who really wishes to neutralize in his mind the offensive associations with evangelical subjects; as he may be assured that one of the most effectual means would be, to make those subjects familiar by often thinking on them.

While remarking on the effect of unpleasing images employed to illustrate christian principles, I cannot help wishing that religious teachers had the good taste to avoid amplifying the metaphors of an undignified order, which may have a kind of coarse fitness for illustration, and are perhaps employed, in a short and transient way, in the Bible. I shall notice only that common one, in which the benefits and pleasures of religion are represented under the image of food. I do not recollect that in the Scriptures this metaphor is ever drawn to a great length. But from the facility of the process, it is not strange that it has been amplified, both in books and discourses, into the most extended parallel descriptions; exhausting the dining-room of images, and ransacking the language for substantives and adjectives, to stimulate the spiritual palate. The figure is combined with so many terms in our language, that it will unavoidably occur; and the analogy briefly and simply suggested may sometimes assist the thought without lessening the subject. But it is degrading to spiritual ideas to be extensively and systematically transmuted, I might say *cooked*, into sensual ones. The analogy between meaner and more dignified things should never be pursued further than one or two points of obviously useful illustration; for, if it be traced to every particular in which a resemblance can be found or fancied, the meaner thing abdicates its humble office of merely indicating some qualities of the great one, and becomes formally its representative and equal By their being made to touch at all points, the meaner is constituted a scale to measure and to limit the magnitude of the superior, and thus the importance of the one shrinks to the insignificance of the other. It will take some time for a man to recover any great degree of solemnity in thinking on the delights or the supports of religion, after he has seen them reduced into all the forms of eating and drinking. In such detailed analogies it often happens, that the most fanciful, or that the coarsest points of the resemblance, remain longest in the thoughts. When the mind has been taught to descend to a low manner of considering divine truth, it will be apt to descend to the lowest. There is no such violent tendency to abstraction and sublimity, in the minds of the generality of readers and hearers, as to render it necessary to take any great pains for the purpose of retaining their ideas in some degree of alliance with matter.

We are to acknowledge, then, the serious disadvantage under which evangelical religion presents itself to persons of mental refinement, with the associations which it has contracted from its uncultivated and injudicious professors. At the same time, it would be unjust not to observe that some christians, of a subordinate intellectual order, are distinguished by such an unassuming simplicity, by so much rectitude of conscience, and by a piety so warm and even exalted, as to leave a cultivated man convicted of a great perversion of feeling, if the faith, of which these are living representatives, did not appear to him in stronger attractive association with their excellence, than in repulsive association with their intellectual inferiority. But I am *supposing* his mind to be in a perverted state, and am far from seeking to defend him. This supposition however being made, I feel no surprise, on surveying the prevailing mental condition of evangelical communities, that this man has acquired an accumulation of prejudices against some of the distinguishing features of the gospel. Permitting himself to feel as if the circumstances which thus diminish or distort an order of christian sentiments, were inseparable from it, he is inclined to regret that there should be any divine sanctions against his framing for himself, on the foundation of some selected principles in christianity which he cannot but admire, but with a qualifying intermixture of foreign elements, a more liberalized scheme of religion.

It was especially unfortunate if, in the advanced stage of this man's perhaps highly cultivated youth, while he was exulting in the conscious enlargement of intellect, and the quickening and vivid perceptiveness of taste, but was still to be regarded as in a degree the subject of *education*, it was his lot to have the principles of religion exhibited and inculcated in a repulsive language and cast of thought by the seniors of his family or acquaintance. In that case, the unavoidable frequency of intercourse must have rendered the counteractive operation of the unpleasing circumstances, associated with christian truth, almost incessant. And it would naturally become continually stronger. For each repetition of that which offended his refined mental habits, would incite him to value and cherish them the more, and to cultivate them according to a standard still more foreign from all congeniality with his instructors. These habits he began and continued to acquire from books of elegant sentiment or philosophical speculation, which he read in disregard of the advice, perhaps to occupy himself much more with works specifically religious. To such literary employment and amusement he has again and again returned, with a delightful rebound from systematic common-places, whether delivered in private or in public instruction; and has felt the full contrast between the force, lustre, and mental richness, brightening and animating the moral speculations or poetical visions of genius, and the manner in which the truths of the gospel had been conveyed. He was not serious and honest enough to make, when in retirement, any deliberate trial of abstracting these truths from the vehicle and combination in which they were thus unhappily set forth, and in a measure disguised, in order to see what they would appear in a better form. This change of form he was competent to effect, or, if he was not, he had but a very small portion of that mental superiority, of which he was congratulating himself that his disgusts were an evidence. But his sense of the duty of doing this was perhaps less cogent, from his perceiving that the evangelical doctrines were inculcated by his relations with no less deficiency of the means of proving them true, than of rendering them interesting; and he could easily discern that his instructors had received the articles of their faith implicitly from a class of teachers, or the standard creed of a religious community, without even perhaps a subsequent exercise of reasoning to confirm what they had thus adopted. They believed these articles through the habit of hearing them, and maintained them by the habit of believing them. The recoil of his feelings, therefore, did not alarm his conscience with the apprehension that it might be absolutely the truth of God, that, under this uninviting form, he was loath to embrace. Unaided by such an impression already existing, and unarmed with a force of argument to work conviction, the seriousness, perhaps sometimes harsh seriousness, of his friends, reiterating the assertion of his mind being in a fatal condition, till he should think and feel exactly as they did, was little likely to conciliate his repugnance. When sometimes their admonitions took the mild or pathetic tone, his respect for their piety, and his gratitude for their affectionate solicitude, had perhaps a momentary effect to make him earnestly wish he could renounce his intellectual fastidiousness, and adopt in pious simplicity all their feelings and ideas. But as the contracted views, the rude figures, and the mixture of systematic and illiterate language, recurred, his mind would again revolt, and compel him to say, This cannot, will not, be my mode of religion.

Now, one wishes there had been some enlightened friend to say to such a man, Why will you not understand that there is no necessity for this to be the *mode* of your religion ? By what want of acuteness do you fail to distinguish between the mode, (a mere extrinsic and accidental mode,) and the substance? In the world of nature you see the same elements wrought into the plainest and the most beautiful, into the most diminutive and the most majestic forms. So the same simple principles of christian truth may constitute the basis of a very inferior, or a very noble, order of ideas. The principles themselves have an essential quality which is not convertible ; but they were not imparted to man to be fixed in the mind as so many bare scientific propositions, each confined to one single mode of conception, without any collateral ideas, and to be always expressed in one unalterable form of words. They are placed there in order to spread out, if I might so express it, into a great multitude and diversity of ideas and feelings. These ideas and feelings, forming round the pure simple principles, will correspond, and will make those principles themselves *seem* to correspond, to the meaner or the more dignified intellectual rank of the mind. Why will you not perceive, that if the subject takes so humble a style in its less intellectual believers, it is not that it cannot unfold greater proportions through a gradation of larger and still larger faculties, and with facility occupy the whole capacity of the amplest, in the same manner as the ocean fills a gulf as easily as a creek! Through this climax it retains an identity of its essential principles, and appears progressively a nobler thing only by gaining a position for more conspicuously displaying itself. Why will you not go with it through this gradation, till you see it presented in a greatness of character adequate to the utmost that you can, without folly, attribute to yourself of large and improved faculty? Never fear lest the gospel should prove not sublime enough for the elevation of your thoughts. If you could attain an intellectual eminence from which you would look with pity on the rank you at present hold, you would still find the dignity of this subject on your level, and rising above it. Do you doubt this? What then do you think of such spirits, for instance, as those of Milton and Pascal? And by how many degrees of the intellectual scale shall yours surpass them, to authorize your feeling that to be little which they felt to be great? They were at times sensible of the magnificence of christian truth, filling, distending, and exceeding, their faculties, and could have wished for even greater powers to do it justice. In their loftiest contemplations, they did not feel their minds elevating the subject, but the subject elevating their minds. Now consider that their views of the gospel were, in essence, the same with those of its meanest sincere disciples; and that therefore many sentiments which, by their unhappy form, have disgusted you so much, bore a faithful though humble analogy to the ideas of these illustrious christians. Why then, while hearing such sentiments, have you not learnt the habit of recognising this analogy, and in pursuance of it casting your thought upward to the highest style of the subject, instead of abandoning the subject itself in the recoil from the unfortunate mode of presenting it? Have you not cause to fear that your dislike goes deeper than this exterior of its exhibition? For, else, would you not anxiously seek, and rejoice to meet, the divine subject in that transfiguration of aspect by which its grandeur would thus be redeemed?

I would make a solemn appeal to the understanding and the conscience of such a man. I would say to him, Is it to the honour of a mind of taste, that it loses, when the religion of Christ is concerned, all the value of its discrimination? Do you not absolutely know that the littleness which you see investing that religion is adventitious? Are you not certain that in hearing the discourse of such men, if they were now to be found, as those I have named, the evangelical truths would appear to you sublime, and that they cannot be less so in fact than they would appear as displayed from those minds? But even suppose that *they* also failed, and that all modern christians, without exception, had conspired to give an unattractive and unimpressive aspect to the subject of their profession, there is still the Christian Revelation—may I not presume that you sometimes read it? But this is to be done in that state of susceptible seriousness, without which you will have no just apprehension of its character; without which you are but like an ignorant clown who, happening to look at the heavens, perceives nothing more awful in that immeasurable wilderness of suns than in the row of lamps along the streets. If you do read that book, in the better state of feeling, I have no comprehension of the constitution of your mind, if the first perception would not be that of a simple venerable dignity, and if the second would not be that of a certain abstract undefinable magnificence; a perception of something which, behind this simplicity, expands into a greatness beyond the compass of your mind; an impression like that with which a thoughtful and imaginative man might be supposed to have looked on the countenance of Newton, feeling a kind of mystical absorption in the attempt to comprehend the magnitude of the soul residing within that form. When in this state of serious susceptibility, have you not also perceived in the character and the manner of the first apostles of this truth, while they were declaring it, an expression of dignity, altogether different from that of other distinguished men, and much more elevated and unearthly? If you examined the cause, you perceived that the dignity arose partly from their being employed as living oracles of this truth, and still more from their whole characters being pervaded by its spirit. And have you not been sometimes conscious, for a moment, that if it possessed your soul in the same manner as it did theirs, it would raise you to be one of the most excellent order of mortals? You would then stand forth in a combination of sanctity, devotion, disinterestedness, superiority to external things, energy, and aspiring hope, in comparison of which the ambition of a conqueror, or the pride of a self-admiring philosopher, would be a very vulgar kind of dignity. You acknowledge these representations to be just; you allow that the kind of sublimity which you have sometimes perceived in the New Testament, that the qualities of the apostolic spirit, and that the intellectual and moral greatness of some modern christians, express the genuine character of the evangelical religion, showing that character to be of great lustre. But then, is it not most disingenuous in you to suffer the meanness which you know to be but associated and separable, to be admitted by your own mind as an excuse for its alienation from what is acknowledged to be in itself the very contrary of meanness? Ought you not to turn on yourself with indignation at that want of rectitude which resigns you to the effect of these associations, or with contempt of the debility which tries in vain to break them? Is it for *you* to be offended at the mental weakness of christians, you, whose intellectual vigour, and whose sense of justice, but leave you to sink helpless in the fastidiousness of sickly taste, and to lament that so many inferior spirits have been consoled and saved by this divine faith as to leave on it a soil which forbids your embracing it, even though your own salvation depend? At the very same time perhaps this weakness takes the form of pride. Let that pride speak out; it would be curious to hear it say, that your mental refinement perhaps *might* have permitted you to take your ground on that eminence of the christian faith where Milton and Pascal stood, *if* so many humbler beings did not disgrace it, by occupying the declivity and the vale.

But after all, what need of referring to illustrious names? as if the claims of that which you acknowledge to be from heaven should be made to depend on the number of those who have received it gracefully; or as if a rational being could calmly wait for his taste to be conciliated, before he would embrace a system by which his immortal interest is to be secured. The Sovereign Authority has signified what the difference shall be in the end, between the consequences of receiving or not receiving the evangelic declaration. Is the difference so announced of such small account that you would not, on serious consideration, be overwhelmed with wonder and shame, that so minor an interference as that of mere taste should so long have made you unjust to yourself in relation to what you are in progress to realize? And if, persisting to decline an exercise of such faithful consideration, you go on a venture to meet a consequence unspeakably disastrous, will an unhallowed and proud refinement appear to have been a worthy cause for which to incur it? You deserve to be disgusted with a divine communication, and to lose all its benefits, if you can thus let every thing have a greater influence on your feelings concerning it than its truth and importance, and if its accidental and separable associations with littleness, can counteract its essential inseparable ones with the Governor and Redeemer of the world, with happiness, and with eternity. With what compassion might you be justly regarded by an illiterate but zealous christian, whose interest in the truths of the New Testament, at once constitutes the best felicity here, and securely carries him toward the kingdom of his Father; while you are standing aloof, and perhaps thinking, that if he and all such as he were dead, you might, after a while, acquire the spirit which should impel you also toward heaven. But why do you not feel your individual concern in this great subject as absolutely as if all men were dead, and you heard alone in the earth the voice of God; or as if you saw, like the solitary exile of Patmos, an awful appearance of Jesus Christ and the visions of hereafter? What is it to you that many christians have given an aspect of littleness to the gospel, or that a few have sustained and exemplified its sublimity?

LETTER III.

ANOTHER cause which I think has tended to render evangelical religion less acceptable to persons of taste, is the *peculiarity of language* adopted in the discourses and books of its teachers, as well as in the religious conversation and correspondence of the majority of its adherents. I do not refer to any past age, when an excessive quaintness deformed the composition of so many writers on religion and all other subjects; my assertion is respecting the diction at present in use.

The works collectively of the best writers in the language, of those especially who may be called the moderns of the language, have created and substantially fixed a standard of general phraseology. If any department is exempted from the authority of this standard, it is the low one of humour and buffoonery, in which the writer may coin and fashion phrases at his whim. But in the language of the higher, and of what may be called middle order of writing, that authority is the law. It does indeed allow indefinite varieties of what is called style, since twenty able and approved writers might be cited, who have each a different style; but yet there is a certain general character of expression which they have mainly concurred to establish. This compound result of all their modes of writing is become sanctioned as the classical manner of employing the language, as the form in which it constitutes the most rectified general vehicle of thought. And though it is difficult to define this standard, yet a well-read person of taste feels when it is transgressed or deserted, and pronounces that no classical writer has employed that phrase, or would have combined those words in such a manner.

The deviations from this standard must be, first, by mean or vulgar diction, which is below it; or secondly, by a barbarous diction, which is *out* of it, or foreign to it; or thirdly, by a diction which, though foreign to it, is yet not to be termed barbarous, because it is elevated entirely above the authority of the standard, by some transcendent force or majesty of thought, or a superhuman communication of truth.

I might make some charge against the language of

divines under the first of these distinctions; but my present attention is to what seems to me to come under the second character of difference from the standard, that of being barbarous.—The phrases peculiar to any trade, profession, or fraternity, are barbarous, if they were not low; they are commonly both. The language of law is felt by every one to be barbarous in the extreme, not only by the huge lumber of its technical terms, but by its very structure, in the parts not consisting of technical terms. The language of science is barbarous, as far as it differs arbitrarily, and in more than the use of those terms which are indispensable to the science, from the pure general model. And I am afraid that, on the same principle, the accustomed diction of evangelical religion also must be pronounced barbarous. For I suppose it will be instantly allowed, that the mode of expression of the greater number of evangelical divines,* and of those taught by them, is widely different from the standard of general language, not only by the necessary adoption of some peculiar terms, but by a continued and systematic cast of phraseology;

* When I say *evangelical divines*, I concur with the opinion of those, who deem a considerable, and, in an intellectual and literary view, a highly respectable class of the writers who have professedly taught christianity, to be *not* strictly evangelical. They might rather be denominated moral and philosophical divines, illustrating and enforcing very ably the generalities of religion, and the christian morals, but not placing the economy of redemption exactly in that light in which the New Testament appears to place it. Some of these have avoided the kind of dialect on which I am animadverting, not only by means of a diction more classical and dignified in the general principles of its structure, but also by avoiding the *ideas* with which the phrases of this dialect are commonly associated. I may however here observe, that it is by no means altogether confined to the specifically evangelical department of writing and discourse, though it there prevails the most, and with the greatest number of phrases. It extends, in some degree, into the majority of writing on religion in general, and may therefore be called the theological, almost as properly as the evangelical, dialect.

insomuch that in reading or hearing five or six sentences of an evangelical discourse, you ascertain the school by the mere turn of expression, independently of any attention to the quality of the ideas. If, in order to try what those ideas would appear in an altered form of words, you attempted to reduce a paragraph to the language employed by intellectual men in speaking or writing well on general subjects, you would find it must be absolutely a version. You know how easily a vast mass of exemplification might be quoted; and the specimens would give the idea of an attempt to create, out of the general mass of the language, a dialect which should be intrinsically spiritual; and so exclusively appropriated to christian doctrine as to be totally unserviceable for any other subject, and to become ludicrous when applied to it.* And this being extracted, like the sabbath from the common course of time, the general range of diction is abandoned, with all its powers, diversities, and elegance, to secular subjects and the use of the profane. It is a kind of popery of language, vilifying every thing not marked with the signs of the holy church, and forbidding any one to minister to religion except in consecrated speech.

Suppose that a heathen foreigner had acquired a full acquaintance with our language in its most classical construction, yet without learning any thing about the gospel, (which it is true enough he might do,) and that he then happened to read or hear an evangelical discourse—he would be exceedingly surprised at the

* This is so true, that it is no uncommon expedient with the would-be wits, to introduce some of the spiritual phrases, in speaking of any thing which they wish to render ludicrous; and they are generally so far successful as to be rewarded by the laugh or the smile of the circle, who probably may never have had the good fortune of hearing wit, and have not the sense or conscience to care about religion.

cast of phraseology. He would probably be arrested and perplexed in such a manner as hardly to know whether he was trying his faculties on the new doctrine, or on the singularity of the diction; whereas the general course of the diction should appear but the same as that to which he had been accustomed. It should be such that he would not even think of *it*, but only of the new subject and peculiar ideas which were coming through it to his apprehension; unless there could be some advantage in the necessity of looking at these ideas through the mist and confusion of the double medium, created by the super-induction of an uncouth special dialect on the general language.—Or if he were *not* a stranger to the subject, but had acquired its leading principles from some author or speaker who employed (with the addition of a very small number of peculiar terms) the same kind of language in which any other serious subject would have been discoursed on, he would still be not less surprised. "Is it possible," he would say, as soon as he could apprehend what he was attending to, " that these are the very same views which lately presented themselves with such lucid simplicity to my understanding? Or is there something more, of which I am not aware, conveyed and concealed under these strange shapings of phrase? Is this another stage of the religion, the school of the adepts, in which I am not yet initiated? And does religion then every where, as well as in *my* country, affect to show and guard its importance by relinquishing the simple language of intelligence, and assuming a sinister dialect of its own? Or is this the diction of an individual only, and of one who really intends but to convey the same ideas that I have elsewhere received in so much more clear and direct a vehicle of words? But then, in what remote corner, placed beyond the authority of criticism and the circulation of literature, where a noble language stagnates into barbarism, did this man study his religion and acquire his phrases? Or by what inconceivable perversion of taste and of labour has he framed, for the sentiments of his religion, a mode of expression so uncongenial with the eloquence of his country, and so calculated to exclude it from all benefit of that eloquence?"

My dear friend, if I were not conscious of a most sincere veneration for evangelical religion itself, I should be more afraid to trust myself in making these observations on the usual manner of expressing its ideas. If my description be exaggerated, I am willing to be corrected. But that there is a great and systematical alienation from the true classical diction, is most palpably obvious: and I cannot help regarding it as an unfortunate circumstance. It gives the gospel too much the air of a professional thing, which must have its peculiar cast of phrases, for the mutual recognition of its proficients, in the same manner as other professions, arts, crafts, and mysteries, have theirs. This is officiously placing the singularity of littleness to draw attention to the singularity of greatness, which in the very act it misrepresents and obscures. It is giving an uncouthness of mien to a beauty which should attract all hearts. It is teaching a provincial dialect to the rising instructor of a world. It is imposing the guise of a cramped formal ecclesiastic on what is destined for an universal monarch.

Would it not be an improvement in the administration of religion, by discourse and writing, if christian truth were conveyed in that neutral vehicle of expression which is adapted indifferently to common serious subjects? But it may be made a question whether it *can* be perfectly conveyed in such language. This point therefore requires a little consideration.—The diction on which I have animadverted, may be described under three distinctions.

The first is a peculiar way of using various common words. And this peculiarity consists partly in expressing ideas by such single words as do not simply and directly belong to them, instead of other single words which do simply and directly belong to them, and in general language are used to express them;* and partly in using such combinations of words as make uncouth phrases. Now what necessity? The answer is immediately obvious as to the former part of the description; there can be no need to use one common word in an affected and forced manner to convey an idea, which there is another common word at hand to express in the simplest and most usual manner. And then as to phrases, consisting of an uncouth combination of words which are common, and have no degree of technicality,—are they necessary? They are not absolutely necessary, unless each of these combinations conveys a thought of so exquisitely singular a turn, that no other conjunction of terms could have expressed it; which was never suggested by one mind to another till these three or four words, falling out of the general order of the language, gathered into a peculiar phrase; which cannot be expressed in the language of another country that has not a correspondent idiom; and which will vanish from the world if ever this phrase shall be forgotten. But these combinations of words have no such pretensions. When you obtain their meaning, you may well wonder why a peculiar apparatus of phrase should have been constructed, to bring and retain such an

---

* As for instance, *walk*, and *conversation*, instead of *conduct*, *actions*, or *deportment*; *flesh*, instead of, sometimes, *body*, sometimes natural inclination.

element of thought within the sphere of your understanding. But indeed the very circumstance of there being nothing extraordinary in the sense, may have been one inducement to the contrivance. There may have been a certain discontent that the import should not appear more significant, more weighty, more sacred, more authoritative, than it could be made to appear as conveyed in common secular language. It could not be trusted to have its proper effect, without some special token borne on its exterior to warn us to pay it reverence. In whatever manner, however, the language came to be perverted into these artificial modes, it would be easy to try whether the ideas, of which they are the vehicles, are such as they exclusively are competent and privileged to convey, insomuch that their rejection would be the forfeiture of a certain portion of religious truth and sentiment, which would thereupon retire beyond the confines of our intelligence, disdaining to stay and make an abode in common forms of language. And it would be found that these phrases, as it is within our familiar experience that all phrases consisting of only common words, and having no relation to art or science, can be exchanged for several different combinations of words, without materially altering the thought or lengthening the expression. Make the experiment on any paragraph written in the manner in question, on any religious topic whatever, and see whether you cannot melt all the uncouth constructions of diction, to be cast in a new and uncanonical shape, without letting any sense there was in them evaporate. I conclude then, that what I have described as the first part of the theological dialect, the peculiar mode of using common words, is not absolutely necessary as a vehicle of christian truths.

The second part of the dialect consists, not in

peculiar mode of using common words, but in a class of words peculiar in themselves, as being seldom used except by divines, but of which the meaning can be expressed, without definition or circumlocution, by other single terms which are in general use. For example, edification, tribulation, blessedness, godliness, righteousness, carnality, lusts, (a term peculiar and theological only in the plural,) could be exchanged for parallel terms too obvious to need mentioning. It is true indeed that there are very few terms, if any, perfectly synonymous. But when there are several words of very similar though not exactly the same signification, and none of them belong to an art or science, the one which is selected is far more frequently used in that *general* meaning by which it is merely equivalent to the others, than in that precise shade of meaning by which it is distinguished from them. The words instruction, improvement, for instance, may not express exactly the sense of edification; but the word edification is probably not often used by a writer or speaker with any recollection of that peculiarity of its meaning by which it differs from improvement or instruction. This is still more true of some other words, as, for example, tribulation and affliction. Whatever small difference of import these words may have in virtue of derivation, it is probable that no man ever wrote tribulation rather than affliction *on account* of such difference. If, in addition to these two, the word distress has offered itself, the selection of any one from the three has perhaps always been determined by habit, or accident, rather than by any perception of a distinct signification. The same remark is applicable to the words blessed, happy, righteous, virtuous, carnal, sensual, and a multitude of others. So that though there are few words strictly synonymous, yet there are very many which are so in *effect*, even by the allowance and sanction of the most rigid laws to which any of the best writers have conformed their composition. Perhaps this is a defect in human thinking; of which the ideal perfection may be, that every conception should be so discriminative and precise, that no two words, which have a definable shade of difference in their meaning, should be equally and indifferently eligible to express that conception. But what writer or speaker will ever even aspire to such perfection of thinking?—not to say that if he did, he would soon find the vocabulary of the most copious language deficient of single direct terms, and indeed of possible combinations of terms, to mark all the sensible modifications of his ideas. If a divine felt that he had such extreme discrimination of thought, that he meant something clearly different by the words carnal, godly, edifying, and so of many others, from what he could express by the words, sensual, pious, religious, instructive, he would certainly do right to adhere to the more peculiar words; but if he does not, he may perhaps improve the vehicle, without hurting the material, of his religious communications, by adopting the general and what may be called classical mode of expression.

The third distinction of the theological dialect consists in words almost peculiar to the language of divines, and for which equivalent terms *cannot* be found, except in the form of definition or circumlocution. Sanctification, regeneration, grace, covenant, salvation, and a few more, may be assigned to this class. These may be called, in a qualified sense, the technical terms of evangelical religion. Now, separately from any religious considerations, it is plainly necessary, in a literary view, that all those terms that express a modification of thought which there are no other words competent to express, without great circumlocution, should be retained. They are requisite to the sufficiency of the language. And then, in considering those terms as connected with the christian truth, I am ready to admit, that it will be of advantage to that truth, for some of those peculiar doctrines, of which it partly consists, to be permanently denominated by certain peculiar words, which shall stand as its technical terms But here several thoughts suggest themselves.

First, the definitions of some of these christian terms are not absolutely unquestionable. The words have assumed the specific formality of technical terms, without having completely the quality and value of such terms. A certain laxity in their sense renders them of far less use in their department, than the terms of science, especially of mathematical science, are in theirs. Technical terms have been the lights of science, but, in many instances, the shades of religion. It is most unfortunate, when, in disquisitions or instructions, the grand leading words, on which the force of all the rest depends, have not a precise and indisputable signification. The effect is similar to that which takes place in the ranks of an army, when an officer has a doubtful opinion, or gives indistinct orders. What I would infer from these observations is, that a christian writer or speaker will occasionally do well, instead of using the peculiar term, to express at length in other words, at the expense of much circumlocution, that idea which he would have wished to convey if he had used that peculiar term. I do not mean that he should do this so often as to render the term obsolete. It might be useful sometimes, especially in verbal instruction, both to introduce the term, and to give such a sentence as I have described. Such an expletive repetition of the idea will more than compensate for the tediousness, by the distinctness and fulness of enunciation.*

Secondly, if the definitions of the christian peculiar terms were even as precise and fixed as those of scientific denominations, yet the nature of the subject is such as to permit an indolent mind to pronounce or to hear these terms without recollecting those definitions. In delivering or writing, and in hearing or reading, a mathematical lecture, both the teacher and the pupil are compelled to form in their minds the exact idea which each technical term has been defined to signify; else the whole train of words is mere sound and inanity. But in religion, a man has a feeling of having some general ideas connected with all the words as he hears them, though he perhaps never studied, or does not retain, the definition of one. I shall have occasion to repeat this remark, and therefore do not enlarge here. The inference is the same as under the former observation; it is, that the technical terms of christianity will contribute little to precision of thought, unless the ideas which they signify be often expressed at length in other words, either in explanation of those terms when introduced, or in substitution for them when omitted.

Thirdly, it is not in the power of single theological terms, however precise their definitions may at any time have been, to secure to their respective ideas an unalterable stability. Unless the ideas themselves, by being often expressed in common words, preserve the signification of the terms, the terms will not preserve the accuracy of the ideas. This is true no doubt of the technical terms of science; but it is true in a much

* It is needless to observe that this would be a superfluous labour with respect to the most simple of the peculiar words, such for instance as *salvation*.

more striking manner of the peculiar words in theology. If the technical terms of science, at least of the strictest kind of science, were to cease to mean what they had been defined to mean, they would cease to mean any thing, and the change would be only from knowledge to blank ignorance. But in the christian theology, the change might be from truth to error; since the peculiar words might cease to mean what they were once defined to mean, by being employed in a different sense. It may not be difficult to conjecture in what sense the terms conversion and regeneration, for example, were used by the reformers, and the men who may be called the fathers of the established church of this country; but what sense have they subsequently borne in the writings of many of its divines? The peculiar words may remain, when the ideas which they were intended to perpetuate are gone. Thus instead of being the signs of those ideas, they become their monuments; and monuments profaned into abodes for the living enemies of the departed. It must indeed be acknowledged, that in some instances innovations of doctrine have been introduced partly by declining the use of the words that designated the doctrines which it was wished to render obsolete; but they have been still more frequently and successfully introduced, under the advantage of retaining the terms while the principles were gradually subverted. And therefore I shall be pardoned for repeating this once more, that since the peculiar words can be kept in one invariable signification only by keeping that signification clearly in sight in another way than the bare use of these words themselves, it would be wise in christian authors and speakers sometimes to express the ideas in common words, either in expletive and explanatory connexion with the peculiar terms, or, occasionally, instead of them. I would still be understood to approve entirely of the use of a few of this class of terms; while the above observations may deduct very much from the usual estimate of their value and importance.

These pages have attempted to show, in what particulars the language adopted by a great proportion of christian divines might be modified, and yet remain faithful to the principles of christian doctrine. Such common words as have acquired an affected cast in theological use, might give place to the other common words which express the ideas in a plain and unaffected manner, and the phrases formed of common words uncouthly combined, may be swept away.—Many peculiar and antique words might be exchanged for other single words, of equivalent signification, and in general use. —And the small number of peculiar terms acknowledged and established as of permanent use and necessity, might, even separately from the consideration of modifying the diction, be often, with advantage to the explicit declaration and clear comprehension of christian truth, made to give place to a fuller expression, in a number of common words, of those ideas of which these peculiar terms are the single signs.

Now such an alteration would bring the language of divines nearly to the classical standard. If evangelical sentiments could be faithfully presented, in an order of words of which so small a part should be of specific cast, they could be presented in what should be substantially the diction of Addison or Pope. And if even Shaftesbury, Bolingbroke, and Hume, could have become christians by some mighty and sudden efficacy of conviction, and had determined to write thenceforth in the spirit of the Apostles, they would have found, if these observations be correct, no radical change necessary in the consistence of their language. An enlightened believer in christianity might have been sorry, if, in such a case, he had seen any of them superstitiously labouring to acquire all the phrases of a school, instead of applying at once to its new vocation a diction fitted for the vehicle of universal thought. Are not *they* yet sufficient masters of language, it might have been asked with surprise, to express all their thoughts with the utmost precision? As their language had been found sufficiently specific to injure the gospel, it would have been strange if it had been too general to serve it. The required alteration would probably have been little more than to introduce familiarly the obvious denominations of the christian topics and objects, such as, redemption, heaven, mediator, Christ, Redeemer, with the others of a similar kind, and a very few of those almost technical words which I have admitted to be indispensable. The habitual use of such denominations would have left the general order of their composition the same. And it would have been striking to observe by how comparatively small a difference of terms a diction which had appeared most perfectly pagan, could be christianized, when the writer had turned to christian subjects, and felt the christian spirit.—On the whole then, I conclude that, with the exception which I have distinctly made, the evangelical principles may be clearly exhibited in what may be called a neutral diction. And if they may, I can imagine some reasons to justify the wish that it were generally employed.

As one of these reasons, I may revert to the consideration of the impression made by the dialect which I have described, on those persons of cultivated taste whom this essay has chiefly in view. I am aware that they are greatly inclined to make an idol of their taste and I am aware also that no species of irreligion can be much worse than to sacrifice to this idol any thing which essentially belongs to christianity. If any part of evangelical religion, all injurious associations being detached, were still of a nature to displease a refined taste, the duty would evidently be to repress its claims and murmurs. We should dread the presumption which would require of the Deity that his spiritual economy should be, both in reality and evidently to our view, correspondent in all parts to the type of order, grandeur, or beauty presented to us in the constitution of the material world, or to those notions of them which have become conventionally established among cultivated minds. But, at the same time, it is a most unwise policy for religion, that the sacrifice of taste which ought, if required, to be submissively made to any part of either its essence or its form as really displayed from heaven, should be exacted to any thing unnecessarily and ungracefully superinduced by man.

As another reason, I would observe, that the disciples of the religion of Christ would wish it to mingle more extensively and familiarly with social converse, and all the serious subjects of human attention. But then it should have every facility, that would not compromise its genuine character, for doing so. And a peculiar phraseology is the direct contrary of such facility, as it gives to what is already by its own nature eminently distinguished from common subjects, an *artificial* strangeness, which makes it difficult for discourse to slide into it, and revert to it and from it, without a formal and uncouth transition. The subject is placed in a condition like that of an entire foreigner in company, who is debarred from taking any share in the conversation, till some one interrupts it by turning directly to him, and beginning to talk with him in the foreign language. You have sometimes observed, when a person has introduced religious topics, in the course of perhaps a tolerably rational conversation on other interesting subjects, that, owing to the cast of expression, fully as much as to the difference of the subject, it was done by an entire change of the whole tenour and bearing of the discourse, and with as formal an announcement as the bell ringing to church. Had his religious diction been more of a piece with the common cast of language of intelligent discourse, he might probably have introduced the subject sooner, and certainly with a much better effect.

A third consideration, is, that evangelical sentiments would be less subject to the imputation of fanaticism, if their language were less contrasted with that of other classes of sentiments. Here it is unnecessary to say, that no pusillanimity were more contemptible than that which, to escape this imputation, would surrender the smallest vital particle of the religion of Christ. We are to keep in solemn recollection his declaration, "Whosoever shall be ashamed of me and of my words, of him also shall the Son of man be ashamed." Any model of terms, which could not be superseded without precluding some idea peculiar to the gospel from the possibility of being faithfully expressed, it would be for his disciples to retain in spite of all the ridicule of the most antichristian age. But I am, at every step, assuming that every part of the evangelical system can be most perfectly exhibited in a diction but little peculiar; and, that being admitted, would it not be better to avert the imputation, as far as this difference of language could avert it? Better, I do not mean, in the way of protective convenience to any cowardly feeling, of the man who is liable to be called a fanatic for maintaining the evangelical principles; he ought,

on the ground both of christian fidelity and of manly
independence, to be superior to caring about the charge;
but better, as to the light in which these principles
might appear to the persons who meet them with this
prejudice. You may have observed that in attributing
fanaticism, they often fix on the phrases, at least as
much as on the absolute substance, of evangelical
doctrines. Now would it not be better to show them
what these doctrines are, as divested of these phrases,
and exhibited clearly in that vehicle in which other
important truths are presented; and thus, at least, to
defeat their propensity to seize on a mode of exhibition
so convertible to the ludicrous, in defence against any
claim made on them for seriousness respecting the substantial matter? If sometimes their grave attention,
their corrected apprehension, their partial approbation
might be gained, it were a still more desirable effect.
And we can recollect instances in which a certain
degree of this good effect has resulted. Persons who
had received unfavourable impressions of some of the
peculiar ideas of the gospel, from having heard them
advanced almost exclusively in the modes of phrase on
which I have remarked, have acknowledged their prejudices to be somewhat diminished, after these ideas
had been presented in the simple general language of
intellect. We cannot indeed so far forget the lessons
of experience, and the inspired declarations concerning
the dispositions of the human mind, as to expect that it
would be more than very partially conciliated by any
possible improvement in the mode of exhibiting christian truth. But it were to be wished that every thing
should be done to bring reluctant minds into doubt, at
least, whether, if they cannot be evangelical, it be
because they are of an order too rectified and refined.

As a further consideration in favour of adopting a

more general language, it may be observed, that hypocrisy would then find a much greater difficulty, as far as speech is concerned, in supporting its imposture. The usual language of hypocrisy, at least of vulgar hypocrisy, is cant; and religious cant is often an affected use of the phrases which have been heard employed as appropriate to evangelical truth; with which phrases the hypocrite has connected no distinct ideas, so that he would be confounded if an intelligent examiner were to require an accurate explanation of them; while yet nothing is more easy to be sung or said. Now were this diction, for the greater part, to vanish from christian society, leaving the truth in its mere essence behind, and were, consequently, the pretender reduced to assume the guise of religion on the more laborious condition of acquiring an understanding of its leading principles, so as to be able to give them forth discriminatively in language of his own, the part of a hypocrite would be much less easily acted, and less frequently attempted. Religion would therefore be seldomer dishonoured by the mockery of a false semblance.

Again, if this alteration of language were introduced, some of the sincere disciples of evangelical religion would much more distinctly feel the necessity of a positive intellectual hold on the principles of their profession. A systematic recurring formality of words tends to prevent a perfect understanding of the subject, by furnishing for complex ideas a set of ready-framed signs, (like stereotype in printing,) which a man learns to employ without really having the ideas of which the combination should consist. Some of the simple ideas which belong to the combination may be totally absent from his mind, the others may be most faintly apprehended; there is no precise construction therefore of the thought; and thus the sign which he uses, stands in fact for nothing. If, on hearing one of these phrases, you were to turn to the speaker, and say, Now what *is* that idea? What do you plainly mean by that expression?—you would often find with how indistinct a conception, with how little attention to the very idea itself, the mind had been contented. And this contentment you would often observe to be, not a humble acquiescence in a consciously defective apprehension of some principle, of which a man feels and confesses the difficulty of attaining more than a partial conception, but the satisfied assurance that he fully understands what he is expressing. On another subject, where there were no settled forms of words to beguile him into the feeling as if he thought and understood, when in fact he did not, and where words must have been selected to define his own formation of the thought, his embarrassment how to express himself would have made him aware that his notion had no shape, and have compelled an intellectual effort to give it one. But it is against all reason that christian truth should be believed and professed with a less concern for precision, and at the expense of less mental exercise, than any other subject would require. And of how little consequence it would seem to be, in *this* mode of believing, whether a man entertains one system of principles or the opposite.

But if such arguments could not be alleged, it would still seem far from desirable, without evident necessity, to clothe evangelical sentiment in a diction varying in more than a few indispensable terms from the general standard, for the simple reason, that it must be barbarous; unless, as I have observed, it be raised quite above the authority of this standard, and of the criticism and the taste which appeal to it, by the venerable dignity of inspiration, which we have no more to expect, or by the intellectual power of a genius almost surpassing human nature. I do not know whether it be absolutely impossible that there should arise a man whose manner of thinking shall be so transcendent in originality and demonstrative vigour, as to authorize him to throw the language into a new order, all his own: but it is questionable whether there ever appeared such a writer, in any language which had been cultivated to its maturity. Even Milton, who might, if ever mortal might, be warranted to sport with all established authority and usage, and to run the language into whatever unsanctioned forms would enlarge his freedom in grand mental enterprise, has been, for presuming in a certain degree to create for himself a peculiar diction, charged by Johnson with writing in a "Babylonish dialect." And Johnson's own mighty force of mind has not defended his Roman dialect from being condemned by all men of taste. The magic of Burke's eloquence is not enough to beguile the perception, that it is of less dignified and commanding tone, has less of the claim to be "for all time," than if the same marvellous affluence of thought and fancy had been conveyed in a language of less arbitrary, capricious, and mannerish character. To revert to the theological peculiarity of dialect; we may look in vain for any theologian of genius so supereminently powerful as might impress on it either a dignity to overawe, or a grace to conciliate, literary taste. But indeed if we had such a one he would not attempt it. If he disregarded the classical standard, and chose to speak in an alien dialect, it would be a dialect of his own, formed in still more complete independence and disregard of the model which so many theological teachers have concurred to establish for the language of religion.

It may be said, perhaps, that any such splendid intervention, in authorization of that model, can be spared; for that the class contains so many of great ability, and so many more of great piety and usefulness, that the peculiar diction will maintain its ground. Probably it will do so, in a considerable degree, for a long time. But no numbers, ability, or piety, will ever redeem it from the character of barbarism.

LETTER IV.

In defence of the diction which I have been describing, it will be said, that it has grown out of the language of the Bible. To a great extent, this is evidently true. Many phrases indeed which casually occurred in the writings of divines, and many which were laboriously invented by those who wished to give to divinity a complete systematic arrangement, and therefore wanted denominations or titles for the multitude of articles in the artificial distribution, have been incorporated in the theological dialect. But a large proportion of its phrases consists partly in such combinations of words as were taken originally from the Bible, and still more in such as have, from familiarity with that book, partly grown in insensible assimilation, and partly been formed intentionally, but rudely, in resemblance, to its characteristic language.

Before proceeding further, I do not know whether it may be necessary, in order to prevent misapprehension, to advert to the high advantage and propriety of often introducing sentences from the Bible, not only in theological, but in any grave moral composition. Passages of the inspired writings must necessarily be cited, in some instances, in proof of the truth of opinions, and may be most happily cited, in many others, to give a venerable and impressive air to serious sentiments which would be admitted as just though unsupported by such a reference to the authority. Both complete sentences, and striking short expressions, consisting perhaps sometimes of only two or three words, may be thus introduced with an effect at once useful and ornamental, while they appear pure and unmodified amidst the composition, as simple particles of scripture, quite distinct from the diction in which they are inserted. When thus appearing in their own genuine quality, as lines or parts of lines taken from a venerable book which is written in a manner very different from our common mode of language, they are read as expressions foreign to the surrounding composition, and, without an effort, referred to the work from which they are brought and of which they retain the unaltered consistence · in the same manner as passages, or striking short expressions, adopted from some respected and well-known classic in our language. Whatever dignity therefore characterizes the great work itself, is possessed also by these detached pieces in the various places where they are inserted, but not, if I may so express it, infused. And if they be judiciously inserted, they impart their dignity to the sentiments which they are employed to enforce. This employment of the sacred expressions may be very frequent, as the Bible contains such an immense variety of ideas, applicable to all manner of interesting subjects. And from its being so familiarly known, its sentences or shorter expressions may be introduced without the formality of noticing, either in terms or by any other mark, from what volume they are drawn.—These observations are more than enough, to obviate any imputation of wanting a due sense of the dignity and force which may b imparted by a judicious introduction of the language of the Bible.

It is a different mode of using biblical language, that constitutes so considerable a part of the dialect which I have ventured to disapprove. When insertions are made from the Bible in the manner here described as effective and ornamental, the composition exhibits two kinds of diction, each bearing its own separate character; the one being the diction which belongs to the author, the other that of the sacred book whence the citations are drawn. We pass along the course of his language with the ordinary feeling of being addressed in a common general phraseology; and when the pure scripture expressions occur, they are recognised in their own peculiar character, and with the sense that we are reading, in small detached portions, just so much of the Bible itself. This distinct recognition of the two separate characters of language prevents any impression of an uncouth heterogeneous consistence. But in the theological dialect, that part of the phraseology which has a biblical cast, is neither the one of these two kinds of language nor the other, but an inseparable though crude amalgam of both. For the expressions resembling those of scripture are blended and moulded into the substance of the diction. I say *resembling;* for though some of them are precisely phrases from the Bible, yet most of them are phrases a little modified from the form in which they occur in the sacred book, by changing or adding words, by compounding two phrases into one, and by fitting the rest of the language to the biblical phrases by an imitative antique construction. In this manner the scriptural expressions, instead of appearing as distinguished points on a common ground, as gems advantageously set in an inferior substance, are reduced to become an ordinary and desecrated ingredient in an uncouth phraseology. They are no longer brought directly from the scriptures, by an act of thought and choice in the person who uses them, and with a recollection of their sacred origin; but merely recur to him in the common usage of the diction, into which they have degenerated in the school of divines. They therefore are now in no degree of the nature of quotations, introduced for their special appositeness in the particular instance, as the expressions of an admired and revered human author would be repeated.

This is the kind of biblical phraseology which I could wish to see less employed,—unless it be either more venerable or more lucid than that which I have recommended. We may be allowed to doubt how far such language can be venerable, after considering, that it gives not the smallest assurance of striking or elevated thought, since in fact a vast quantity of most inferior writing has appeared in this kind of diction; that it is not *now* actually drawn from the sacred fountains; that the incessant repetition of its phrases in every kind of religious exercise and performance has worn out any solemnity it might ever have had; and that it is the very usual concomitant and sign of a servilely systematic and cramped manner of thinking. It may be considered also, that, from whatever high origin any modes and figures of speech may be drawn, they are reduced, 'n point of dignity, to the quality of the material with which they become interfused; so that if the whole character of the dialect of divines is not adapted to excite veneration, the proportion of it which gives a colour of scripture-phraseology, not standing out distinct from the composition, will have lost the virtue to excite it. And again, let it be considered, that in almost all cases, an attempt to imitate the peculiarity of form in which a venerable object is presented, not only fails to excite veneration, but provokes the contrary sentiment; especially when all things in the form of the venerable model are homogeneous, while the imitation exhibits some features of resemblance incongruously combined with what is mainly and unavoidably of a different cast. A grand ancient edifice, of whatever order, or if it were of a construction peculiar to itself, would be an impressive object; but a modern little one raised in its neighbourhood, of a conformation for the greatest part glaringly vulgar, but with a number of antique windows and angles in imitation of the grand structure, would be a grotesque and ridiculous one.

Scriptural phrases then can no longer make a solemn impression, when modified and vulgarized into the texture of a language which, taken altogether, is the reverse of every thing that can either attract or command. Such idioms may indeed remind one of prophets and apostles, but it is a recollection which prompts to say, Who are these men that, instead of respectfully introducing at intervals the direct words of those revered dictators of truth, seem to be mocking the sacred language by a barbarous imitative diction of their own? They may affect the forms of a divine solemnity, but there is no fire from heaven. They may show something like a burning bush, but it is without an angel.

As to perspicuity, there will not be a question whether that be one of the recommendations of this corrupt modification of the biblical phraseology. Without our leave, the mode of expression habitually associated with the general exercise of our intelligence, conveys ideas to us the most easily and the most clearly. And not unfrequently even in citing the pure expressions of scripture, especially in doctrinal subjects, a religious instructor will find it indispensable to add a sentence in order to expose the sense in a plainer manner; and that not as comment, but as explanation. He has many occasions for seeing that unless he do this, there will not be, in the minds of the persons to be instructed, exactly and definitively the idea which he understands to be expressed in the cited passage. Even to possess *himself* of a clear apprehension, there is, he might perceive in his mind, a kind of translating operation, embodying the idea in more common language, equivalent to the biblical.

But would not the disuse of a language which seems to bear a constant reference to the Bible, by this intimate blending of its phraseology, tend to put the Bible out of remembrance? It may be answered, that the Bible, as a book which will be read beyond all comparison more than any other, will keep *itself* in remembrance, among the serious part of mankind. Besides, it may be presumed that religious teachers and writers, however secularized the language they may adopt, will too often bring the sacred book in view by direct reference and citation, to admit any danger, from them, of its being forgotten. And though its distinct unmodified expressions should be introduced much seldomer in the course of their sentences, than the half-scriptural phrases are recurring in the diction under consideration, they would remind us of the Bible in a more advantageous manner, than a dialect which has lost the dignity of a sacred language without acquiring the grace of a classical one. I am sensible in how many points the illustration would be defective, but it would partly answer my purpose to observe, that if it were wished to promote the study of some venerated human author of a former age, suppose Hooker, the way would not be to attempt incorporating a great number of his turns of expression into the essential structure of our own diction, which would generally have a most uncouth effect, but to make respectful references, and often to insert in our composition sentences, and parts of sentences, distinctly *as his*, while our own cast of diction was conformed to the general modern standard.

Let the oracles of inspiration be cited continually, both as authority and illustration, in a manner that shall make the mind instantly refer each expression that is introduced to the venerable book whence it is taken; but let *our* part of religious language be simply ours, and let those oracles retain their characteristic form of expression unimitated, unparodied, to the end of time.*

An advocate for the theological diction, who should hesitate to maintain its necessity or utility on the ground

---

* In the above remarks, I have not made any distinction between the sacred books in their own language, and as translated. It might not however be improper to notice, that though there is a great peculiarity of language in the original, yet a certain proportion of the phraseology, as it stands in the translated scriptures, does not properly belong to the structure of the original composition, but is to be ascribed to the complexion of the language at the time when the translation was made. A translation, therefore, made now, and conformed to the present state of the language, in the same degree in which the earlier translation was conformed to the state of the language at that time, would make an alteration in some parts of that phraseology which the theological dialect has attempted to incorporate and imitate. If therefore it *were* the duty of divines to take the biblical mode of expression for their model, it would still be quite a work of supererogation to take this model in a wider degree of difference from the ordinary language suited to serious thoughts than as it would appear in such a later version. This would be a homage, not to the real diction of the sacred scriptures, but to the earlier cast of our own language. At the same time it must be admitted, both that the change of expression which a later version might, on merely philological principles, be justified by the progress and present standard of our language for making, would not be great: and that every sentiment of prudence and devotional taste that a considerable proportion of it has grown out of the language of scripture, may yet think it has become necessary in consequence of so many people having been so long accustomed to it. I cannot but be aware, that many respectable teachers of christianity would find a very great difficulty to depart from their inveterate usage. Nor could they acquire, if the change were attempted, a happy command of a more general language, without being considerably conversant with good writers on general subjects, and sedulously exercising themselves to throw their thoughts into a somewhat similar current of language. Unless, therefore, this study has been cultivated, or is intended to be cultivated, it will perhaps be better for *them*, especially if far advanced in life, to retain the accustomed mode of expression with all disadvantages. Younger theological students, however, are supposed to become

---

forbids to make quite so much alteration as those principles might warrant. All who have long venerated the scriptures in their somewhat antique version, would protest against their being laboriously modernized into every nice conformity with the present standard of the language, and against any other than a very literal translation. If it could be supposed that our language had not yet attained a fixed state, but would progressively change for ages to come, it would be desirable that the translation of the Bible should always continue, except in what might essentially affect the sense, a century or two behind, for the sake of that venerable air which a shade of antiquity confers on the form, of what is so sacred and authoritative in substance. But I cannot allow that the same law is to be extended to the language of divines. *They* have no right to assume the same ground and the same distinctions as the Bible; they ought not to affect to keep it company. There is no solemn dignity in their writings, which can claim to be invested with a venerable peculiarity. Imitate the Bible or not, their composition is merely of the ordinary human quality, and subject to the same rules as that of their contemporaries who write on other subjects. And if they remain behind the advanced state of the classical diction, those contemporaries will not allow them to excuse themselves by pretending to identify themselves with the Bible.

acquainted with those authors who have displayed the utmost extent and powers of language in its freest form : and it is right for them to be told that evangelical doctrine would incur no necessary corruption or profanation by being conveyed in so liberal, diversified, and what I may call *natural* a diction ; a language which may be termed the day-light of thought, as compared with the artificial lights of the peculiar dialect.—With regard also to a considerable proportion of christian readers and hearers, I am sensible that a reformed language would be excessively strange to them. But may I not allege, without any affectation of paradox, that its being so strange to them would be a proof that it is quite time it were adopted ? For the manner in which some of them would receive this altered dialect, would prove that the customary phraseology had scarcely given them any clear notions. It would be found, as I have observed before, that to them the peculiar phrases had been not so much the vehicles of ideas, as substitutes for them. So undefined has been their understanding of the sense, while they mechanically chimed to the sound, that if they hear the very ideas which these phrases signify, or did or should signify, expressed ever so plainly in other language, they do not recognise them ; and are instantly on the alert with the epithets, sound, orthodox, and all the watch-words of ecclesiastical suspicion. For such christians, the diction is the convenient asylum of ignorance, indolence, and prejudice.

But I have enlarged far beyond my intention, which was only to represent, with a short illustration, that this peculiar dialect is unfavourable to a cordial reception of evangelical doctrines in minds of cultivated taste. This I know o be a fact from many observations in real life, especially among intellectual young persons, not altogether regardless of serious subjects, and not seduced, though not out of danger of being so, by the cavils against the divine authority of christianity itself.

After dismissing the consideration of the language, which has unfortunately been made the canonical garb of religion, I meant to have taken a somewhat more general view of the accumulation of bad writing, under which the evangelical theology has been buried; and which has contributed to bring its principles in disfavour with too many persons of accomplished mental habits. A large proportion of that writing may be sentenced as bad, on more accounts than merely the peculiarity of dialect. But this is an invidious topic, and I shall make only a few observations.

Proofs of an intellect considerably above the common level, with a literary execution disciplined to great correctness, and partaking somewhat of elegance, are requisite on the lowest terms of acceptance for good writing, with cultivated readers. Superlatively strong sense will indeed command attention, and even admiration, in the absence of all the graces, and notwithstanding much incorrectness or clumsiness in the workmanship of the composition. But when thus standing the divested and sole excellence, it must be pre-eminently conspicuous to have this power. Below this pitch of single or of combined merit, a book cannot please persons of discerning judgment and refined taste, though its subject be the most interesting on earth; and for acceptableness, therefore, the subject is unfortunate in coming to those persons in that book. A disgusting cup will spoil the finest element which can be conveyed in it, though that were the nectar of immortality.

Now, in this view, I suppose it will be acknowledged that the evangelical cause has been, on the whole, far from happy in its prodigious list of authors. A number of them have displayed a high order of excellence; but one regrets as to a much greater number, that they did not revere the dignity of their religion too much, to beset and suffocate it with their superfluous offerings. To you I need not expatiate on the character of the collective christian library. It will have been obvious to you that there is a multitude of books which form the perfect vulgar of religious authorship; a vast exhibition of the most subordinate materials that can be called thought, in language too grovelling to be called style. Some of these writers seem to have concluded that the greatness of the *subject* was to do every thing, and that they had but to pronounce, like David, the name of " the Lord of Hosts," to give pebbles the force of darts and spears. Others appear to have really wanted the perception of any great difference, in point of excellence, between the meaner and the superior modes of writing. If they had read alternately Barrow's or South's pages and their own, they probably might have doubted on which side to assign the palm. A number of them, citing, in a perverted sense, the language of St. Paul, " not with excellency of speech," " not with enticing words of man's wisdom," " not in the words which man's wisdom teacheth," expressly disclaim every thing that belongs to fine writing, not exactly as what they could not have attained, but as what they judge incompatible with the simplicity of evangelical truth and intentions. In the books of these several but kindred classes you are mortified to see how low religious thought and expression *can* sink; and you almost wonder how it was possible for the noblest ideas that are known to the sublimest intelligences, the ideas of God, of Providence, of redemption, of eternity, to shine on a serious human mind without imparting some small occasional degree of dignity to the strain of thought. The indulgent feelings, which you entertain for the intellectual and literary deficiency of humble christians in their religious communications in private, are with difficulty extended to those who make for their thoughts this demand on public attention: it was necessary for them to be christians, but what made it their duty to become authors? Many of the books are indeed successively ceasing, with the progress of time, to be read or known; but the new supply continually brought forth is so numerous, that a person who turns his attention to religious reading is certain to meet a variety of them. Now only suppose a man who has been conversant and enchanted with the works of eloquence, glowing poetry, finished elegance, or strong reasoning, to meet a number of these books in the outset of his more serious inquiries; in what light would the religion of Christ appear to him, if he did not find some happier illustrations of it?

There is another large class of christian books, which bear the marks of learning, correctness, and an orderly understanding; and by a general propriety leave but little to be censured; but which display no invention, no prominence of thought, or living vigour of expression; all is flat and dry as a plain of sand. It is perhaps the thousandth iteration of common-places, the listless attention to which is hardly an action of the mind; you seem to understand it all, and mechanically assent while you are thinking of something else. Though the author has a rich immeasurable field of possible varieties of reflection and illustration around him, he seems doomed to tread over again the narrow space of ground long since trodden to dust, and in all his movements appears clothed in sheets of lead.

There is a smaller class that might be called mock-eloquent writers. These saw the effect of brilliant expression in those works of eloquence and poetry where it was dictated and animated by energy of thought; and very reasonably wished that christian sentiments might assume a language as impressive as any subject had ever employed to fascinate or command. But unfortunately they forgot that eloquence resides essentially in the thought, and that no words can make genuine eloquence of that which would not be such in the plainest that could fully express the sense. Or probably, they were quite confident of the excellence of the thoughts that were demanding to be so finely sounded forth. Perhaps they concluded them to be vigorous and sublime from the very circumstance, that they disdained to show themselves in plain language. The writers would be but little inclined to suspect of poverty or feebleness the thoughts which seemed so naturally to be assuming, in their minds and on their page, such a magnificent style. A gaudy verbosity is always eloquence in the opinion of him that writes it; but what is the effect on the reader?* Real eloquence strikes with immediate force, and leaves not the possibility of asking or thinking whether it *be* eloquence; but the sounding sentences of these writers leave you cool enough to examine with doubtful curiosity a language that seems threatening to move or astonish you, without actually doing so. It is something like the case of a false alarm of thunder; where a sober man, who is not apt to startle at sounds, looks out to see whether it be not the rumbling of a cart. Very much at your ease, you contrast the pomp of the expression with the

* I should be accurate, and say, the reader of disciplined judgment and good taste; for it is true enough that readers are not wanting, nor few, who can be taken with glare and bombast.

quality of the thoughts; and then read on for amusement, or cease to read from disgust. In a serious hour, indeed, the feelings both of amusement and disgust give place to the regret, that it should be in the power of bad writing to bring the most important subjects in danger of something worse than failing to interest. The unpleasing effect it has on your own mind will lead you to apprehend its having a very injurious one on many others.

A principal device in the fabrication of this style, is, to multiply epithets, dry epithets, laid on the surface, and into which no vitality of the sentiment is found to circulate. You may take a number of the words out of each page, and find that the sense is neither more nor less for your having cleared the composition of these epithets of chalk of various colours, with which the tame thoughts had submitted to be dappled and made fine.

Under the denomination of mock-eloquence may also be placed the mode of writing which endeavours to excite the passions, not by presenting striking ideas of the object of passion, but by the appearance of an emphatical enunciation of the writer's own feelings concerning it. You are not made to perceive how the thing itself has the most interesting claims on your heart; but are required to be affected in mere sympathy with the author, who attempts your feelings by frequent exclamations, and perhaps by an incessant application to his fellow-mortals, or to their Redeemer, of all the appellations and epithets of passion, and sometimes of a kind of passion not appropriate to the object. To this last great Object, especially, such forms of expression are occasionally applied, as must excite a revolting emotion in a man who feels that he cannot meet the same being at once on terms of adoration and of caressing equality

It would be going beyond my purpose, to carry my remarks from the literary merits, to the moral and theological characteristics, of christian books; else a very strange account could be given of the injuries which the gospel has suffered from its friends. You might often meet with a systematic writer, in whose hands the whole wealth, and variety, and magnificence, of revelation, shrink into a meagre list of doctrinal points, and who will let no verse in the Bible tell its meaning, or presume to have one, till it has taken its stand by one of those points. You may meet with a christian polemic, who seems to value the arguments for evangelical truth as an assassin values his dagger, and for the same reason; with a descanter on the invisible world, who makes you think of a popish cathedral, and from the vulgarity of whose illuminations you are glad to escape into the solemn twilight of faith ; or with a grim zealot for such a theory of the divine attributes and government, as seems to delight in representing the Deity as a dreadful king of furies, whose dominion is overshaded with vengeance, whose music is the cries of victims, and whose glory requires to be illustrated by the ruin of his creation.

It is quite unnecessary to say, that the list of excellent christian writers would be very considerable. But as to the vast mass of books that would, by the consenting adjudgment of all men of liberal cultivation, remain after this deduction, one cannot help deploring the effect which they must have had on unknown thousands of readers. It would seem beyond all question that books which, though even asserting the essential truths of christianity, yet utterly preclude the full impression of its character ; which exhibit its claims on admiration and affection with insipid feebleness of sentiment; or which cramp its simple majesty into an artificial form at once distorted and mean; must be seriously prejudicial to the influence of this sacred subject, though it be admitted that many of them have sometimes imparted a measure both of instruction and of consolation. This they might do, and yet at the same time convey extremely contracted and inadequate ideas of the subject.* There are a great many of them into which an intelligent christian cannot look without rejoicing that *they* were not the books from which he received his impressions of the glory of his religion. There are many which nothing would induce him, even though he did not materially differ from them in the leading articles of his belief, to put into the hands of an inquiring young person; which he would be sorry and ashamed to see on the table of an infidel; and some of which he regrets to think may still contribute to keep down the standard of religious taste, if I may so express it, among the public instructors of mankind. On the whole it would appear, that a profound veneration for christianity would induce the wish, that, after a judicious selection of books had been made, the Christians also had their Caliph Omar, and their General Amrou.

LETTER V.

THE injurious causes which I have thus far considered, are associated immediately with the *object*, and, by misrepresenting it, render it less acceptable to refined taste; but there are others, which operate by perverting the very principles of this taste itself, so as

* It is true enough that on every other subject, on which a multitude of books have been written, there must have been many which in a literary sense were bad. But I cannot help thinking that the number coming under this description, bear a larger proportion to the excellent ones in the religious department than any other. One

to put it in antipathy to the religion of Christ, even though presented in its own full and genuine character, cleared of all these associations. I shall remark chiefly on one of these causes.

I fear it is incontrovertible, that what is denominated Polite Literature, the grand school in which taste acquires its laws and refined perceptions, and in which are formed, much more than under any higher austerer discipline, the moral sentiments, is, for the far greater part, hostile to the religion of Christ; partly, by introducing insensibly a certain order of opinions unconsonant, or at least not identical, with the principles of that religion; and still more, by training the feelings to a habit alien from its spirit. And in this assertion, I do not refer to writers palpably irreligious, who have laboured and intended to seduce the passions into vice, or the judgment into the rejection of divine truth; but to the general community of those elegant and ingenious authors who are read and admired by the christian world, held essential to a liberal education and to the progressive accomplishment of the mind in subsequent life, and studied often without an apprehension, or even a thought, of their injuring the views and temper of spirits advancing, with the New Testament for their chief instructor and guide, into another world.

It is *modern* literature that I have more particularly in view; at the same time, it is obvious that the writings of heathen antiquity have continued to operate till now, in the very presence and sight of christianity, with their own proper influence, a correctly heathenish

---

chief cause of this has been, the mistake by which many good men, professionally employed in religion, have deemed their respectable mental competence to the office of public speaking, the proof of an equal competence to a work which is subjected to much severer literary and intellectual laws.

influence, on the minds of many who have never thought of denying or doubting the truth of that religion. This is just as if an eloquent pagan priest had been allowed constantly to accompany our Lord in his ministry, and had divided with him the attention and interest of his disciples, counteracting, of course, as far as his efforts were successful, the doctrine and spirit of the Teacher from heaven.*

The few observations which the subject may require to be made on ancient literature, will be directed to the part of it most immediately descriptive of what may be called human reality, representing character, sentiment, and action. For it will be allowed, that the purely speculative part of that literature has in a great measure ceased to interfere with the intellectual discipline of modern times. It obtains too little attention, and too little deference, to contribute materially to the formation of the mental habits, which are adverse to the christian doctrines and spirit. Divers learned and

* It is however no part of my object in these letters to remark on the influence, in modern times, of the fabulous religion that infested the ancient works of genius. That influence is at the present time, I should think, extremely small, from the fables being so stale : all readers are sufficiently tired of Jupiter, Apollo, Minerva, and the rest. As long however as they could be of the smallest service, they were piously retained by the christian poets of this and other countries, who are now under the necessity of seeking out for some other mythology, the northern or the eastern, to support the languishing spirit of poetry. Even the ugly pieces of wood, worshipped in the South Sea Islands, will probably at last receive names that may more commodiously hitch into verse, and be invoked to adorn and sanctify the belles lettres of the next century. The Mexican abominations and infernalities have already received from us their epic tribute. The poet has no reason to fear that the supply of gods may fail; it is at the same time a pity, one thinks, that a creature so immense should have been placed in a world so small as this, where all nature, all history, all morals, all true religion, and the whole resources of innocent fiction, are too little to furnish materials enough for the wants and labours of his genius.

fanatical devotees to antiquity and paganism, have indeed made some effort to recall the long departed veneration for the dreams and subtleties of ancient philosophy. But they might with as good a prospect of success recommend the building of temples or a pantheon, and the revival of the institutions of idolatrous worship. The greater number of intelligent, and even learned men, would feel but little regret in consigning the largest proportion of that philosophy to oblivion; unless they may be supposed to like it as heathenism more than they admire it as wisdom; or unless their pride would wish to retain a reminiscence of it for contrast to their own more rational philosophizing.

The ancient speculations of the religious order include indeed some splendid ideas relating to a Supreme Being; but these ideas impart no attraction to that immensity of inane and fantastic follies from the chaos of which they stand out, as of nobler essence and origin. For the most part they probably were traditionary remains of divine communications to man in the earliest ages. A few of them were, possibly, the utmost efforts of human intellect, at some happy moments excelling itself. But in whatever proportions they be referred to the one origin or the other, they stand so distinguished from the accumulated multifarious vanities of pagan speculation on the subject of Deity, that they throw contempt on those speculations. They throw contempt on the greatest part of the theological dogmas and fancies of even the very philosophers who would cite and applaud them. They rather direct our contemplation and affection toward a religion divinely revealed, than obtain any degree of favour for those notions of the Divinity, which sprang and indefinitely multiplied from a melancholy combination of ignorance and depraved imagination. As to the apparent analogy between certain particulars in the pagan religions, and some of the most specific articles of christianity, those notions are presented in such fantastic, and varying, and often monstrous shapes, that they can be of no prejudice to the christian faith, either by pre-occupying in our minds the place of the christian doctrines, or by indisposing us to admit them, or by perverting our conception of them.

As to the ancient metaphysical speculation, whatever may be the tendency of metaphysical study in general, or of the particular systems of modern philosophers, as affecting the cordial and simple admission of christian doctrines, the ancient metaphysics may certainly be pronounced inoperative and harmless. If it were possible to analyze the mass of what may be termed our *effective* literature, so as to ascertain what elements and interfusions in it have been of influential power, and in what respective proportions, in forming our habits of thinking and feeling, it is probable that a very small share would be found derived from the ideal theories of the old philosophers. It is probable also, that in future not one of a thousand men, cultivated in a respectable degree, will ever take the trouble of a resolute and persisting effort to master those speculations. Besides the too prevailing and still increasing indisposition to metaphysical study in *any* school, there is a settled conviction that those speculations were baseless and useless, and that whoever aspires to the high and abstracted wisdom must learn it from the later philosophers. And as the only thing we can seek and value in pure abstracted speculations is truth, when the persuasion of their truth is gone their attraction and influence are extinct. That which could please the imagination or interest the affections, might in a considerable degree continue to please and interest them, though convicted of much fallacy. But that which is too subtile and intangible to please the imagination, loses all its power when it is rejected by the judgment. This is the predicament to which time has reduced the metaphysics of the old philosophers. The captivation of their systems seems almost as far withdrawn from us as the songs of their Syrens, or the enchantments of Medea.

While these thin speculations have been suspended in air, taking all the forms and colours of clouds or rainbows, meteors or fogs, the didactic morality of some of the ancient philosophers, faithfully keeping to the solid ground of human interests, has doubtless had a considerable influence on the moral sentiments of cultivated men, progressively on to the present time. A certain quality, derived from it into literature, has perpetuated its operation indirectly on many who are not conversant with it immediately at its origin. But it may have a considerable direct influence on those who are in acquaintance with the great primary moralists themselves. After a long detention among the vagaries and monsters of mythology, or a bewildered adventure in the tenebrious and fantastic region of ancient metaphysics, in chase of that truth which the pursuer sometimes thinks, though doubtfully, that he sees, but which still eludes him, the student of antiquity is gratified at meeting with a sage who leads him among interesting realities, and discourses to him in plain and impressive terms of direct instruction concerning moral principles and the means of happiness. And since it is necessarily the substantial object of this instruction to enforce virtue, excellence, goodness, he feels little apprehension of any vitiating effect on his moral sentiments. He entirely forgets that moral excellence, or virtue, has been defined and enforced by another authority; and that though a large portion of the scheme must be, as matter of practice, mainly the same in the dictates of that authority, and in the writings of Epictetus, or Cicero, or Antoninus, yet there is a specific difference of substance in certain particulars, and a most important one in the principles that constitute the general basis. While he is admiring the beauty of virtue as displayed by one accomplished moralist, and its lofty independence as exhibited by another, he is not admonished to suspect that any thing in their sentiments, or his animated coalescence with them, can be wrong.

But the part of ancient literature which has had incomparably the greatest influence on the character of cultivated minds, is that which has turned, if I may so express it, moral sentiments into real beings and interesting companions, by displaying the life and actions of eminent individuals. A few of the personages of fiction are also to be included. The captivating spirit of Greece and Rome dwells in the works of the biographers; in so much of the history as might properly be called biography, from its fixing the whole attention and interest on a few signal names; and in the works of the principal poets.

No one, I suppose, will deny, that both the characters and the sentiments, which are the favourites of the poet and the historian, become the favourites also of the admiring reader; for this would be a virtual denial of the excellence of the performance, in point of eloquence or poetic spirit. It is the high test and proof of genius that a writer can render his subject interesting to his readers, not merely in a general way, but in the *very same manner* in which it interests himself. If the great works of antiquity had not this power, they would long since have ceased to charm. We could not long tolerate what caused a revolting of our moral feelings, while it was designed to please them. But if their characters and sentiments really do thus fascinate the heart, how far will this influence be coincident with the spirit and with the design of christianity?*

Among the poets, I shall notice only the two or three pre-eminent ones of the Epic class. Homer, you know, is the favourite of the whole civilized world; and it is many centuries since there needed one additional word of homage to the prodigious genius displayed in the Iliad. The object of inquiry is, what kind of predisposition will be formed toward christianity in a young and animated spirit, that learns to glow with enthusiasm at the scenes created by the poet, and to indulge an ardent wish, which that enthusiasm will probably awaken, for the possibility of emulating some of the principal characters? Let this susceptible youth, after having mingled and burned in imagination among heroes, whose valour and anger flame like Vesuvius, who wade in blood, trample on dying foes, and hurl defiance against earth and heaven; let him be led into the company of Jesus Christ and his disciples, as displayed by the evangelists, with whose narrative, I will suppose, he is but slightly acquainted before. What must he, what can he, do with his feelings in this transition? He will find himself flung as far as "from the centre to the utmost pole;" and one of these two opposite exhibitions of character will inevitably excite his aversion. Which of them is that likely to be, if he is become thoroughly possessed with the Homeric passions?

* It may be noticed here that a great part of what could be said on heathen literature as opposed to the religion of Christ, must necessarily refer to the peculiar *moral spirit* of that religion. It would border on the ridiculous to represent the martial enthusiasm of ancient historians and poets as counteracting the peculiar *doctrines* of the gospel, meaning by the term those dictates of truth that do not directly involve moral distinctions.

Or if, reversing the order, you will suppose a person to have first become profoundly interested by the New Testament, and to have acquired the spirit of the Saviour of the world, while studying the evangelical history; with what sentiments will *he* come forth from conversing with heavenly mildness, weeping benevolence, sacred purity, and the eloquence of divine wisdom, to enter into a scene of such actions and characters, and to hear such maxims of merit and glory, as those of Homer? He would be still more confounded by the transition, had it been possible for him to have entirely escaped that deep depravation of feeling which can think of crimes and miseries with little emotion, and which we have all acquired from viewing the prominent portion of the world's history as composed of scarcely any thing else. He would find the mightiest strain of poetry employed to represent ferocious courage as the greatest of virtues, and those who do not possess it as worthy of their fate, to be trodden in the dust. He will be taught, at least it will not be the fault of the poet, if he be not taught, to forgive a heroic spirit for finding the sweetest luxury in insulting dying pangs, and imagining the tears and despair of distant relations. He will be incessantly called upon to worship revenge, the real divinity of the Iliad, in comparison of which the Thunderer of Olympus is but a subaltern pretender to power. He will be taught that the most glorious and enviable life is that, to which the greatest number of other lives are made a sacrifice; and that it is noble in a hero to prefer even a short life attended by this felicity, to a long one which should permit a longer life also to others. The terrible Achilles, a being whom, if he had really existed, it had been worth a temporary league of the tribes then called nations to reduce to the quietness of a dungeon or a tomb, is

rendered interesting even amidst the horrors of revenge
and destruction, by the intensity of his affection for
his friend, by the melancholy with which he appears in
the funeral scene of that friend, by one momentary
instance of compassion, and by his solemn references
to his own impending and inevitable doom. A reader who
has even passed beyond the juvenile ardour of life, feels
himself interested, in a manner that excites at intervals
his own surprise, in the fate of this fell exterminator;
and he wonders, and he wishes to doubt, whether the
moral that he is learning, be, after all, exactly no other
than that the grandest employment of a great spirit is
the destruction of human creatures, so long as revenge,
ambition, or even caprice, may choose to regard them
under an artificial distinction, and call them *enemies*.
But this, my dear friend, is the real and effective moral
of the Iliad, after all that critics have so gravely written
about lessons of union, or any other subordinate moral
instructions, which they discover or imagine in the
work. Who but critics ever thought or cared about
any such drowsy lessons? Whatever is the chief and
grand impression made by the whole work on the
ardent minds which are most susceptible of the influence of poetry, *that* shows the real moral; and
Alexander, and Charles XII. through the medium of
" Macedonia's madman," correctly received the genuine
inspiration.

If it be said, that such works stand on the same
ground, except as to the reality or accuracy of the
facts, with an eloquent history, which simply *exhibits*
the actions and characters, I deny the assertion. The
actions and characters are presented in a *manner* which
prevents their just impression, and empowers them to
make an opposite one. A transforming magic of genius
displays a number of atrocious savages in a hideous

slaughter-house of men, as demi-gods in a temple of glory. No doubt an eloquent history might be so written as to give the same aspect to such men, and such operations; but that history would deserve to be committed to the flames. A history that should give a faithful representation of miseries and slaughter, would set no one, who had not attained the last depravation, on fire to imitate the principal actors. It would excite in a degree the same emotion as the sight of a field of dead and dying men after a battle is over; a sight at which the soul would shudder and revolt, and earnestly wish that this might be the last time the sun should behold such a spectacle: but the tendency of the Homeric poetry, and of a great part of epic poetry in general, is to insinuate the glory of repeating such a tragedy. I therefore ask again, how it would be possible for a man whose mind was first completely assimilated to the spirit of Jesus Christ, to read such a work without a most vivid antipathy to what he perceived to be the moral spirit of the poet? And if it were not too strange a supposition, that the most characteristic parts of the Iliad had been read in the presence and hearing of our Lord, and by a person animated by a fervid sympathy with the work—do you not instantly imagine Him expressing the most emphatical condemnation? Would not the reader have been made to know, that in the spirit of that book he could never become a disciple and a friend of the Messiah? But then, if he believed this declaration, and were serious enough to care about being the disciple and friend of the Messiah, would he not have deemed himself extremely unfortunate to have been seduced, through the pleasures of taste and imagination, into habits of feeling which rendered it impossible, till their predominance should be destroyed, for him to receive the only true religion, and the only Redeemer of the world ? To show *how* impossible it would be, I wish I may be pardoned for making another strange and indeed a most monstrous supposition, namely, that Achilles, Diomede, Ulysses, and Ajax had been real persons, living in the time of our Lord, and had become his disciples, and yet, (excepting the mere exchange of the notions of mythology for christian opinions,) had retained entire the state of mind with which their poet has exhibited them. It is instantly perceived that Satan, Beelzebub, and Moloch might as consistently have been retained in heaven. But here the question comes to a point : if these great examples of glorious character pretending to coalesce with the transcendent Sovereign of virtues, would have been probably the most enormous incongruity existing, or that ever had existed, in the creation, what harmony can there be between a man who has acquired a considerable degree of congeniality with the spirit of these heroes, and that paramount Teacher and Pattern of excellence ? And who will assure me that the enthusiast for heroic poetry does *not* acquire a degree of this congeniality ? But unless I can be so assured, I necessarily persist in asserting the noxiousness of such poetry.

Yet the work of Homer is, notwithstanding, the book which christian poets have translated, which christian divines have edited and commented on with pride, at which christian ladies have been delighted to see their sons kindle into rapture, and which forms an essential part of the course of a liberal education, over all those countries on which the gospel shines. And who can tell how much that passion for war which, from the universality of its prevalence, might seem inseparable from the nature of man, may have been, in the civilized world, reinforced by the enthusiastic admiration with which young men have read Homer, and similar poets, whose genius transforms what is, and ought always to appear purely horrid, to an aspect of grandeur? Should it be asked, What ought to be the practical consequence of such observations? I may surely answer that I cannot justly be required to assign that consequence. I cannot be required to do more than exhibit in a simple light an important point of truth. *If* such works do really impart their own spirit to the mind of an admiring reader, and *if* this spirit be totally hostile to that of christianity, and *if* christianity ought really and in good faith to be the supreme regent of all moral feeling, then it is evident that the Iliad, and all books which combine the same tendency with great poetical excellence, are among the most mischievous things on earth. There is but little satisfaction, certainly, in illustrating the operation of evils without proposing any adequate method of contending with them. But in the present case, I really do not see what a serious observer of the character of mankind can offer. To wish that the works of Homer, and some other great authors of antiquity, should cease to be read, is just as vain as to wish they had never been written. As to the far greater number of readers, it were equally in vain to wish that pure christian sentiments might be sufficiently recollected, and loved, to accompany the study, and constantly prevent the injurious impression, of the works of pagan genius. The few maxims of christianity to which the student may have assented without thought, and for which he has but little veneration, will but feebly oppose the influence; the spirit of Homer will vanquish as irresistibly as his Achilles vanquished. It is also most perfectly true, that as long as pride, ambition, and vindictiveness, hold so mighty a prevalence in the character and in the nature of our species, they would still amply display themselves, though the stimulus of heroic poetry were withdrawn, by the annihilation of all those works which have invested the worst passions and the worst actions with a glare of grandeur. With or without the infections of heroic poetry, men and nations will continue to commit offences against one another, and to avenge them; to assume an arrogant precedence, and account it and laud it as noble spirit; to celebrate their deeds of destruction, and call them glory; to idolize the men who possess, and can infuse, the greatest share of an infernal fire; to set at nought all principles of virtue and religion in favour of some thoughtless vicious mortal who consigns himself in the same achievement to fame and perdition; to vaunt in triumphal entries, or funeral pomps, or bombastic odes, or strings of scalps, how far human skill and valour can surpass the powers of famine and pestilence; men and nations will continue thus to act, till a mightier intervention from heaven shall establish the dominion of christianity. In that better season, perhaps the great works of ancient genius will be read in such a disposition of mind as can receive the intellectual improvement derivable from them, and at the same time as little coincide or be infected with their moral spirit, as in the present age we venerate their mythological vanities.

In the mean time, one cannot believe that any man, who seriously reflects how absolutely the religion of Christ claims a conformity of his whole nature, will without regret feel himself animated with a class of sentiments, of which the habitual prevalence would be the total preclusion of christianity.

And it seems to show how little this religion is really understood, or even considered, in any of the countries denominated christian, that so many who profess to adopt it never once thought of guarding their own minds, and those of their children, against the eloquent seductions of so opposite a spirit. Probably they would be more intelligent and vigilant, if any other interest than that of their professed religion were endangered. But a thing which injures them only in *that* concern, is sure to meet with all possible indulgence.

With respect to religious parents and preceptors, whose children and pupils are to receive that liberal education which must inevitably include the study of these great works, it will be for them to accompany the youthful readers throughout, with an effort to show them, in the most pointed manner, the inconsistency of many of the sentiments, both with moral rectitude in general, and with the special dictates of christianity. And in order to give the requisite force to those dictates, it will be an important duty to illustrate to them the amiable tendency, and to prove the awful authority, of this dispensation of religion. This careful effort will often but partially prevent the mischief; but it seems to be all that can be done.

Virgil's work is a kind of lunar reflection of the ardent effulgence of Homer; surrounded, if I may extend the figure, with a beautiful halo of elegance and tenderness. So much more refined an order of sentiment might have rendered the heroic character far more attractive, to a mind that can soften as well as glow, if there had actually been a hero in the poem. But none of the personages intended for heroes take hold enough of the reader's feelings to assimilate them in moral temper. No fiction or history of human characters and actions will ever powerfully transfuse its spirit, without some one or some very few individuals of signal peculiarity or greatness, to concentrate and embody the whole energy of the work. There would be no danger therefore of any one's becoming an idolater of the god of war through the inspiration of the Æneid, even if a larger proportion of it had resounded with martial enterprise. Perhaps the chief counteraction to christian sentiments which I should apprehend to an opening susceptible mind, would be a depravation of its ideas concerning the other world, from the picturesque scenery which Virgil has opened to his hero in the regions of the dead, and the imposing images with which he has shaded the avenue to them. Perhaps also the affecting sentiments which precede the death of Dido, might tend to lessen, especially in a pensive mind, the horror of that impiety which would throw back with violence the possession of life, as if in reproach to its great Author, for having suffered that there should be unhappiness in a world where there is sin.

LETTER VI.

In naming Lucan, I am not unaware that an avowal of high admiration may hazard all credit for correct discernment. I must, however, confess that, in spite of his rhetorical ostentation, and all the offences of a too inflated style, he does in my apprehension greatly surpass all the other ancient poets in direct force of the ethical spirit; and that he would have a stronger influence to seduce my feelings, in respect to moral greatness, into a discordance from christian principles. His leading characters are widely different from those of Homer, and of an eminently superior order. The mighty genius of Homer appeared and departed in a rude age of the human mind, a stranger to the intellectual enlargement which would have enabled him to combine in his heroes the dignity of thought, instead of mere physical force, with the energy of passion. For want of this, they are great heroes without being great *men*. They appear to you only as tremendous fighting and destroying animals; a kind of human mammoths. The prowess of personal conflict is all they can understand and admire, and in their warfare their minds never reach to any of the sublimer views and results even of war; their chief and final object seems to be the mere savage glory of fighting, and the annihilation of their enemies. When the heroes of Lucan, both the depraved and the nobler class, are employed in war, it seems but a small part of what they can do, and what they intend; they have always something further and greater in view than to evince their valour, or to riot in the vengeance of victory. Ambition as exhibited in Pompey and Cæsar seems almost to become a grand passion, when compared to the contracted and ferocious aim of Homer's chiefs; while this passion, even thus elevated, serves to exalt by comparison the far different and nobler sentiments and objects of Cato and Brutus. The contempt of death, which in the heroes of the Iliad often seems like an incapacity or an oblivion of thought, is in Lucan's favourite characters the result, or at least the associate, of high philosophic spirit; and this strongly contrasts their courage with that of Homer's warriors, which is, (according indeed to his own frequent similes,) the reckless daring of wild beasts. Lucan sublimates martial into moral grandeur. Even if you could deduct from his great men all that which forms the specific martial display of the hero, you would find their greatness little diminished; they would still retain their

commanding and interesting aspect. The better class
of them, amidst war itself, hate and deplore the spirit
and destructive exploits of war. They are indignant
at the vices of mankind for compelling *their virtue* into
a career in which such sanguinary glories can be acquired. And while they deem it their duty to exert
their courage in conflict for a just cause, they regard
camps and battles as vulgar things, from which their
thoughts often turn away into a train of solemn and
presaging reflections, in which they approach sometimes
the most elevated sublimity. You have a more absolute
impression of grandeur from a speech of Cato, than
from all the mighty exploits that epic poetry ever bla-
zoned. The eloquence of Lucan's moral heroes does
not consist in images of triumphs and conquests, but
in reflections on virtue, sufferings, destiny, and death;
and the sentiments expressed in his own name have
often a melancholy tinge which renders them irresistibly interesting. He might seem to have felt a
presage, while musing on the last of the Romans, that
their poet was soon to follow them. The reader becomes
devoted both to the poet, and to these illustrious men;
but, under the influence of this attachment, he adopts
all their sentiments, and exults in the sympathy; forgetting, or unwilling, to reflect, whether this state of
feeling be concordant with the religion of Christ, and
with the spirit of the apostles and martyrs. The most
captivating of Lucan's sentiments, to a mind enamoured
of pensive sublimity, are those concerning death. I
remember the very principle which I would wish to
inculcate, that is, the necessity that a believer of the
gospel should preserve the christian tenour of feeling
predominant in his mind, and clear of incongruous
mixture, having struck me with great force amidst the
enthusiasm with which I read many times over the

memorable account of Vulteius, the speech by which he inspired his gallant band with a passion for death, and the reflections on death with which the poet closes the episode. I said to myself, at the suggestion of conscience, What are these sentiments with which I am glowing? Are these the just ideas of death? Are they such as were taught by the Divine Author of our religion? Is this the spirit with which St. Paul approached his last hour? And I felt a painful collision between this reflection and the passion inspired by the poet. I perceived clearly that the kind of interest which I felt was no less than a real adoption, for the time, of the very same sentiments with which he was animated.

The epic poetry has been selected for the more pointed application of my remarks, from the belief that it has had a much greater influence on the moral sentiments of succeeding ages than all the other poetry of antiquity, by means of its impressive display of individual great characters. And it will be admitted that the moral spirit of the epic poets, taken together, is as little in opposition to the christian theory of moral sentiments as that of the collective poetry of other kinds. Some just and fine sentiments to be found in the Greek tragedies are in the tone of the best of the pagan didactic moralists. And they infuse themselves more intimately into our minds when thus coming warm in the course of passion and action, and speaking to us with the emphasis imparted by affecting and dreadful events; but still are of less vivid and penetrating charm, than as emanating from the insulated magnificence of such striking and sublime individual characters as those of epic poetry. The mind of the reader does not, from those dramatic scenes, retain for months and years an animated recollection of some personage whose name constantly recalls the sentiments which he uttered, or with which his conduct inspired us. The Greek drama is extremely deficient in both grand and interesting characters, in any sense of the epithets that should imply an imposing or a captivating moral power. Much the greatest number of the persons and personages brought on the scene are such as we care nothing about, otherwise than merely on account of the circumstances in which we see them acting or suffering. With few exceptions they come on the stage, and go off, without possessing us with either admiration or affection. When therefore the maxims or reflections which we hear from them have an impressive effect, it is less from any commanding quality in the persons, than from the striking, and sometimes portentous and fearful situations, that the sentiments have their pathos. There are a few characters of greater power over our respect and our sympathies, who draw us, by virtue of personal qualities, into a willing communion with them, at times, in moral principles and emotions. We are relieved and gratified, after passing through so much wickedness, misfortune, and inane common-place moralizing, to be greeted with fine expressions of justice, generosity, and fidelity to a worthy purpose, by persons whom we can regard as living realizations of such virtues. It is like finding among barbarous nations, (as sometimes happens,) some individual or two eminently and unaccountably above the level of their tribe, whose intelligence and virtues have, by the contrast and the surprise, a stronger attraction than similar qualities meeting us in a cultivated community. But the delight sometimes kindled by sentiments of magnanimous or gentle virtue, is exceedingly repressed, and often quenched, in the reader of the Greek drama, by the incessant intrusion of a hideous moral barbarism;

T

especially by the implication of the morality with an execrable mythology. There is an odious interference of "the gods," sometimes by their dissensions with one another perplexing and confounding the rules of human obligation; often contravening the best intentions and efforts; depriving virtue of all confidence and resource; despising, frustrating, or punishing it; turning its exertions and sacrifices to vanity or disaster; and yet to be the objects of devout homage, a homage paid with intermingled complaints and reproaches, extorted from defeated or suffering virtue, which is trying to be better than the gods. Nothing can be more intensely dreary than the moral economy as represented in much of that drama. Let any one contemplate it as displayed for example, in the Prometheus Chained, or the whole stories of Œdipus and Orestes. On the whole I have conceded much in saying, that a small portion of the morality of that drama may have a place with that of the best of the didactic moralists.

I shall not dwell long on the biography and history, since it will be allowed that their influence is very nearly coincident with that of the epic poetry. The work of Plutarch, the chief of the biographers, (a work so necessary, it would seem, to the consolations of a christian, that I have read of some learned man declaring, and without any avowed rejection of the Bible, that if he were to be cast on a desert island, and could have one book, and but one, it should be this,) the work of Plutarch delineates a greatness partly of the same character as that celebrated by Homer, and partly of the more dignified and intellectual kind which is so commanding in the great men of Lucan, several of whom indeed are the subjects also of the biographer. Various distinctions might, no doubt, be remarked in the impression made by great characters as illustrated in poetry, and as exposed in the plainness of historical record: but I am persuaded that the habits of feeling which will grow from admiring the one or the other, will be substantially the same as affecting the temper of the mind in regard to christianity.

A number of the men exhibited by the biographers and historians, rose so eminently above the general character of the human race, that their names have become inseparably associated with our ideas of moral greatness. A thoughtful student of antiquity enters this majestic company with an impression of mystical awfulness, resembling that of Ezekiel in his vision. In this select and revered assembly we include only those who were distinguished by elevated virtue, as well as powerful talents and memorable actions. Undoubtedly the magnificent powers and energy without moral excellence, so often displayed on the field of ancient history, compel a kind of prostration of the soul in the presence of men, whose surpassing achievements seem to silence for a while, and but for a while, the sense of justice which must execrate their ambition and their crimes; but where greatness of mind seems but secondary to greatness of virtue, as in the examples of Phocion, Epaminondas, Aristides, Timoleon, Dion, Cimon, and several more, the heart applauds itself for feeling an irresistible captivation. This number indeed is small, compared with the whole galaxy of renowned names; but it is large enough to fill the mind, and to give as venerable an impression of pagan greatness, as if none of its examples had been the heroes whose fierce brilliance lightens through the blackness of their depravity; or the legislators, orators, and philosophers, whose wisdom was degraded by imposture, venality, or vanity.

A most impressive part of the influence of ancient character on modern feelings, is derived from the accounts of two or three of the greatest philosophers, whose virtue, protesting and solitary in the times in which they lived, whose intense devotedness in the pursuit of wisdom, and whose occasional sublime glimpses of apprehension, received from beyond the sphere of error in which they were enclosed and benighted, present them to the mind with something like the venerableness of the prophets of God. Among the exhibitions of this kind, it is unnecessary to say that Xenophon's Memoir of Socrates stands unrivalled and above comparison.

Sanguine spirits without number have probably been influenced in modern times by the ancient history of mere heroes ; but persons of a reflective disposition have been incomparably more affected by the contemplation of those men whose combination of mental power with illustrious virtue constitutes the supreme glory of heathen antiquity.—And why do I deem the admiration of this noble display of moral excellence pernicious to these reflective minds, in relation to the religion of Christ ? For the simplest possible reason ; because the principles of that excellence are not identical with the principles of this religion ; as I believe every serious and self-observant man who has been attentive to them both, will have verified in his own experience. He has felt the animation which pervaded his soul, in musing on the virtues, the sentiments, and the great actions, of these dignified men, suddenly expiring, when he has attempted to prolong or transfer it to the virtues, sentiments, and actions, of the apostles of Jesus Christ. Sometimes he has, with mixed wonder and indignation, remonstrated with his own feelings, and has said, I know there is the highest excellence in the religion of the Messiah, and in the characters of his most magnanimous followers; and surely it is ex-

cellence also that attracts me to those other illustrious men; why then cannot I take a full delightful interest in them both? But it is in vain; he finds this amphibious devotion impossible. And he will always find it so; for, antecedently to experience, it would be obvious that the order of sentiments which animated the one form of excellence, is extremely diverse from that which is the vitality of the other. If the whole system of a christian's sentiments is required to be exactly adjusted to the economy of redemption, they must be widely different from those of the men, however wise or virtuous, who never thought or heard of the Saviour of the world; else where is the peculiarity or importance of this new dispensation, which does however both avow and manifest a most signal peculiarity, and with which heaven has connected the signs and declarations of infinite importance? If, again, a christian's grand object and solicitude is to please God, this must constitute his moral excellence, (even though the *facts*, the mere actions, were the same,) of a very different nature from that of the men who had not in firm faith any god that they cared to please, and whose highest glory it might possibly become, that they boldly differed from their deities; as Lucan undoubtedly intended it as the most emphatical applause of Cato, that he was the inflexible patron and hero of the cause which was the aversion of the gods.* If humility is required as a characteristic of a christian's mind, he is here again placed in a state of contrariety to that self-idolatry, the love of glory which accompanied, and was applauded as a virtue while it accompanied, almost all the moral greatness of the heathens. If a christian lives for eternity, and advances towards death with the certain expectation of judgment, and of a new and awful world,

* Victrix causa Diis placuit, sed victa Catoni.

how different must be the essential quality of his serious sentiments, as partly created, and wholly pervaded, by this mighty anticipation, from the order of feeling of the virtuous heathens, who had no positive or sublime expectations beyond death. The interior essences, if I may so speak, of the two kinds of excellence, sustained or produced by these two systems of principles, are so different, that they will hardly be more convertible or compatible in the same mind than even excellence and turpitude.—Now it appears to me that the enthusiasm, with which a mind of deep and thoughtful sensibility dwells on the history of sages, virtuous legislators, and the worthiest class of heroes of heathen antiquity, will be found to beguile that mind into an order of sentiments congenial with theirs, and therefore thus seriously different from the spirit and principles of christianity.* It is not exactly that the judgment admits distinct pagan propositions, but the heart insensibly acquires an unison with many of the sentiments which *imply* those propositions, and are wrong unless those propositions be right. It forgets that a different state of feeling, corresponding to a greatly different scheme of principles, is appointed by the Sovereign Judge of all things as (with relation to *us*) an indispensable preparation for entering the eternal paradise;†

* Should it be pretended that, in admiring pagan excellence, the mind takes the mere *facts* of that excellence, separately from the principles, and as far as they are identical with the facts of christian excellence, and then, connecting christian principles with them, converts the whole ideally into a christian character before it cordially admires, I appeal to experience that this is not true. If it were, the mind would be able to turn with full complacency from an affectionate admiration of an illustrious heathen, to admire, in the same train of feeling and with still warmer emotion, the excellence of St. Paul; which is not the fact.

† I hope none of these observations will be understood to insinuate the impossibility of the future happiness of virtuous heathens. But a question on that subject would here be out of place.

and that now, no moral distinctions, however splendid, are excellence in his sight, if not conformed to his declared standard. It slides into a persuasion that, under *any* economy, to be like one of those heathen examples should be a competent fitness for any world to which good spirits are to be assigned. The devoted admirer contemplates them as the most enviable specimens of his nature, and almost wishes he could have been one of them; without reflecting that this would probably have been under the condition, among many other circumstances, of adoring Jupiter, Bacchus, or Æsculapius, and yet despising the deities that he adored; and under the condition of being a stranger to the Son of God, and to all that he has disclosed and accomplished for the felicity of our race. It would even throw an ungracious chill on his ardour, if an evangelical monitor should whisper, " Remember Jesus Christ," and express his regret that these illustrious men could not have been privileged to be elevated into christians. If precisely the word " elevated" were used, the admonished person might have a feeling, at the instant, as if it were not the *right* word. But this state of mind is no less in effect than hostility to the gospel, which these feelings are practically pronouncing to be at least unnecessary; and therefore that noblest part of ancient literature which tends to produce it, is inexpressibly injurious. It had been happy for many cultivated and aspiring minds, if the men whose characters are the moral magnificence of the classical history, had been such atrocious villains, that their names could not have been recollected without execration. Nothing can be more disastrous than to be led astray by eminent virtue and intelligence, which can give a sense of congeniality with grandeur in the deviation.

It will require a very affecting impression of the

christian truth, a decided conception of the christian character, and a habit of thinking with sympathetic admiration of the most elevated class of christians, to preserve the genuine evangelical spirit amidst this ideal society with personages who might pardonably have been esteemed of the noblest form of human nature, if a revelation had not been received from heaven. Some views of this excellence it were in vain for a christian to forbid himself to admire; but he must learn to admire under a discriminative restriction, else the emotion involves a desertion of his cause. He must learn to assign these men in thought to another sphere, and to regard them as beings under a different economy with which our relations are dissolved; as wonderful examples of a certain imperfect kind of moral greatness, formed on a model foreign to true religion, and which is crumbled to dust and given to the winds.—At the same time, he may well, while beholding some of these men, deplore that if so much excellence could be formed on such a model, the sacred system which gives the acknowledged exemplar for his own character should not have far more assimilated him to heaven.—So much for the effect of the most interesting part of ancient literature.

In the next letter I shall make some observations on modern polite literature, in application of the same rule of judgment. Many of them must unavoidably be very analogous to those already made; since the greatest number of the modern fine writers acquired much of the character of their minds from those of the ancient world. Probably indeed the ancients have exerted a much more extensive influence in modern times by means of the modern writers to whom they have communicated their moral spirit, than immediately by their own works.

LETTER VII.

To a man who had long observed the influences which tyrannize over human passions and opinions, it would not perhaps have appeared strange, that when the Grand Renovator came on earth, and during the succeeding ages, a number of the men whose superior talents were to carry on the course of literature, and promote and guide the progress of the human mind, should reject his religion. These I have placed out of the question, as it is not my object to show the injuries done to christianity by its avowed enemies. But it might have been expected, that all the intelligent men, from that hour to the end of time, who should really admit the truth of this religion, would perceive the sovereignty and universality of its claims, feel that every thing unconsonant with it ought instantly to vanish from the whole system of approved sentiments and the whole school of literature, and to keep as clearly aloof as the Israelites from the boundary that guarded the sanctity of Mount Sinai. It might have been presumed, that all principles which the new dispensation rendered obsolete, or declared or implied to be wrong, should no more be regarded as belonging to the system of principles to be henceforward received and taught, than dead bodies in their graves belong to the race of living men. To retain or recall them would therefore be as offensive to the judgment, as to take up these bodies and place them in the paths of men would be offensive to the senses; and as absurd as the practice of the ancient Egyptians, who made their embalmed ancestors their companions at their festivals. It might have been supposed, that whatever christianity had actually substituted, abolished, or supplied, would therefore be *practically* regarded by these believers of it as substituted, abolished, or supplied; and that they would, in all their writings, be at least as careful of their fidelity in this great article, as an adherent to the Newtonian philosophy would be certain to exclude, from his scientific discourse, all notions that seriously implied the Ptolemaic or the Tychonic system to be true. Necessarily, a number of these literary believers would write on subjects so completely foreign to what comes within the cognizance of christianity, that a pure neutrality, which should avoid all interference with it, would be all that could be claimed from them in its behalf; though at the same time, one should feel some degree of regret, to see a man of enlarged mind exhausting his ability and his life on these foreign subjects, without devoting some short interval to the service of that which he believes to be of far surpassing moment.*

But the great number who chose to write on subjects

* I could not help feeling a degree of this regret in reading lately the memoirs of the admirable and estimable Sir William Jones. Some of his researches in Asia have incidentally served the cause of religion; but did he think that nothing more remained possible to be done in service to christianity, that his accomplished mind was left at leisure for hymns to the Hindoo gods? Was not this even a violation of the neutrality, and an offence, not only against the gospel, but against theism itself? I know what may be said about personification, license of poetry, and so on; but should not a worshipper of God hold himself under a solemn obligation to abjure all tolerance of even poetical figures that can seriously seem, in any way whatever, to recognise the pagan divinities—or abominations, as the prophets of Jehovah would have called them? What would Elijah have said to such an employment of talents in his time? It would have availed little to have told him that these divinities were only personifications (with their appropriate representative idols) of objects in nature, of elements, or of abstractions. He would have sternly replied, And was not Baal, whose prophets I destroyed, the same?

that come within the relations of the christian system, as on the various views of morals, the distinctions and judgments of human character, and the theory of happiness, with almost unavoidable references sometimes to our connexion with Deity, to death, and to a future state, ought to have written every page under the recollection, that these subjects are not left free for careless or arbitrary sentiment since the time that "God has spoken to us by his Son;" and that the finest composition would be only so much eloquent impiety, if essentially discordant with the dictates of the New Testament. Had this been a habitual and influential recollection with the admired writers of the christian world, an ingenuous mind might have been conversant alternately with their works and those of evangelists and apostles, without being confounded in the conflict of antipathy between the inspirations of genius and the inspirations of heaven.

I confine my view chiefly to the elegant literature of our own country. And there is a presumption in its favour, independently of actual comparison, that it is much less exceptionable than the belles lettres of the other countries of modern Europe; for this plain reason, that the extended prevalence of the happy light of the Reformation through almost the whole period of the production of our works of genius and taste, must necessarily, by presenting the religion of Christ in an aspect more true to its genuine dignity, have compelled from the intellectual men who did not deny its truth, and could not be entirely ignorant of its most essential properties, a kind and degree of respect which would not be felt by the same order of men in popish countries, whose belief in christianity was no more than a deference to the authority of the church, and whose occasional allusions or testimonies to it would recognise it in no higher character than that in which it appears as degraded into a superstition; so that there would be only a fallacious or equivocal glimmer of christianity thrown occasionally on their pages of moral sentiment.

In this assumption in favour of our polite literature, against that of the popish countries, I set out of view, on both sides, that portion which is of directly immoral or infidel tendency; since it is not at all my object to comment on the antichristian effect of the palpably vicious part of our literature, but to indicate a certain moral and religious insalubrity in much of that which, in general account, is for the most part tolerably accordant, and in many instances actively subservient, to truth and virtue.

Going over from the vicious and irreligious to the directly opposite quarter, neither do I include in the literature on which I am animadverting any class of authors formally theological, not even the most admired sermon writers in our language; because it is probable that works specifically theological have not been admitted to constitute more than a small part of that school of thinking and taste, in which the generality of cultivated men have acquired the moral habitude of their minds. That school is composed of poets, moral philosophers, historians, essayists, and you may add the writers of fiction. If the great majority of these authors have injured, and still injure, their pupils in the most important of all their interests, it is a very serious consideration, both in respect to the accountableness of the authors, and the final effect on their pupils. I maintain that they are guilty of this injury.

On so wide a field, my dear friend, it would be in vain to attempt making particular references and selections to verify all these remarks. I must appeal for their truth to your own acquaintance with our popular fine writers.

In the first place, and as a general observation, the alleged injury has been done, to a great extent, by Omission, or rather it should be called Exclusion. I do not refer so much to that unworthy care, maintained through the works of our ingenious authors to avoid *formally* treating on any topics of an expressly evangelical kind, as to the absence of that christian tinge and modification, (rendered perceptible partly by a plain recognition occasionally of some great christian truth, and partly by a solicitous, though it were a tacit, conformity to every principle of the christian theory,) which should pervade universally the sentiments regarding man as a moral being. Consider how small a portion of the serious subjects of thought can be detached from all connexion with the religion of Christ, without narrowing the scope to which he meant it to extend, and repelling its intervention where he required it should intervene. The book which unfolds it, has exaggerated its comprehensiveness, and the first distinguished christians had a delusive view of it, if it does not actually claim to mingle its principles with the whole system of moral ideas, so as to give them a special modification ; as the principle of fire, interfused through the various forms and combinations of the elements, contributes essentially to constitute that condition by which they are adapted to their important uses, which condition and adaptation therefore they would lose if that principle were no longer inherent.

And this claim for the extensive interference of the christian principles, made as a requirement from authority, appears to be just in virtue of their own nature. For they are not of a nature which necessarily restricts them to a peculiar department, like the principles appropriate to some of the sciences. We should at once perceive the absurdity of a man who should be pretending to adjust all his ideas on general subjects according to the rules of geometry, and should maintain (if any man could do so preposterous a thing) that geometrical laws ought to be taken as the basis of our reasoning on politics and morals. Or, if this be too extreme a supposition, let any other class of principles, foreign to moral subjects, be selected, in order to show how absurd is the effect of an attempt to stretch them beyond their proper sphere, and force them into some connexion with ideas with which they have no natural relation. Let it be shown how such principles can in no degree modify the subject to which they are attempted to be applied, nor mingle with the reasons concerning it, but refuse to touch it, like magnetism applied to brass. I would then show, on the contrary, that the christian principles are of a quality which puts them in relation with something in the nature of almost all serious subjects. Their introduction into those subjects therefore is not an arbitrary and forced application of them; it is merely permitting their cognizance and interfusion in whatever has some quality of a common nature with them. It must be evident in a moment that the most general doctrines of christianity, such as those of a future judgment, and immortality, have a direct relation with every thing that can be comprehended within the widest range of moral speculation and sentiment. It will also be found that the more particular doctrines, such as those of the moral pravity of our nature, an atonement made by the sacrifice of Christ, the interference of a special divine influence in renewing the human mind, and conducting it through the discipline for a future state, together with all the inferences, conditions, and motives resulting from them, cannot be admitted and religiously regarded, without combining in numberless instances with a man's ideas on moral subjects. That writer must therefore have retired beyond the limits of an immense field of important and most interesting speculations, indeed beyond the limits of all the speculation most important to man, who can say that nothing in the religion of Christ bears, in any manner, on any part of his subject, any more than if he were a philosopher of Saturn.

In thus habitually interfering and combining with moral sentiments and speculations, the christian principles will greatly modify them. The ideas infused from those principles to be combined with the moral sentiments, will not appear as simply *additional* ideas in the train of thought, but as also affecting the character of the rest. A writer whose mind is so possessed with the christian principles that they continually suggest themselves in connexion with his serious speculations, will unavoidably present a moral subject in a somewhat different aspect, even when he makes no express references to the gospel, from that in which it would be presented by another writer, whose habits of thought were clear of evangelical recollections. Now in every train of thinking in which the recognition of those principles would effect this modification, it ought to be effected; so that the very last idea within the compass of speculation which would have a different cast as a ray of the gospel falls, or does not fall, upon it, should be faithfully presented in that light. The christian principles cannot be true, without determining what shall be true in the mode of representing every subject in which there is any thing belonging to them by essential relation. Obviously, as far as the gospel can go, and does by such relation with things claim to go, with a modifying action, it cannot be a matter of indifference whether it *do* go or not; for nothing on which its application would have this effect, would be equally right as so modified and as not so modified. That which is made precisely correct by this qualified condition, must therefore, separately from it, be incorrect. He who has sent a revelation to declare the theory of sacred truth, and to order the relations of all moral sentiment with that truth, cannot give his sanction at once to this final constitution, and to that which refuses to be conformed to it. He therefore disowns that which disowns the religion of Christ. And what he disowns he condemns; thus placing all moral sentiments in the same predicament with regard to the christian economy, in which Jesus Christ placed his contemporaries, "He that is not with me is against me."—The order of ideas dissentient from the christian system, presumes the existence, or attempts the creation, of some other economy.

Now, in casting a recollective glance over our elegant literature, as far as I am acquainted with it, I cannot help thinking that much the greater part falls under this condemnation. After a comparatively small number of names and books are excepted, what are called the British Classics, with the addition of very many works of great literary merit that have not quite attained that rank, present an immense vacancy of christianized sentiment. The authors do not give signs of having ever deeply studied christianity, or of having been aware that any such thing is a duty. Whatever has strongly occupied a man's attention, affected his feelings, and filled his mind with ideas, will even unintentionally show itself in the train and cast of his discourse; these writers do not in this manner betray that their faculties have been occupied and interested by the special views unfolded in the evangelic dispensation. Of their coming from the contemplation of these views you discover no notices analogous, for instance, to those which appear in the writing or discourse of a man, who has been passing some time amidst the wonders of Rome or Egypt, and who shows you, by almost unconscious allusions and images occurring in his language even on other subjects, how profoundly he has been interested in beholding triumphal arches, temples, pyramids, and cemeteries. Their minds are not naturalized, if I may so speak, to the images and scenery of the kingdom of Christ, or to that kind of light which the gospel throws on all objects. They are somewhat like the inhabitants of those towns within the vast salt mines of Poland, who, seeing every object in their region by the light of lamps and candles only, have in their conversation hardly any expressions describing things in such aspects as never appear but under the lights of heaven. You might observe, the next time that you open one of these works, how far you may read, without meeting with an idea of such a nature, or so expressed, as could not have been unless Jesus Christ had come into the world;* though the subject in hand may be one of those which he came in a special manner to illuminate, and to enforce on the mind by new and most cogent arguments. And where so little of the light and rectifying influence of these communications has been admitted into the habits of thought, there will be very few cordially reverential and animated references to the great Instructor himself. These will perhaps occur not oftener than a traveller in some parts of Africa, or Arabia, comes to a spot of green vegetation in the desert. You might have read

* Except perhaps in respect to humanity and benevolence, on which subject his instructions have improved the sentiments of infidels themselves, in spite of the rejection of their divine authority.

a considerable number of volumes, without becoming clearly apprised of the existence of the dispensation, or that such a sublime Minister of it had ever appeared among men. And you might have diligently read, for several years, and through several hundred volumes without discovering its nature or importance, or that the writers, when alluding to it, acknowledged any peculiar and essential importance as belonging to it. You would only have conjectured it to be a scheme of opinions and discipline which had appeared, in its day, as many others had appeared, and left us, as the others have left us, to follow our speculations very much in our own way, taking from those schemes, indifferently, any notions that we may approve, and facts or fictions that we may admire.

You would have supposed that these writers had heard of one Jesus Christ, as they had heard of one Confucius, as a teacher whose instructions are admitted to contain many excellent things, and to whose system a liberal mind will occasionally advert, well pleased to see China, Greece, and Judea, as well as England, producing their philosophers, of various degrees and modes of illumination, for the honour of their respective countries and periods, and for the concurrent promotion of human intelligence. All the information which they would have supplied to your understanding, and all the conjectures to which they might have excited your curiosity, would have left you, if not instructed from other sources, to meet the real religion itself, when at length disclosed to you, as a thing of which you had but slight recognition, further than its name; as a wonderful novelty. How little you would have expected, from their literary and ethical glimpses, to find the case to be, that the system so insignificantly and carelessly acknowledged in the course of their fine sentiments, is the actual and sole economy by the provisions of which their happiness can be secured, by the laws of which they will be judged, which has declared the relations of man with his Creator, and specified the exclusive ground of acceptance; which is therefore of infinite consequence to you, and to them, and to all their readers, as fixing the entire theory of the condition and destinies of man on the final principles, to which all theories and sentiments are solemnly required to be " brought into obedience."

Now, if the fine spirits, who have thus preserved an ample, rich, diversified, crowded province of our literature, clear of evangelical intrusion, are really the chief instructors of persons of taste, and form, from early life, their habits of feeling and thought, the natural result must be a state of mind very uncongenial with the gospel. Views habitually presented to the mind in its most susceptible periods, and during the prolonged course of its improvements, in the varied forms and lights of sublimity and beauty, with every fascination of the taste, ingenuity, and eloquence, which it has admired still more each year as its faculties have expanded, will have become the settled order of its ideas. And it will feel the same complacency in this intellectual order, that we feel, as inhabitants of the material world, in the great arrangement of nature, in the green blooming earth, and the splendid hemisphere of heaven.

LETTER VIII.

It will be proper to specify, somewhat more distinctly, several of the particulars in which I consider the majority of our fine writers as at variance with the tenour of the christian revelation, and therefore beguiling their readers into a complacency in an order of sentiments that sometimes virtually, and sometimes directly, disowns it.

One thing extremely obvious to remark is, that the *good man*, the man of virtue, who is necessarily coming often in view in the volumes of these writers, *is not a christian*. His character could have been formed though the christian revelation had never been opened on the earth, or though the New Testament had perished ages since, and it might have been a fine spectacle, but of no striking peculiarity. It has no such complexion and aspect as would have appeared foreign and unaccountable in the absence of the christian truth, and have excited wonder what it should bear relation to, and on what model, or in what school, such a conformation of principles and feelings could have taken its consistence. Let it only be said, that this man of virtue had been conversant whole years with such oracles and examples as Socrates, Plato, Cicero, Antoninus, and Seneca, selecting what in any of them appeared the wisest or best, and all would be explained; there would be nothing to suggest the question, " But if so, with whom has he conversed *since*, to lose so strangely the proper character of his school, under the broad impression of some other mightier influence?"

The good man of our polite literature never talks with affectionate devotion of Christ, as the great High Priest of his profession, as the exalted friend and lord, whose injunctions are the laws of his virtues, whose work and sacrifice are the basis of his hopes, whose doctrines guide and awe his reasonings, and whose example is the pattern which he is earnestly aspiring to resemble. The last intellectual and moral designations in the world by which it would occur to you to describe him, would be those by which the apostles so much

exulted to be recognised, a disciple, and a servant, of
Jesus Christ; nor could you imagine him as at all
gratified by being so described. You do not hear him
express, that he accounts the habitual remembrance of
Christ essential to the nature of that excellence which
he is cultivating. He rather seems, with the utmost
coolness of choice, adopting virtue as according with
the dignity of a rational agent, than to be in the least
degree impelled to the high attainment by any relations
with the Saviour of the world.

If you suppose a person of such character to have
fallen into the company of St. Paul, you can easily
imagine the total want of congeniality. Though both
avowedly devoted to truth, to virtue, and perhaps to
religion, the difference in the cast of their sentiments
would have been as great as that between the physical
constitution and habitudes of a native of the country
at the equator, and those of one from the arctic regions.
Would not that determination of the apostle's mind, by
which there was a continual intervention of ideas concerning one great object, in all subjects, places, and
times, have appeared to this man of virtue and wisdom
inconceivably mystical? In what manner would he have
listened to the emphatical expressions respecting the
love of Christ constraining us, living not to ourselves,
but to him that died for us and rose again, counting all
things but loss for the knowledge of Christ, being ardent
to win Christ and be found in him, and trusting that
Christ should be magnified in our body, whether by
life or by death? Perhaps St. Paul's energy of temperament, evidently combined with a vigorous intellect,
might have awed him into silence. But amidst that
silence, he must have decided, in order to defend his
self-complacency, that the apostle's mind had fallen,
notwithstanding its strength, under the dominion of an

irrational association; for he would have been conscious that no such ideas had ever kindled his affections, and that no such affections had ever animated his actions; and yet *he* was indubitably a good man, according to a generally approved standard, and could, in another style, be as eloquent for goodness as St. Paul himself. He would therefore have assured himself, either that it was not necessary to be a christian, or that this order of feelings was not necessary to that character. But if the apostle's sagacity had detected the cause of this reserve, and the nature of his associate's reflections, he would most certainly have declared to him with emphasis that both these things were necessary—or that he had been deceived by inspiration; and he would have parted from this self-complacent man with admonition and compassion. Would St. Paul have been wrong? But if he would have been right, what becomes of those authors, whose works, whether from neglect or design, tend to satisfy their readers of the perfection of a form of character which he would have pronounced essentially unsound?

Again, moral writings are instructions on the subject of happiness. Now the doctrine of this subject is declared in the evangelical testimony: it had been strange indeed if it had not, when the happiness of man was expressly the object of the communication. And what, according to this communication, are the essential requisites to that condition of the mind without which no man ought to be called happy; without which ignorance or insensibility alone can be content, and folly alone can be cheerful? A simple reader of the christian scriptures will reply that they are—a change of heart, called conversion, the assurance of the pardon of sin through Jesus Christ, a habit of devotion approaching so near to intercourse

with the Supreme Object of devotion that revelation
has called it "communion with God," a process, named
sanctification, of improvement in all internal and external virtue, a confidence in the divine Providence
that all things shall work together for good, and a
conscious preparation for another life, including a firm
hope of eternal felicity. And what else can he reply?
Did the lamp of heaven ever shine more clearly since
omnipotence lighted it, than these ideas display themselves through the christian revelation? *Is* this then
absolutely and exclusively the true account of happiness? It is not that which our accomplished writers
in general have chosen to sanction. Your recollection
will tell you that they have most certainly presumed to
avow, or to insinuate, a doctrine of happiness which
implies much of the christian doctrine to be a needless
intruder on our speculations, or an imposition on our
belief; and I wonder that this grave fact should so
little have alarmed the christian students of elegant
literature. The wide difference between the dictates
of the two authorities is too evident to be overlooked;
for the writers in question have very rarely, amidst an
immense assemblage of sentiments concerning happiness, made any reference to what the inspired teachers
so explicitly declare to be its constituent and vital
principles. How many times you might read the sun
or the moon to its repose, before you would find an
assertion or a recognition, for instance, of a change of
the mind being requisite to happiness, in any terms
commensurate with the significance which this article
seems to bear, in all the varied propositions and notices
respecting it in the New Testament! Some of these
writers appear hardly to have admitted or to have
recollected even the maxim, that happiness must essentially consist in something so fixed in the mind itself,

as to be substantially independent of worldly condition for their most animated representations of it are merely descriptions of fortunate combinations of external circumstances, and of the feelings so immediately depending on them, that they will expire the moment that these combinations are broken up. The greater number, however, have fully admitted so plain a truth, and have given their illustrations of the doctrine of happiness accordingly. And what appears in these illustrations as the brightest image of happiness? It is, probably, that of a man feeling an elevated complacency in his own excellence, a proud consciousness of rectitude; privileged with freedom of thought, and extended views, cleared from the mists of prejudice and superstition; displaying the generosity of his nature in the exercise of beneficence, without feeling, however, any grateful incitement from remembrance of the transcendent generosity of the Son of Man; maintaining, in respect to the events and bustle of the surrounding scene, a dignified indifference, which can let the world go its own way, undisturbed by its disordered course; temperately enjoying whatever good grows on his portion of the field of life, and living in a cool resignation to fate, without any strong expressions of a specific hope, or even solicitude, with regard to the termination of life and to all futurity. Now, notwithstanding a partial coincidence of this description with the christian theory of happiness,* it is evident that on the whole the two modes are so different that no man can realize them both. The consequence is

---

* No one can be so absurd as to represent the notions which pervade the works of polite literature as *totally*, and at all points, opposite to the principles of christianity; what I am asserting is, that in some important points they are substantially and essentially different, and that in others they disown the christian modification.

clear; the natural effect of incompetent and fallacious schemes, prepossessing the mind by every grace and force of genius, will be an aversion to the christian scheme; which will be seen to place happiness in elements and relations much less flattering to what will be called a noble pride; to make it consist in something of which it were a vain presumption for the man to fancy that *himself* can be the sovereign creator.

It is, again, a prominent characteristic of the christian revelation, that having declared this life to be but the introduction to another, it systematically preserves the recollection of this great truth through every representation of every subject; so that the reader is not allowed to contemplate any of the interests of life in a view which detaches them from the grand object and conditions of life itself. An apostle could not address his friends on the most common concerns, for the length of a page, without the final references. 'He is like a person whose eye, while he is conversing with you about an object, or a succession of objects, immediately near, should glance every moment toward some great spectacle appearing on the distant horizon. He seems to talk to his friends in somewhat of that manner of expression with which you can imagine that Elijah spoke, if he remarked to his companion any circumstance in the journey from Bethel to Jericho, and from Jericho to the Jordan; a manner betraying the sublime anticipation which was pressing on his thoughts. The correct consequence of conversing with our Lord and his apostles would be, that the thought of immortality should become almost as habitually present and familiarized to the mind as the countenance of a domestic friend; that it should be the grand test of the value of all pursuits, friendships, and speculations; and that it should mingle a certain nobleness with every thing which it permitted to occupy our time. Now, how far will the discipline of modern polite literature coincide?

I should be pleased to hear a student of that literature seriously profess that he is often and impressively reminded of futurity; and to have it shown that ideas relating to this great subject are presented in sufficient number, and in a proper manner, to produce an effect which should form a respectable proportion of the *whole* effect produced by these authors on susceptible minds. But there is no ground for expecting this satisfaction.

It is true that the idea of immortality is so exceedingly grand, that many writers of genius who have felt but little genuine interest in religion, have been led by their perception of what is sublime to introduce an allusion which is one of the most powerful means of elevating the imagination: and, in point of energy and splendour, their language has been worthy of the subject. In these instances, however, it is seldom found that the idea is presented in that light which, while displaying it prominent in its individual grandeur, shows also its extensive necessary connexion with other ideas: it appears somewhat like a majestic tower, which a traveller in some countries may find standing in a solitary scene, no longer surrounded by the great assemblage of buildings, the ample city, of which it was raised to be the centre, the strength, and the ornament. Immortality has been had recourse to in one page of an ingenious work as a single topic of sublimity, in the same manner as a magnificent phenomenon, or a brilliant achievement, has been described in another. The author's object might rather seem to have been to supply an occasional gratification to taste, than to reduce the mind and all its feelings under the dominion of a grand practical principle.

It is true also, that a graver class of fine writers, who have expressed considerable respect for religion and for christianity, and who, though not writing systematically on morals, have inculcated high moral principles, have made references to a future state as the hope and sanction of virtue. But these references are made less frequently, and with less enforcement and emphasis, than the connexion between our present conduct and a future life must be acknowledged to claim. The manner in which they are made seems to betray either a deficiency of interest in the great subject, or a pusillanimous anxiety not to offend those readers who would think it too directly religious. It is sometimes adverted to as if rather from a compelling sense, that if there is a future state, moral speculation must be defective, even to a degree of absurdity, without some allusions to it, than from feeling a profound delight in the contemplation. When the idea of another life is introduced to aggravate the force of moral principles, and the authority of conscience, it is done so as to appear like a somewhat *reluctant* acknowledgment of the deficiency of inferior sanctions. The consideration comes and vanishes in transient light, after the writer has eloquently expatiated on every circumstance by which the present life can supply motives to goodness. In some instances, a watchful reader will also perceive what appears too much like care to divest the idea, when it *must* be introduced, of all direct references to that sacred Person who first completely opened the prospect of immortality, or to some of those other doctrines which he taught in immediate connexion with this great truth. There seems reason to suspect the writer of being pleased that, though it is indeed to the gospel alone that we owe the positive assurance of immortality, yet it was a subject so much in the conjectures and speculation of the heathen sages, that he may mention it without therefore so expressly recognising the gospel, as he must in the case of introducing some truth of which not only the evidence, but even the first explicit conception, was communicated by that dispensation.

Taking this defective kind of acknowledgment of a future state, together with that entire oblivion of the subject which prevails through an ample portion of elegant literature, I think there is no hazard in saying, that a reader who is satisfied without any other instructions, will learn almost every lesson sooner than the necessity of habitually living for eternity. Many of these writers seem to take as much care to guard against the inroad of ideas from that solemn quarter, as the inhabitants of Holland do against the irruption of the sea; and their writings do really form a kind of moral dyke against the invasion from the other world. They do not instruct a man to act, to enjoy, and to suffer, as a being that may by to-morrow have finally abandoned this orb: every thing is done to beguile the feeling of his being a "stranger and a pilgrim on the earth." The relation which our nature bears to the circumstances of the present state, and which individuals bear to one another, is mainly the ground on which their considerations of duty proceed and conclude. And their schemes of happiness, though formed for beings at once immortal and departing, include little which avowedly relates to that world to which they are removing, nor reach beyond the period at which they will properly but begin to live. They endeavour to raise the groves of an earthly paradise, to shade from sight that vista which opens to the distance of eternity.

Another article in which the anti-christian tendency

of a great part of our productions of taste and genius is apparent, is, the kind of consolation administered to distress, old age, and death. Things of a mournful kind make so large a portion of the lot of humanity, that it is impossible for writers who take human life and feelings for their subject to avoid, (nor indeed have they endeavoured to avoid,) contemplating man in those conditions in which he needs every benignant aid to save him from despair. And here, if any where, we may justly require an absolute coincidence of all moral instructions with the religion of Christ: since consolation is eminently its distinction and its design; since a being in distress has peculiarly a right not to be trifled with by the application of unadapted expedients; and since insufficient consolations are but to mock it, and deceptive ones are to betray. It should then be clearly ascertained by the moralist, and never forgotten, what are the consolations provided by this religion, and under what condition they are offered.

Christianity offers even to the irreligious, who relent amidst their sufferings, the alleviation springing from inestimable promises made to penitence: any other system, which should attempt to console them, simply as suffering, and without any reference to the moral and religious state of their minds, would be mischievous, if it were not inefficacious. What are the principal sources of consolation to the pious, is immediately apparent. The subjects of adversity and sorrow are assured that God exercises his paternal wisdom and kindness in afflicting his children: that this necessary discipline is to refine and exalt them by making them "partakers of his holiness;" that he mercifully regards their weakness and pains, and will not let them suffer beyond what they shall be able to bear; that their great Leader has suffered for them more than they can suffer, and compassionately sympathizes with them still; that this short life was far less designed to confer a present happiness, than to mature them to a fitness for being happy for ever; and that patient constancy shall receive a resplendent crown. An aged christian is soothed by the assurance that his Almighty Friend will not despise the enfeebled exertions, nor desert the oppressed and fainting weakness, of the last stage of his servant's life. When advancing into the shade of death itself, he is animated by the faith that the great sacrifice has taken the malignity of death away; and that the divine presence will attend the dark steps of this last and lonely enterprise, and shew the dying traveller and combatant that even this melancholy gloom is to him the utmost limit of the dominion of evil, the very confine of paradise, the immediate access to the region of eternal life.

Now, in the greater number of the works under review, what are the modes of consolation which sensibility, reason, and eloquence, have most generally exerted themselves to apply to the mournful circumstances of life, and to its close? You will readily recollect such as these: a man is suffering—well, it is the common destiny, every one suffers sometimes, and some much more than he; it is well it is no worse. If he is unhappy now, he *has* been happy, and he could not expect to be so invariably. It were folly to complain that his nature was constituted capable of suffering, or placed in a world where it is exposed to the infliction. If it were not capable of pain, it would not of pleasure. Would he be willing to lose his being, to escape these ills? Or would he consent, if such a thing were possible, to be any person else?—The sympathy of each kind relation and friend will not be wanting. His condition may probably change for the better; there is hope in every situation; and meanwhile, it is an opportunity for displaying manly fortitude. A strong mind can proudly triumph over the oppression of pain, the vexations of disappointment, and the tyranny of fortune. If the cause of distress is some irreparable deprivation, it will be softened by the lenient hand of time.*

The lingering months of an aged man are soothed almost, it is pretended, into cheerfulness, by the respectful attention of his neighbours; by the worldly prosperity and dutiful regard of the family he has brought up; by the innocent gaiety and amusing activity of their children; and by the consideration of his fair character in society. If he is a man of thought, he has the added advantage of some philosophical considerations; the cares and passions of his former life are calmed into a wise tranquillity; he thinks he has had a competent share of life; it is as proper and necessary for mankind to have their "exits," as their "entrances;" and his business will now be to make a "well-graced retreat from the stage, like a man that has properly acted his part, and may retire with applause.

As to the means of sustaining the spirit in death, the general voice of these authors asserts the chief and only all-sufficient one to be the recollection of a well-spent life. Some minor repellents of fear are added; as for instance, that death is in fact a far less tremendous thing than that dire form of it by which imagination and superstition are haunted; that the sufferings in death

* Can it be necessary to notice here again, that every system of moral sentiments must inevitably contain some principles not disclaimed by christianity; with whose dictates various particulars in this assemblage of consolations are not inconsistent if held in a subordinate rank? But the enumeration taken altogether, and exclusively of the grand christian principles, forms a scheme of consolation essentially different from that so beneficently displayed in the religion of Christ.

are less than men often endure in the course of life; that it is only like one of those transformations with which the world of nature abounds; and that it is easy to conceive, and reasonable to expect, a more commodious vehicle and habitation. It would seem almost unavoidable to glance a thought toward what revelation has signified to us of "the house not made with hands," of the " better country, that is, the heavenly." But the greater number of the writers of taste advert to the scene beyond this world with apparent reluctance, unless it can be done, on the one hand, in the manner of pure philosophical conjecture, or on the other, under the form of images, bearing some analogy to the visions of classical poetry.*

The arguments for resignation to death are not so much drawn from future scenes, as from a consideration of the evils of the present life; the necessity of yielding to a general and irreversible law; the dignity of submitting with that calmness which conscious virtue is entitled to feel; and the improbability (as these writers sometimes intimate) that any formidable evils are to be apprehended after death, except by a few of the very worst of the human race. Those arguments are in general rather aimed to quiet fear than to animate hope. The pleaders of them seem more concerned to convey the dying man in peace and silence out of the world, than to conduct him to the celestial felicity. Let us but see

* I am very far from disliking philosophical speculation, or daring flights of fancy, on this high subject. On the contrary, it appears to me strange that any one firmly holding the belief of a life to come, should not have both the intellectual faculty and the imagination excited to the utmost effort in the trial, however unavailing, to give some outlines of definite form to the unseen realities. What I mean to censure in the mode of referring to another life, is, the care to avoid any direct resemblance or recognition of the ideas which the New Testament has given to guide, in some small, very small degree, our conjectures.

him embarked on his unknown voyage in fair weather, and we are not accountable for what he may meet, or whither he may be carried, when he is gone out of sight. They seldom present a lively view of the distant happiness, especially in any of those images in which the christian revelation has intimated its nature. In which of these books, and by which of the real or fictitious characters whose last hours and thoughts they sometimes display, will you find, in terms or in spirit, the apostolic sentiments adopted, " To depart and be with Christ is far better;" " Willing rather to be absent from the body, and present with the Lord?" The very existence of that sacred testimony which has given the only genuine consolations in death, and the only just conceptions of what is beyond it, seems to be scarcely recollected; while the ingenious moralists are searching the exhausted common places of the stoic philosophy, or citing the treacherous maxims of a religion perverted to accordance with the corrupt wishes of mankind, or even recollecting the lively sayings of the few whose wit has expired only in the same moment with life, to fortify the pensive spirit for its last removal. "Is it not because there is not a God in Israel, that ye have sent to inquire of Baalzebub the God of Ekron?"

Another order of sentiments concerning death, of a character too bold to be called consolations, has been represented as animating one class of human beings. In remarking on Lucan, I noticed that desire of death which has appeared in the expressions of great minds, sometimes while merely indulging solemn reflections when no danger or calamity immediately threatened, but often in the conscious approach towards a fatal catastrophe. Many writers of later times have exerted their whole strength, and have even excelled themselves, in representing the high sentiments in which this desire has displayed itself; genius has found its very gold mine in this field. If this grandeur of sentiment had been of the genuine spirit to animate piety while it exalts the passions, some of the poets would have ranked among our greatest benefactors. Powerful genius, aiding to inspire a christian triumph in the prospect of death, might be revered as a prophet, might be almost loved as a benignant angel. Few men's emotions can have approached nearer to enthusiasm than mine, in reading the sentiments made to be uttered by sages and reflective heroes in this prospect. I have felt these passages as the last and mightiest of the enchantments of poetry, of power to inspire for a little while a contempt of all ordinary interests, of the world which we inhabit, and of life itself. While the enthusiast is elated with such an emotion, nothing may appear so captivating as some noble occasion of dying; such an occasion as that when Socrates died for virtue; or that when Brutus at Philippi fell with falling liberty.* Poetry has delighted to display personages of this high order, in the same fatal predicament; and the situation of such men has appeared inexpressibly enviable, by means of those sublime sentiments by which they illuminated the gloom of death. The reader has loved to surround himself in imagination with that gloom, for the sake of irradiating it with that sublimity. All other greatness has been for a while eclipsed by the greatness of thought displayed by these contemplative and magnanimous

* Poetry will not easily exceed many of the expressions which mere history has recorded. I should little admire the capability of feeling, or greatly admire the christian temper, of the man who could without emotion read, for instance, the short observations of Brutus to his friend, (in contemplation even of a *self-inflicted* death,) on the eve of the battle which extinguished all hope of freedom: "We shall either be victorious, or pass away beyond the power of those that are so. We shall deliver our country by victory, or ourselves by death."

spirits, though untaught by religion, when advancing to meet their fate.

But the christian faith recalls the mind from this enchantment, to recollect that the christian spirit in dying can be the only right and noble one, and to consider whether these examples be not exceedingly different Have not the most enlightened and devout christians, whether they have languished in their chambers, or passed through the fire of martyrdom, manifested their elevation of mind in another strain of eloquence? The examples of greatness in death, which poetry has exhibited, generally want all those sentiments respecting the pardon of sin, and a Mediator who has accomplished and confers the deliverance, and often the explicit idea of meeting the Judge, with which a christian contemplates his approaching end. Their expressions of intrepidity and exultation have no analogy with the language of an incomparable saint and hero, " O death, where is thy sting? O grave, where is thy victory? Thanks be to God, who giveth us the victory through our Lord Jesus Christ." The kind of self-authorized confidence of taking possession of some other state of being, as monarchs would talk of a distant part of their empire which they were going to enter; the proud apostrophe to the immortals, to prepare for the great and rival spirit that is coming; their manner of consigning to its fate a good but falling cause, which will sink when they are gone, there not being virtue enough on earth to support, or in heaven to vindicate it; their welcoming the approach of death in an exultation of lofty and bitter scorn of a hated world and a despicable race—are not the humility, nor the benevolence, nor the reverential submission to the Supreme Governor, with which it is in the proper character of a christian to die. If a christian will partly unite with these high spirits in being weary of a world of dust and trifles, in defying the pains of death, in panting for an unbounded liberty, it will be at the same time with a most solemn commitment of himself to the divine mercy, which *they* forget, or were never instructed, to implore. And as to the vision of the other world, you will observe a great difference between the language of sublime poetry and that of revelation, in respect to the nature of the sentiments and triumphs of that world, and still more perhaps in respect to the associates with whom the departing spirit expects soon to mingle. The dying magnanimity of poetry anticipates high converse with the souls of heroes, and patriots, and perhaps philosophers; a christian feels himself going, (I may accommodate the passage,) to "an innumerable company of angels, to the general assembly and church of the firstborn, to God the Judge of all, to the spirits of just men made perfect, and to Jesus the Mediator of the new covenant."

In defence of those who have thus given attractions to the image of death by means foreign and opposite to the evangelical principles, it may be said, that many of the personages whom their scenes exhibit in the contemplation of death, or in the approach to it, were necessarily, from the age or country in which they lived or are feigned to have lived, unacquainted with christianity; and that therefore it would have been absurd to represent them as animated by christian sentiments. Certainly. But then I ask, on what ground men of genius will justify themselves for *choosing*, with a view to the improvement of the heart, as they will profess, examples of which they cannot preserve the consistency, without making them pernicious? Where is the conscience of that man, who is anxiously careful that every sentiment expressed by the historical or fictitious personage, in the fatal season, should be harmonious with every principle of the character,—but feels not the smallest concern about the consistency of selecting or creating the character itself, with his conviction of the absolute authority of the religion of Christ? In glancing forward, he knows that his favourite is to die, and that he cannot die as a christian; yet he is to depart in a splendour of moral dignity. Would it not therefore be a dictate of conscience to warn his readers, that 'he expects to display the exit with a commanding sublimity, of which the natural effect is to be, a complacency, or an elation, in the idea of such a death as a christian cannot die. But how would he feel while giving such a warning? Might it not be said to him, And are *you* then willing to die otherwise than as a christian? If you are, you virtually pronounce christianity an imposture, and, to be consistent, should avow the rejection. If you are not, how can you endeavour to seduce your readers into an enthusiastic admiration of such a death as you wish may now be yours? How can you endeavour to infect your reader with sentiments which you could not hear him utter in his last hours without alarm for the state of his mind? Is it *necessary* to the pathos and sublimity of poetry, to introduce characters which cannot be justly represented without falsifying our view of the most serious of all subjects? If this *be* necessary, it would be better that poetry with all its charms were exploded, than that the revelation of God should be frustrated in the great object and demand of fixing its own ideas of death, clearly and alone, in the minds of beings whose manner of preparing for it is of infinite consequence. But there is no such dilemma; since many examples could be found, and an unlimited number may with rational probability be imagined, of christian greatness in death. Are not then the preference of examples adverse to christianity, and that temper of the poet's mind which is in such full sympathy with them, empowering him to personate them with such entireness and animation, and to express for them all the appropriate feelings, a worse kind of infidelity, as it is far more injurious, than that of the cold dealer in cavils and quibbles against the gospel? What is the christian belief of that poet worth, who would not on reflection feel self-reproach for the affecting scene, which may for a while have betrayed some of his readers to regard it as a more dignified thing to depart in the character of Socrates or Cato, than of St. John or a christian martyr? What would have been thought of the pupil of an apostle, who, after hearing his master describe the spirit of a christian's departure from the world, in language which he believed to be of conclusive authority, and which asserted or clearly implied that this alone was greatness in death, should have taken the first occasion to expatiate with enthusiasm on the closing scene of a philosopher, or on the exit of a stern hero, that, acknowledging within the visible creation no object for either confidence or fear, departed with the aspect of a being who should be going to summon his gods to judgment for the misfortunes of his life? And how will these careless men of genius give their account to the Judge of the world, for having virtually taught many aspiring minds that, notwithstanding his first coming was to conquer for man the king of terrors, there needs no recollection of him, in order to look toward death with noble defiance or sublime desire?

Some of their dying personages are so consciously uninformed of the realities of the invisible state, that the majestic sentiments which they disclose on the verge of life, can only throw a faint glimmering on unfathomable darkness; but some anticipate the other world, as I have already observed, in very defined images. I recollect one of them, after some just reflections on the vanity and wretchedness of life, thus expressing his complacency in view of the great deliverer:

> " Death joins us to the great majority;
> 'Tis to be born to Platos and to Cæsars;
> 'Tis to be great for ever.
> 'Tis pleasure, 'tis ambition then, to die."

Another, an illustrious female, in a tragedy which I lately read, welcomes death with the following sentiments:

> ——" Oh 'tis wondrous well!
> Ye gods of death, that rule the Stygian gloom!
> Ye who have greatly died, I come! I come!
> The hand of Rome can never touch me more;
> Hail! perfect freedom, hail!"

> " My free spirit should ere now have join'd
> That great assembly, those devoted shades,
> Who scorn'd to live till liberty was lost!
> But, ere their country fell, abhorr'd the light."

> " Shift not thy colour at the sound of death;
> It is to me perfection, glory, triumph.
> Nay, fondly would I choose it, though persuaded
> It were a long dark night without a morning;
> To bondage far prefer it, since it is
> Deliverance from a world where Romans rule."

> ——" Then let us spread
> A bold exalted wing, and the last voice we hear,
> Be that of wonder and applause."

> " And is the sacred moment then so near?
> The moment when yon sun, those heavens, this earth,
> Hateful to me, polluted by the Romans,
> And all the busy slavish race of men,
> Shall sink at once, and straight another state
> Rise on a sudden round?
> Oh to be there!"*

---

* This is not perhaps one of the best specimens: it is the last that has come under my notice. I am certain of having read many, but have not recollection enough to know where to find them

You will recollect to have read many equally improper to engage a christian's full sympathy, and therefore, convicting the poetic genius which produced them of treachery to the true faith, in such efforts to seduce our feelings. It is a pernicious circumstance in passages of this strain, that the special thoughts and images which are alien from the spirit of christianity, are implicated with those *general* sentiments of anticipation, those emotions aspiring to greatness and felicity in indefinite terms, which a dying christian may energetically express; so that through the animated sympathy with the general, and as it were elementary sentiments, the reader's mind is beguiled into complacency in the more special ones of an antichristian spirit.

Sometimes even very bad men are made to display such dignity in death, as at once to impart an attraction to their false sentiments, and to mitigate the horror of their crimes. I recollect the interest with which I read, many years since, in Dr. Young's Busiris, the proud magnanimous speech at the end of which the tyrant dies: these are some of the lines:

"I thank these wounds, these raging pains, which promise
An interview with equals soon elsewhere.
Great Jove, I come!"

Even the detestable Zanga, in the prospect of death, while assured by his conscience that "to receive him hell blows all her fires," rises to a certain imposing greatness, by heroic courage tempered to a kind of moral dignity, through the relenting of revenge and the ingenuous manifestation of sentiments of justice. To create an occasion of thus compelling us to do homage to the dying magnanimity of wicked men, is unfaithfulness to the religion which condemns such magnanimity as madness. It is no justification to say that such instances have been known, and therefore such representations are only vividly reflected images of reality; for if the laws of criticism do not enjoin, in works of genius, a careful adaptation of all examples and sentiments to the purest moral purpose, as a far higher duty than the study of resemblance to the actual world, the laws of piety most certainly do. Let the men who have so much literary conscience about this verisimilitude, content themselves with the office of mere historians, and then they may relate without guilt, provided the relation be simple and unvarnished, all the facts, and speeches of depraved greatness within the memory of the world. But when they choose the higher office of inventing and combining, they are accountable for the consequences. They create a new person, and, in sending him into society, they can choose whether his example shall tend to improve or to pervert the minds that will be compelled to admire him.

It is an immense transition from such instances as those I have been remarking on, to Rousseau's celebrated description of the death of his Eloisa, which would have been much more properly noticed in an earlier page. It is long since I read that scene, one of the most striking specimens probably of original conception and interesting sentiment that ever appeared; but though the representation is so extended as to include every thing which the author thought needful to make it perfect, there is no explicit reference to the peculiarly evangelical causes of complacency in death. Yet the representation is so admirable, that the serious reader is tempted to suspect even his own mind of fanaticism, while he is expressing to his friends the wish that they, and that himself, may be animated, in the last day of life, by a class of ideas which that eloquent writer would have been ashamed to introduce.

LETTER IX.

Does it not appear to you, my dear friend, that an approving reader of the generality of our ingenious authors will acquire an opinion of the moral condition of our species very different from that which is dictated by the divine declarations? The Governor of all intelligent creatures has spoken of this nation or family of them, as exceedingly remote from conformity to that standard of perfection which alone can ever be his rule of judgment. And this is pronounced not only of vicious individuals, who are readily given up to condemnation by those who entertain the most partial or the proudest estimate of human nature, but of the constitutional quality of that nature itself. The moral part of the constitution of man is represented as placing him immensely below that rank of dignity and happiness to which, by his intellectual powers, and his privilege of being immortal, he would otherwise have seemed adapted to belong. The descriptions of the human condition are such as if the nature had, by a dreadful convulsion, been separated off at each side from a pure and happy system of the creation, and had fallen down an immeasurable depth, into depravation and misery. In this state man is represented as loving, and therefore practically choosing, the evils which subject him to the condemnation of God; and it is affirmed that no expedient, but that very extraordinary one which christianity has revealed, can change this condition, and avert this condemnation with its formidable consequences.

Every attempt to explain the wisdom and the exact ultimate intention of the Supreme Being, in constituting a nature subject in so fatal a degree to moral evil, will fail. But even if a new revelation were given to turn this dark inquiry into noonday, it would make no difference in the actual state of things. An extension of knowledge could not reverse the fact, that the human nature has displayed, through every age, the most aggravated proofs of being in a deplorable and hateful condition, whatever were the reasons for giving a moral agent a constitution which it was foreseen would soon be found in this condition. Perhaps, if there were a mind expanded to a comprehension so far beyond all other created intelligences, that it could survey the general order of a great portion of the universe, and look into distant ages, it might understand in what manner the melancholy fact could operate to the perfection of the vast system; and according to what principles, and in reference to what ends, all that has taken place within the empire of the Eternal Monarch is right. But in this contemplation of the whole, it would also take account of the separate condition of each part; it would perceive that this human world, whatever are its relations to the universe, has its own distinct economy of interests, and stands in its own relation and accountableness to the righteous Governor; and that, regarded in this exclusive view, it is an awful spectacle. Now, to this exclusive sphere of our own condition and interests revelation confines our attention; and pours contempt, though not more than experience pours, on all presumption to reason on those grand unknown principles according to which the Almighty disposes the universe; all our estimates therefore of the state and relations of man must take the subject on this insulated ground. Considering man in this view, the sacred oracles have represented him as a more melancholy object than Nineveh or Babylon in ruins; and an infinite aggregate of obvious facts confirms the doctrine. This doctrine then is absolute authority in our speculations on human nature. But to this authority the writers in question seem to pay, and to teach their readers to pay, but little respect. And unless those readers are pre-occupied by the grave convictions of religious truth, rendered still more grave by painful reflection on themselves, and by observation on mankind; or unless they are capable of enjoying a malicious or misanthropic pleasure, like Mandeville and Swift, in detecting and exposing the degradation of our nature, it is not wonderful that they should be prompt to entertain the sentiments which insinuate a much more flattering estimate. Our elegant and amusing moralists no doubt copiously describe and censure the follies and vices of mankind; but many of these, they maintain, are accidental to the human character, rather than a disclosure of intrinsic qualities. Others do indeed spring radically from the nature; but they are only the wild weeds of a virtuous soil. Man is still a very dignified and noble being, with strong dispositions to all excellence, holding a proud eminence in the ranks of existence, and (if such a Being is adverted to) high in the favour of his Creator. The measure of virtue in the world vastly exceeds that of depravity; we should not indulge a fanatical rigour in our judgments of mankind; nor be always reverting to an ideal perfection; nor accustom ourselves to contemplate the Almighty always in the dark majesty of justice.—None of their speculations seem to acknowledge the gloomy fact which the New Testament so often asserts or implies, that all men are "by nature children of wrath."

It is quite of course that among sentiments of this order, the idea of the redemption by Jesus Christ (if any allusion to it should occur,) can but appear with equivocal import, and "shorn of the beams" which constitute the peculiar light of his own revelation.

While man is not considered as lost, the mind canno' do justice to the expedient, or to "the only name under heaven," by which he can be redeemed. Accordingly the gift of Jesus Christ does not appear to be habitually recollected as the most illustrious instance of the beneficence of God that has come within human knowledge, and as the fact which has contributed more than all others to relieve the oppressive awfulness of the mystery in which our world is enveloped. No thankful joy seems to awake at the thought of so mighty an interposition, and of him whose sublime appointment it was to undertake and accomplish it. When it is difficult to avoid making some allusion to him, he is acknowledged rather in any of his subordinate characters, than as absolutely a Redeemer; or if the term Redeemer, or, our Saviour, is introduced, it is done as with a certain inaptitude to pronounce a foreign appellative; as with a somewhat irksome feeling at falling in momentary contact with language so specifically of the christian school. And it is done in a manner which betrays, that the author does not mean all that he feels some dubious intimation that such a term should mean. Jesus Christ is regarded rather as having added to our moral advantages, than as having conferred that without which all the rest were in vain; rather as having made the passage to a happy futurity somewhat more commodious, than as having formed the passage itself over what was else an impassable gulf. Thus that comprehensive sum of blessings, called in the New Testament Salvation, or Redemption, is shrunk into a comparatively inconsiderable favour, which a less glorious messenger might have brought, which a less magnificent language than that dictated by inspiration might have described, and which a less costly sacrifice might have secured.

It is consistent with this delusive idea of humar

nature, and these crude, and faint, and narrow conceptions of the christian economy, that these writers commonly represent felicity hereafter as the pure reward of merit. I believe you will find this, as far as any allusions are made to the subject, the prevailing opinion through the school of polite literature. You will perceive it to be the real opinion of many writers who do sometimes advert, in some phrase employed by way of respectful ceremony to *our national creed*, to the work or sacrifice of Christ.

I might remark on the antichristian motives to action which are sanctioned and inspirited by many of these authors: I will only notice one, the love of glory; that is, the desire of being distinguished, admired, and praised.

No one will think of such a thing as bringing the christian laws in absolute prohibition of our desire to possess the favourable opinion of our fellow men. In the first place, a material portion of human happiness depends on the attachment of relations and friends, and it is right for a man to wish for the happiness resulting from such attachment. And since the degree in which he will obtain it, must depend very much on the higher or lower estimate which these persons entertain of his qualities and abilities, it is right for him to wish, while he endeavours to deserve, that their estimate may be high, in order that he may enjoy a large share of their affection.

In the next place, it is too plain to be worth an observation, that if it were possible for a man to desire the respect and admiration of mankind purely as a mean of giving a greater efficacy to his efforts for their welfare, and for the promotion of the cause of heaven, while he would be equally gratified that any other man, in whose hands this mean would have exactly the same effect, should obtain the admiration instead of himself, this would be something eminently more than innocent; it would be the apotheosis of a passion which in its ordinary quality deserves no better denomination than vanity. But where is the example?

In the third place, as the Creator has included this desire in the essential constitution of our nature, he intended its gratification, in some limited degree, to be a direct and immediate cause of pleasure. The good opinion of mankind, expressed in praise, or indicated by any other signs, pleases us by a law of the same order as that which constitutes mutual affection a pleasure, or that which is the cause that we are gratified by music, or the beauties and gales of spring. The indulgence of this desire is thus authorized, to a certain extent, by its appointment to be a source of pleasure.

But to what extent? It is notorious that this desire has, if I may so express it, an immense voracity. It has within itself no natural principle of limitation, since it is incapable of being gratified to satiety. A whole continent applauding or admiring has not satisfied some men's avarice of what they called glory. To what extent, I repeat, may the desire be indulged? Evidently not beyond that point where it begins to introduce its evil accessories, envy, or ungenerous competition, or resentful mortification, or disdainful comparison, or self-idolatry. But I appeal to each man who has deeply reflected on himself, or observed those around him, whether this desire under even a considerably limited degree of indulgence be not very apt to introduce some of these accessories; and whether, in order to preclude them from his own mind, he have not at times felt it necessary to impose on this desire a restraint almost as unqualified as if he had been aiming to suppress it altogether. In wishing to prohibit an *excess* of its indulgence, he has perceived that even what had seemed to him a small degree has amounted, or powerfully tended, to that excess—except when the desire has been operating under the kindly and approved modification, of seeking to engage the affection of relations or a few friends. The measure therefore of this passion, compatible with the best condition of the mind, will be found to be exceedingly limited.

Again, the desire cannot be cherished without becoming a motive of action exactly in the degree in which it is cherished. Now if the most authoritative among a good man's motives of action must be the wish to please God, it is evident that the passion which supplies another motive, ought not to be allowed in a degree that will empower the motive thus put in force to contest, in the mind, the supremacy of the pious motive. But here, again, I appeal to the reflective man of conscience, whether he have not found that the desire of human applause, indulged in only such a degree as he had not, for a while, suspected of being immoderate, may be a motive strong enough not only to maintain a rivalry with what should be the supreme motive, but absolutely to prevail over it. In each pursuit or performance in which he has excelled, or endeavoured to excel, has he not sometimes been forced to observe, with indignant grief, that his thoughts much more promptly adverted to human praise, than to divine approbation? And when he has been able in some measure to repress the passion, has he not found that a slight stimulus was competent to restore its impious ascendency?—Now what is it that should follow from these observations? What can it be, as a general inference, but plainly this, that though the desire of human applause, if it could be a calm, closely limited, and subordinate feeling, would be consistent with christian virtue; yet, since it so mightily tends to an excess, destructive of the very essence of that virtue, it ought, (excepting in the cases where human estimation is sought as a mean toward some valuable end,) to be opposed and repressed in a manner NOT MUCH LESS general and unconditional than if it were purely evil? The special inference, available to the design of this essay, is, that so much of our literature as, on the contrary, tends to animate the passion with new force, is most pernicious.

These assertions are certainly in the spirit of the New Testament, which, not exacting a total extinction of the love of human applause, yet alludes to most of its operations with censure, exhibits, probably, no approved instance of its indulgence, and abounds with emphatically cogent representations, both of its pernicious influence when it predominates, and of its powerful tendency to acquire the predominance. The honest disciple of that divine school, being at the same time a self-observer, will be convinced that the degree beyond which the passion is not tolerated by the christian law, is a degree which it will be sure to reach and to exceed in his mind in spite of the most systematical opposition. The most resolute and persevering repression will still leave so much of this passion as christianity will pronounce a fault or a vice. He will be anxious to assemble, in aid of the repressive discipline, all the arguments of reason, all striking examples, and all the interdictions of the Bible.

Now I think I cannot be mistaken in asserting, that a great majority of our fine writers have gone directly counter to any such doctrine and discipline. No advocate will venture to deny, that they have commended and instigated the love of applause, of fame, of glory, or whatever it may be called, in a degree which, if the preceding representation be just, places them in pointed hostility to the christian religion. Sometimes, indeed, when it was the planetary hour for high philosophy, or when they were in a splenetic mood, occasioned perhaps by some chagrin of disappointed vanity, they have acknowledged, and even very rhetorically exposed, the inanity of this same glory. Most of our ingenious authors have, in one place or another, been moral or satirical at the expense of what Pope so aptly denominates the "fool to fame." They perceived the truth, but as the truth did not make them free, they were willing after all to dignify a passion to which they felt themselves irretrievable slaves. And they have laboured to do it by celebrating, with every splendid epithet, the men who were impelled by this passion through the career in which they were the idols of servile mankind and their own; by describing glory as the best incentive to noble actions, and their worthiest reward; by placing the temple of Virtue (proud station of the goddess) in the situation to be a mere introduction to that of Fame ; by lamenting that so few, and their unfortunate selves not of the number, can "climb the steep where that proud temple shines afar:" and by intimating a charge of meanness of spirit against those, who have no generous ardour to distinguish themselves from the crowd, by deeds calculated and designed to pitch them aloft in gazing admiration. If sometimes the ungracious recollection strikes them, and seems likely to strike their readers, that this admiration is provokingly capricious and perverse, since men have gained it without rightful claims, and lost it without demerit, and since all kinds of fools have offered the incense to all kinds of villains, they escape from the disgust and from the benefit of this recollection by saying, that it is *honourable* fame that noble spirits seek ; for they despise the ignorant multitude, and seek applause by none but worthy actions, and from none but worthy judges. Almost every one of these writers will sometimes, perhaps, advert to the approbation of the Supreme Being, as what wise and good men will value most; but such an occasional acknowledgment feebly counteracts the effect of many glowing sentiments and descriptions of a contrary tendency.—If this be a correct animadversion on our popular fine writers, there can be no question whether they be likely to animate their readers with christian motives of action.

I will remark only on one particular more, namely, the culpable license, careless, if not sometimes malignant, taken by the lighter order of these writers, and by some even of the graver, in their manner of ridiculing the cant and extravagance by which hypocrisy, fanaticism, or the peculiarities of a sect or a period, may have disgraced or falsified christian doctrines. Sometimes, indeed, they have selected and burlesqued modes of expression which were *not* cant, and which ignorance and impiety alone would have dared to ridicule. And often, in exposing to contempt the follies of notion or language or manners, by which a christian of good taste deplores that the profession of the gospel should ever have been deformed, they take not the smallest care to preserve a clear separation between what taste and sense have a right to explode, and what piety bids to reverence. By this criminal carelessness, (to give it no stronger denomination,) they have fixed repulsive and irreverent associations on the evangelical truth itself, for which many persons, when afterwards they have yielded their faith and affection to that truth, have had cause to wish that certain volumes had gone into the fire, instead of coming into their hands. Many others, who have not thus become its converts, retain the bad impression unabated, and cherish the disgust. Gay writers ought to know that this is dangerous ground.

I am sorry that this extended censure on works of genius and taste could not be prosecuted with a more marked application, and with more discriminative references than the continual repetition of the expressions, " elegant literature," and " these writers." It might be a service of some value to the evangelical cause, if a work were written containing a faithful estimate, individually, of the most popular writers of the last century and a half, in respect to the important subject of these comments; with formal citations from some of their works, and a candid statement of the general tendency of others. In an essay like this it is impossible to make an enumeration of names, or pass a judgment, except in a very cursory manner, on any particular author. Even the several *classes* of authors, which I mentioned some time back, as coming under the accusation, shall detain you but a short time.

The Moral Philosophers for the most part seem anxious to avoid every thing that might render them liable to be mistaken for Christian Divines. They regard their department as a science complete in itself; and they investigate the foundation of morality, define its laws, and affix its sanctions, in a manner generally so much apart from christianity, that the reader would almost conclude that religion to be *another* science complete in itself.* An *entire* separation, it is true,

* When it happens sometimes, that a moral topic hardly *can* be disposed of without some recognition of its involving, or being intimately connected with, a *theological* doctrine, it is curious to notice, with what an air of indifference, somewhat partaking of contempt, one of these writers will observe, that *that* view of the matter is the business of the *divines*, with whose department he does not pretend to interfere.

cannot well be preserved; since christianity has decided some moral questions on which reason was dubious or silent; and since that final retribution, which the New Testament has so luminously foreshown, brings evidently the greatest of sanctions. To make *no* reference in the course of inculcating moral principles, to a judgment to come, if there be an understood admission that it is actually revealed, would look like systematic irreligion. But still it is striking to observe how small a portion of the ideas, (relative to this and other points of the greatest moral interest,) which distinguish the New Testament from other books, many moral philosophers have thought indispensable to a theory in which they professed to include the sum of the duty and interests of man. A serious reader is constrained to feel that either there is too much in *that* book, or too little in theirs. He will perceive that, in the inspired book, the moral principles are intimately interwoven with all those doctrines which could not have been known but through revelation. He will find also in this superior book, a vast number of ideas avowedly designed to interest the *affections* in favour of all moral principles and virtues. The " quickening spirit," thus breathed among what might else be dry and lifeless, is drawn from considerations of the divine mercy, the compassion of the Redeemer, the assurance of aid from heaven in the difficult strife to *be* what the best principles prescribe, the relationship subsisting between good men on earth and those who are departed; and other kindred topics, quite out of the range to which the mere moral preceptors appear to hold themselves limited. The system of morals, as placed in the temperature of such considerations, has the character and effect of a different zone. Thus, while any given virtue, equally prescribed in the treatise of the moral philosopher and the christian code, would in mere definition be the same in both, the manner in which it bears on the heart and conscience must be greatly different.

It is another difference also of momentous consequence, if it be found that the christian doctrine declares the virtues of a good man not to be the cause of his acceptance with God, and that the philosophic moralists disclaim any other On the whole it must be concluded, that there cannot but be something very defective in that theory of morality which makes so slight an acknowledgment of the religion of Christ, and takes so little of its peculiar character. The philosophers place the religion in the relation of a diminutive satellite to the sphere of moral interests; useful as throwing a few rays on that side of it on which the solar light of human wisdom could not directly shine; but that it can impart a vital warmth, or claims to be acknowledged paramount in dignity and influence, some of them seem not to have a suspicion.

No doubt, innumerable reasonings and conclusions may be advanced on moral subjects which shall be *true* on a foundation of their own, equally in the presence of the evangelical system and in its absence. Independently of that system, it were easy to illustrate the utility of virtue, the dignity which it confers on a rational being, its accordance to the "reason and fitness of things," its conformity and analogy to much of what may be discerned in the order of the universe. It would also have been easy to pass from virtue in the abstract, into an illustration and enforcement of the several distinct virtues, as arranged in a practical system. And if it should be asked, Why may not some writers employ their speculations on those parts and views of moral truth which are thus independent of the gospel, leaving it to other men to christianize the whole by the addition of the evangelical relations, motives, and conditions?—I readily answer, that this may sometimes very properly be done. An author may render good service by demonstrating, for instance, the utility of virtue in general, or of any particular virtue, as shown in its effect on the prosperity of states, of smaller communities, and of individuals; in its conduciveness to health, mental tranquillity, social confidence, and the like. In doing this, he would expressly take a marked ground, and aim at a specific object. He would not (or should not) let it be imagined for a moment that such particular views embrace all that is of essential interest in the reasons and relations of moral rectitude. It would be plainly understood that other considerations, of the highest importance, recognising, in all our obligations to virtue, our relations with God, with a spiritual economy, with a future life, are indispensable to a complete moral theory. But the charge against the moral philosophers is meant to be applied to those who, not professing to have any such specific and limited scope, but assuming the office of moralist in its most comprehensive character, and making themselves responsible as teachers of virtue in its whole extent, have yet quite forgotten the vital implication of ethical with evangelical truth.

When I mention our Historians, it will instantly occur to you, that the very foremost names in this department import every thing that is deadly to the christian religion itself, as a divine communication, and therefore lie under a condemnation of a different kind. But may not many others, who would have repelled the imputation of being enemies to the christian cause, be arraigned of having forgotten what was due from its friends? The historian intends his work to have the effect of a series of moral estimates of the persons whose actions he records; now, if he believes that a Judge of the world will come at length, and pronounce on the very characters that his work adjudges, it is one of the plainest dictates of good sense, that all the awards of the historian should be faithfully coincident with the judgments which may be expected ultimately from that supreme authority. Those distinctions of character which the historian applauds as virtues, or censures as vices, should be exactly the same qualities, which the language already heard from that Judge certifies us that he will approve or condemn. It is worse than foolish to erect a literary court of morals and human character, of which the maxims, the language, the decisions, and the judges, will be equally the objects of contempt before Him, whose intelligence will instantly distinguish and place in light the right and the wrong of all time. What a wretched abasement will overwhelm on that day some of the pompous historians, who were called by others, and accounted by themselves, the high authoritative censors of an age, and whose verdict was to fix on each name perpetual honour or infamy, if they shall find many of the questions and the decisions of that tribunal proceed on principles which they would have been ashamed to apply, or never took the trouble to understand! How will they be confounded, if some of the men whom they had extolled, are consigned to ignominy, and some that they had despised, are applauded by the voice at which the world will tremble and be silent! But such a sad humiliation may, I think, be apprehended for many of the historians, by every serious christian reader who shall take the hint of this subject along with him through their works. He will not seldom feel that the writers seem uninformed, while they remark and decide on actions and characters, that a final Lawgiver has come from heaven, or that he will come, or on what account he will come, yet once more. Their very diction often abjures the plain christian denominations of good and evil; nor do I need to recount the specious and fallacious terms which they have employed in their place. How then can a mind which learns to think in *their* manner, learn at the same time to think in *his* from whom it will, however, be found no light matter to have dissented, when his judgment shall be declared for the last time in this world?

The various interesting sets of short Essays, with the Spectator and Rambler at their head, must have had a very considerable influence, during a season at least, and not yet entirely extinct, on the moral taste of the public. Perhaps, however, it is too late in the day for any interest to be taken in religious animadversions which might with propriety have been ventured upon the Spectator, when it was the general and familiar favourite with the reading portion of the community.* A work of such wide compass, and avowedly assuming the office of guardian and teacher of all good principles, gave fair opportunities for a christian writer to in-

* Within the thirty or forty years antecedent to the date of the present edition, and even within the shorter interval since the slight remarks in the text were written, there has been a surprising change in the tone of our literature, and in the public taste which it both consults and forms. The smooth elegance, the gentle graces, the amusing, easy, and not deep current of sentiment, of which Addison is our finest example, have come to be regarded as languid, and almost insipid; and the passion is for force, energy, bold developement of principles, and every kind of high stimulus. This has been the inevitable accompaniment of the prodigious commotion in the state of the world, the rousing of the general mind from its long lethargy, to an activity and an exertion of power which nothing can quell, which is destined to a continually augmenting operation till the condition of the world be changed. This new spirit of our lite-

troduce, excepting what is strictly termed science, a little of every subject affecting the condition and happiness of men. Why then was it fated that the stupendous circumstance of the redemption by the Messiah, of which the importance is commensurate with the whole interests of man, with the value of his immortal spirit, with the government of his Creator in this world, and with the happiness of eternity, should not a few times, in the long course and extensive moral jurisdiction of that work, be set forth in the most explicit, uncompromising, and solemn manner, in the full aspect and importance which it bears in the christian revelation, with the directness and emphasis of apostolic fidelity? Why should not a few of the most peculiar of the doctrines, comprehended in the primary one of salvation by the Mediator, have been clothed with the fascinating elegance of Addison, from whose pen many persons would have received an occasional evangelical lesson with incomparably more candour than from any professed divine? A pious and benevolent man, such as the avowed advocate of christianity ought to be, should not have been contented that so many thousands of minds as his writings were adapted to instruct

rature is a great advantage gained; but gained at a grievous cost: for we have in its train an immense quantity of affectation: all sorts and sizes of authors must be aiming at vigour, point, bold strokes, originality. The consequence is, an ample exhibition of contortion. tricks of surprise, paradox, headlong dash, factitious fulmination. and turgid inanity. In some of the grossest instances, this ape of mental force and freedom stares and swaggers, and spouts a half-drunken rant. One wonders to see how much even some of the ablest among the writers of the present times have gone into the bad fashion, have discarded the masculine simplicity so graceful to intellectual power, and spoiled compositions admirable for vigorous thinking by a continual affectation, which carries them along in a dashing capering sort of style, as if determined that the " march of intellect" shall be a dance to a fiddle.

and to charm, should have been left, for any thing that he very unequivocally attempted to the contrary in his most popular works, to end a life which he had contributed to refine, acquainted but slightly with the grand security of happiness after death. Or if it could not be deemed his duty to introduce in a formal manner any of the most specifically evangelical subjects, it might at least have been expected, that some of the many serious essays scattered through the Spectator should have more of a christian strain, more recognition of the great oracle, in the speculations concerning the Deity, and the gravest moral subjects. There might, without hazard of symbolizing with the dreaded *fanaticism* of the preceding age, have been more assimilation of what may be called, as it now stands, a *literary* fashion of religion, to the spirit of the New Testament. From him also, as a kind of dictator among the elegant writers of the age, it might have been expected that he would set himself, with the same decision and virtuous indignation which he made his Cato display against the betrayers of Roman liberty and laws, to denounce that ridicule which has wounded religion by a careless or by a crafty manner of holding up its abuses to scorn: but of this impropriety (to use an accommodating term,) the Spectator itself is not free from examples.

Addison wrote a book expressly in defence of the religion of Christ; but to be the dignified advocate of a cause, and to be its humble disciple, may be very different things. An advocate has a feeling of making himself important; he seems to *confer* something on the cause; but as a disciple, he must surrender to feel littleness, humility, and submission. Self-importance might find more to gratify it in becoming the *patron* of a beggar, than the *servant* of a potentate. Addison was, moreover, very unfortunate, for any thing like justice to genuine christianity, in the class of persons with whom he associated, and among whom he did not hold his pre-eminence by any such imperial tenure, as could make him careless of the policy of pleasing them by a general conformity of sentiment. One can imagine with what a perfect storm of ridicule he would have been greeted, on entering one of his celebrated coffee-houses of wits on the day after he should have published in the Spec-tator a paper, for instance, on the necessity of being devoted to the service of Jesus Christ. The friendship of the world ought to be a " pearl of great price," for its cost is very serious.

The powerful and lofty spirit of Johnson was far more capable of scorning the ridicule, and defying the opposition, of wits and worldlings. And yet his social life must have been greatly unfavourable to a deep and simple consideration of christian truth, and the cultivation of christian sentiment. Might not even his imposing and unchallenged ascendency itself betray him to admit, insensibly, an injurious influence on his mind? He associated with men of whom many were very learned, some extremely able, but comparatively few made any decided profession of piety; and perhaps a considerable number were such as would in other society have shown a strong propensity to irreligion. This however dared not to appear undisguisedly in Johnson's presence; and it is impossible not to revere the strength and noble severity that made it so cautious. But this constrained abstinence from overt irreligion had the effect of preventing the repugnance of his judgment and religious feelings to the frequent society of men from whom he would have recoiled, if the real temper of their minds, in regard to the most important subjects, had been unreservedly forced on his view. Decorum toward religion being preserved, he would take no rigorously judicial account of the internal character of those who brought so finely into play his mental powers and resources, in conversations on literature, moral philosophy, and general intelligence; and who could enrich every matter of social argument by their learning, their genius, or their knowledge of mankind. But if, while every thing unequivocally hostile to christianity was kept silent in his company, there was nevertheless a latent impiety in possession of the heart, it would inevitably, however unobviously, infuse something of its spirit into the communications of such men. And, through the complacency which he felt in the high intellectual intercourse, some infection of the noxious element would insinuate its way into his own ideas and feelings. For it is hardly possible for the strongest and most vigilant mind, under the genial influence of eloquence, fancy, novelty, and bright intelligence, interchanged in amicable collision, to avoid admitting some effluvia (if I may so express it) breathing from the most interior quality of such associates, and tending to produce an insensible assimilation; especially if there should happen to be, in addition, a conciliating exterior of accomplishment, grace, and liberal manners. Thus the very predominance by which Johnson could repress the direct irreligion of statesmen, scholars, wits, and accomplished men of the world, might, by retaining him their intimate or frequent associate, subject him to meet the influence of that irreligion acting in a manner too indirect and refined to excite either hostility or caution.

But indeed if his caution was excited, there might still be a possibility of self-deception in the case. The great achievement and conscious merit of upholding, by his authority, a certain standard of good principles among such men, and compelling an acquiescence at least, wherever he was present, might tend to make himself feel satisfied with that order of sentiments, though materially lower than the standard which his conscientious judgment must have adopted, if he had formed it under the advantage of long and thoughtful retirement and exemption from the influence of such associates. It would be difficult for him to confess to himself that what was high enough for a repressive domination over impiety, might yet be below the level of true christianity. It is hard for a man to suspect himself deficient in that very thing in which he not only excels other men, but mends them. Nothing can well be more unfortunate for christian attainments, even in point of right judgment, than to be habitually in society where a man will feel as if he held a saintly eminence of character in merely securing a decent neutrality, or a semblance of slight partial assent, in other words a forbearance of hostility, to that divine law of faith and morals, which is set up over that society and all mankind, as the grand distinguisher between those who are in light and those who are in darkness, those who are approved and those who are condemned; and which has been sent on earth with a demand, not of this worthless non-aggression, but of cordial entire addiction and devoted zeal.

If there be any truth in the representations which make so large a part of this essay, Johnson's continual immersion in what is denominated polite literature, must have subjected him to the utmost action and pervasion of an influence of which the antichristian effect cannot be neutralized, without a more careful study than we have reason to believe he gave, or even had time to give, to the doctrine of religion as a distinct independent subject.

It must however be admitted that this illustrious

author, who, though here mentioned only in the class of essayists, is to be ranked among the greatest moral philosophers, is less at variance with the essentials of the christian economy, than the very great majority of either of these classes of authors. His speculations tend in a far less degree to beguile the approving and admiring reader into a spirit, which feels repelled in estrangement and disgust on turning to the instructions of Christ and his apostles; and he has more explicit and solemn references to the grand purpose of human life, to a future judgment, and to eternity, than almost any other of our elegant moralists has had the piety or the courage to make. There is so much that most powerfully coincides and cooperates with christian truth, that the disciple of christianity the more regrets to meet occasionally a sentiment, respecting, perhaps, the rule to judge by in the review of life, the consolations in death, the effect of repentance, or the terms of acceptance with God, which he cannot reconcile with the evangelical theory, nor with those principles of christian faith in which Johnson avowed his belief. In such a writer he cannot but deem such deviations a matter of grave culpability.

Omission is his other fault. Though he did introduce in his serious speculations more distinct allusions to religious ideas, than most other moralists, yet he did not introduce them so often as may be claimed from a writer who frequently carries seriousness to the utmost pitch of solemnity. There scarcely ever was an author, not formally theological, in whose works a large proportion of explicit christian sentiment was more requisite for a consistent entireness of character, than in the moral writings of Johnson. No writer ever more completely exposed and blasted the folly and vanity of the greatest number of human pursuits. The visage of Medusa could not have darted a more fatal glance against the tribe of gay triflers, the competitors of ambition, the proud exhibiters in the parade of wealth, the rhapsodists on the sufficiency of what they call philosophy for happiness, the grave consumers of life in useless speculations, and every other order of "walkers in a vain show." His judicial sentence is directed, as with a keen and mephitic blast, on almost all the most favourite pursuits of mankind. But it was so much the more peculiarly his duty to insist, with fulness and emphasis, on that one model of character, that one grand employment of life, which is enjoined by heaven, and will stand the test of that unshrinking severity of judgment, which should be exercised by every one who looks forward to the test which he is finally to abide. No author has more impressively displayed the misery of human life; he laid himself under so much the stronger obligation to unfold most explicitly the only effectual consolations, the true scheme of felicity as far as it is attainable on earth, and that delightful prospect of a better region, which has so often inspired exultation in the most melancholy situations. No writer has more expressively illustrated the rapidity of time, and the shortness of life; he ought so much the more fully to have dwelt on the views of that great futurity at which his readers are admonished by the illustration that they will speedily arrive. No writer can make more poignant reflections on the pains of guilt; was it not indispensable that he should oftener have directed the mind suffering this bitterest kind of distress to that great sacrifice once offered for sin? No writer represents with more striking, mortifying, humiliating truth the failure of human resolutions, and the feebleness of human efforts, in the contest with corrupt propensity, evil habit, and adapted temptation; why did not this melancholy observation and experience prompt a very frequent recollection, and emphatical expression of the importance of that assistance from on high, without which the divine word has so often repeated the warning that our labours will fail?

In extending the censure to the Poets, it is gratifying to meet an exception in the most elevated of all their tribe. Milton's consecrated genius might harmoniously have mingled with the angels that announced the Messiah to be come, or that, on the spot and at the moment of his departure, predicted his coming again; might have shamed to silence the muses of paganism; or softened the pains of a christian martyr. Part of the poetical works of Young, those of Watts, and of Cowper, have placed them among the permanent benefactors of mankind; as owing to them there is a popular poetry in the true spirit of christianity; a poetry which has imparted, and is destined to impart, the best sentiments to innumerable minds. Works of great poetical genius that should be thus faithful to true religion, might be regarded as trees by the side of that "river of the water of life," having in their fruit and foliage a virtue to contribute to "the healing of the nations."—But on the supposition that there were a man sufficiently discerning, impartial, and indefatigable for a research throughout the general body of our poetical literature, it would be curious to see what kind of religious system, and what account of the state of man, as viewed under moral estimate, and in relation to the future destiny, would be afforded by a digested assemblage of all the most marked sentiments, supplied by the vast majority of the poets, for such a scheme of moral and religious doctrine.—But if it would be exceedingly amusing to observe the process and the fantastic result, it would in the next place be very sad to consider, that these fallacies have been insinua'ed by the charms of poetry into countless thousands of minds, with a beguilement that has, first, diverted them from a serious attention to the gospel, then confirmed them in a habitual dislike of it, and finally operated to betray some of them to the doom which, beyond the grave, awaits the neglect or rejection of the religion of Christ.

You have probably seen Pope cited as a christian poet, by some pious authors, whose anxiety to impress reluctant genius into an appearance of favouring christianity, has credulously seized on any occasional verse, which seemed an echo of the sacred doctrines. No reader can exceed me in admiring the discriminative thought, the shrewd moral observation, the finished and felicitous execution, and the galaxy of poetical beauties, which combine to give a peculiar lustre to the writings of Pope. But I cannot refuse to perceive, that almost every allusion in his lighter works to the names, the facts, and the topics, that specially belong to the religion of Christ, is in a style and spirit of profane banter; and that, in most of his graver ones, where he meant to be dignified, he took the utmost care to divest his thoughts of all the mean vulgarity of christian associations. "Off, ye profane!" might seem to have been his signal to all evangelical ideas, when he began his Essay on Man; and they were obedient, and fled; for if you detach the detail and illustrations, so as to lay bare the outline and general principles of the work, it will stand confest an elaborate attempt to redeem the whole theory of the condition and interests of man, both in life and death, from all the explanations imposed on it by an unphilosophical revelation from heaven. And in the happy riddance of the despised though celestial light, it exhibits a sort of moon-light vision, of thin impalpable abstractions, at which a speculatist may gaze, with a dubious wonder whether they be realities or phantoms; but which a practical man will in vain try to seize and turn to account ; and which an evangelical man will disdain to accept in exchange for those forms of truth which his religion brings to him as real living friends, instructors, and consolers; which present themselves to him, at his return from a profitless adventure in that shadowy dreary region, with an effect like that of meeting the countenances of his affectionate domestic associates, on his awaking from the fantastic succession of vain efforts and perplexities, among strange objects, incidents, and people, in a bewildering dream.—But what deference to christianity was to be expected, when such a man as Bolingbroke was the genius whose imparted splendour was to illuminate, and the demigod* whose approbation was to crown, the labours which, according to the wish and presentiment of the poet, were to conjoin these two venerable names in endless fame.?

I it be said for some parts of these dim speculations, that though christianity comes forward as the practical dispensation of truth, yet there must be, in remote abstraction behind, some grand, ultimate, elementary truths, which this dispensation does not recognise, but even intercepts from our view by a system of less refined elements, in which doctrines of a more contracted. palpable, and popular form, of comparatively local purport and relation, are imposed in substitution for the higher and more general and abstracted truths—I answer, And what did the poet, or "the master of the poet and the song," know about those truths, and how did they come by their information.

* He is so named somewhere in Pope's Works.

A serious observer must acknowledge with regret, that such a class of productions as novels, in which folly has tried to please in a greater number of shapes than the poet enumerates in the Paradise of Fools, is capable of producing a very considerable effect on the moral taste of the community. A large proportion of them however are probably of too slight and insipid a consistence to have any more specific counteraction to christian principles than that of mere folly in general; excepting indeed that the most flimsy of them will occasionally contribute their mite of mischief, by alluding to a christian profession, in a manner that identifies it with the cant by which hypocrites have aped it, or the extravagance with which fanatics have inflated or distorted it. But a great and direct force of counteracting influence is emitted from those, which eloquently display characters of eminent vigour and virtue, when it is a virtue having no basis in religion; a factitious thing resulting from the mixture of dignified pride with generous feeling; or constituted of those philosophical principles which are too often accompanied, in these works, by an avowed or strongly intimated contempt of the interference of any religion, especially the christian. If the case is mended in some of these productions into which an awkward religion has found its way, it is rather because the characters excite less interest of any kind, than because any which they *do* excite is favourable to religion. No reader is likely to be impressed with the dignity of being a christian by seeing, in one of these works, an attempt to combine that character with the fine gentleman, by means of a most ludicrous apparatus of amusements and sacraments, churches and theatres, morning-prayers and evening-balls. Nor will it perhaps be of any great service to the christian cause, that some others of them profess to exemplify and defend, against the cavils and scorn of infidels, a religion of which it does not appear that the writers would have discovered the merits, had it not been established by law. One may doubt whether any one will be more than amused by the venerable priest, who is introduced probably among libertine lords and giddy girls, to maintain the sanctity of terms, and attempt the illustration of doctrines, which these well-meaning writers do not perceive that the worthy gentleman's college, diocesan, and library, have but very imperfectly enabled him to understand. If the reader even wished to be more than amused, it is easy to imagine how much he would be likely to be instructed and affected, by such an illustration or defence of the christian religion, as the writer of a fashionable novel would deem a graceful or admissible expedient for filling up his plot.

One cannot close such a review of our fine writers without melancholy reflections. That cause which will raise all its zealous friends to a sublime eminence on the last and most solemn day the world has to behold, and will make them great for ever, presented its claims full in sight of each of these authors in his time. The very lowest of those claims could not be less than a conscientious solicitude to beware of every thing that could in any point injure the sacred cause. This claim has been slighted by so many as have lent attraction to an order of moral sentiments greatly discordant with its principles. And so many are gone into eternity under the charge of having employed their genius, as the magicians their enchantments against Moses, to counteract the Saviour of the world.

Under what restrictions, then, ought the study of polite literature to be conducted? I cannot but have foreseen that this question must return at the end of these observations; and I am sorry to have no better answer to give than before, when the question came in the way, inconveniently enough, to perplex the conclusion to be drawn from the considerations on the tendency of the classical literature. Polite literature will necessarily continue to be a large department of the grand school of intellectual and moral cultivation. The evils therefore which it may contain, will as certainly affect in some degree the minds of the successive pupils, and teachers also, as the hurtful influence of the climate, or of the seasons, will affect their bodies. To be thus affected, is a part of the destiny under which they are born, in a civilized country. It is indispensable to acquire the advantage; it is inevitable to incur the evil. The means of counteraction will amount, it is to be feared, to no more than palliatives. Nor can these be proposed in any specific method. All that I can do, is, to urge on the reader of taste the very serious duty of continually recalling to his mind, and if he be a parent or preceptor, of cogently representing to those he instructs, the real character of religion as exhibited in the christian revelation, and the reasons which command an inviolable adherence to it.

FINIS.

COMPLETE CATALOGUE

OF

BOHN'S LIBRARIES,

CONTAINING

STANDARD WORKS OF EUROPEAN LITERATURE IN THE ENGLISH LANGUAGE, ON HISTORY, BIOGRAPHY, TOPOGRAPHY, ARCHÆOLOGY, THEOLOGY, ANTIQUITIES, SCIENCE, PHILOSOPHY, NATURAL HISTORY, POETRY, ART, FICTION, WITH DICTIONARIES, AND OTHER BOOKS OF REFERENCE. THE SERIES COMPRISES TRANSLATIONS FROM THE FRENCH, GERMAN, ITALIAN, SPANISH, SCANDINAVIAN, ANGLO-SAXON, LATIN, AND GREEK. PRICE 3s. 6d. OR 5s. PER VOLUME (WITH EXCEPTIONS). A COMPLETE SET IN 627 VOLUMES, PRICE £140 2s.

Catalogues sent Post-free on Application.

LONDON:
GEORGE BELL AND SONS, YORK STREET,
COVENT GARDEN.
1881.

May, 1881.

COMPLETE CATALOGUE
OF
BOHN'S LIBRARIES.

STANDARD LIBRARY.

A SERIES OF THE BEST ENGLISH AND FOREIGN AUTHORS, PRINTED IN POST 8VO.

260 Vols. at 3s. 6d. each, excepting those marked otherwise.

Addison's Works. With the Notes of Bishop HURD, much additional matter, and upwards of 100 Unpublished Letters. Edited by H. G. BOHN. *Portrait and 8 Engravings on Steel.* In 6 vols.

Alfieri's Tragedies, including those published posthumously. Translated into English Verse, and edited with Notes and Introduction, by EDGAR A. BOWRING, C.B. 2 vols.

Bacon's Essays, Apophthegms, Wisdom of the Ancients, New Atlantis, and Henry VII., with Introduction and Notes. *Portrait.*

Ballads and Songs of the Peasantry of England. Edited by ROBERT BELL.

Beaumont and Fletcher, a popular Selection from. By LEIGH HUNT.

Beckmann's History of Inventions, Discoveries, and Origins. Revised and enlarged. *Portraits.* In 2 vols.

Bremer's (Miss) Works. Translated by MARY HOWITT. *Portrait.* In 4 vols.
Vol. 1. The Neighbours and other Tales.
Vol. 2. The President's Daughter.
Vol. 3. The Home, and Strife and Peace.
Vol. 4. A Diary, the H—— Family, &c.

British Poets, from Milton to Kirke WHITE. Cabinet Edition. In 4 vols.

Browne's (Sir Thomas) Works. Edited by SIMON WILKIN. In 3 vols.

Burke's Works. In 6 Volumes.
Vol. 1. Vindication of Natural Society, On the Sublime and Beautiful, and Political Miscellanies.
Vol. 2. French Revolution, &c.
Vol. 3. Appeal from the New to the Old Whigs; the Catholic Claims, &c.
Vol. 4. On the Affairs of India, and Charge against Warren Hastings.

Burke's Works—*continued.*
Vol. 5. Conclusion of Charge against Hastings; on a Regicide Peace, &c.
Vol. 6. Miscellaneous Speeches, &c. With a General Index.

Burke's Speeches on Warren Hastings; and Letters. With Index. In 2 vols. (forming vols. 7 and 8 of the works).

—— **Life.** By PRIOR. New and revised Edition. *Portrait.*

Butler's (Bp.) Analogy of Religion, and Sermons, with Notes. *Portrait.*

Camoëns' Lusiad, Mickle's Translation. Edited by E. R. HODGES.

Cary's Translation of Dante's Heaven, Hell, and Purgatory. Copyright edition, being the only one containing Cary's last corrections and additions.

Carafas (The) of Maddaloni: and Naples under Spanish Dominion. Translated from the German of Alfred de Reumont.

Carrel's Counter Revolution in England. Fox's History and Lonsdale's Memoir of James II. *Portrait.*

Cellini (Benvenuto), Memoirs of Translated by ROSCOE. *Portrait.*

Cervantes' Galatea, Translated by GORDON GYLL.

Chaucer's Works. Edited by ROBERT BELL. New Edition, improved. With Introduction by W. W. SKEAT. 4 vols.

Coleridge's (S. T.) Friend. A Series of Essays on Morals, Politics, and Religion.

—— **(S. T.) Biographia Literaria,** and two Lay Sermons.

Commines. (*See Philip de Commines.*)

18

Condé's Dominion of the Arabs in Spain. Translated by Mrs. Foster. 1r. 3 vols.

Cowper's Complete Works. Edited, with Memoir of the Author, by Southey. Illustrated with 50 Engravings. In 8 vols.
Vols. 1 to 4. Memoir and Correspondence.
Vols. 5 and 6. Poetical Works. Plates.
Vol. 7. Homer's Iliad. Plates.
Vol. 8. Homer's Odyssey. Plates.

Coxe's Memoirs of the Duke of Marlborough. Portraits. In 3 vols.
. An Atlas of the plans of Marlborough's campaigns, 4to. 10s. 6d.

—— History of the House of Austria. Portraits. In 4 vols.

Cunningham's Lives of Eminent British Painters. New Edition by Mrs. Heaton. 3 vols.

Defoe's Works. Edited by Sir Walter Scott. In 7 vols.

De Lolme on the Constitution of England. Edited, with Notes, by John Macgregor.

Emerson's Works. 2 vols.

Foster's (John) Life and Correspondence. Edited by J. E. Ryland. In 2 vols.
—— Lectures at Broadmead Chapel. Edited by J. E. Ryland. In 2 vols.

Foster's (John) Critical Essays. Edited by J. E. Ryland. In 2 vols.
—— Essays—On Decision of Character, &c. &c.
—— Essays—On the Evils of Popular Ignorance, &c.
—— Fosteriana: Thoughts, Reflections, and Criticisms of the late John Foster, selected from periodical papers, and Edited by Henry G. Bohn (nearly 600 pages). 5s.

Fuller's (Andrew) Principal Works. With Memoir. Portrait.

Gibbon's Roman Empire. Complete and Unabridged, with Notes; including, in addition to the Author's own, those of Guizot, Wenck, Niebuhr, Hugo, Neander, and other foreign scholars; and an elaborate Index. Edited by an English Clergyman. In 7 vols.

Goethe's Works, Translated into English. In 8 vols.
Vols. 1. and 2. Autobiography, 20 Books; and Travels in Italy, France, and Switzerland. Portrait.
Vol. 3. Faust. Two Parts. By Miss Swanwick.

Goethe's Works—continued.
Vol. 4. Novels and Tales.
Vol. 5. Wilhelm Meister's Apprenticeship.
Vol. 6. Conversations with Eckermann and Soret. Translated by John Oxenford.
Vol. 7. Poems and Ballads, including Hermann and Dorothea. Translated by E. A. Bowring, C.B.
Vol. 8. Götz von Berlichingen, Tor quato Tasso, Egmont, Iphigenia, Clavigo, Wayward Lover, and Fellow Culprits. By Sir Walter Scott, Miss Swanwick, and E. A. Bowring, C.B. With Engraving.

—— Correspondence with Schiller. See Schiller.

Greene, Marlowe, and Ben Jonson, Poems of. Edited by Robert Bell. With Biographies. In 1 vol.

Gregory's (Dr.) Evidences, Doctrines, and Duties of the Christian Religion.

Guizot's Representative Government. Translated by A. R. Scoble.
—— History of the English Revolution of 1640. Translated by William Hazlitt. Portrait.
—— History of Civilisation. Translated by William Hazlitt. In 3 vols. Portrait.

Hazlitt's Table Talk. A New Edition in one volume.
—— Lectures on the Comic Writers, and on the English Poets.
—— Lectures on the Literature of the Age of Elizabeth, and on Characters of Shakespeare's Plays.
—— Plain Speaker.
—— Round Table; the Conversations of James Northcote, R.A.; Characteristics, &c.
—— Sketches and Essays, and Winterslow (Essays Written there). New Edition.

Hall's (Rev. Robert) Miscellaneous Works and Remains, with Memoir by Dr. Gregory, and an Essay on his Character by John Foster. Portrait.

Hawthorne's Tales. In 2 vols.
Vol. 1. Twice Told Tales, and the Snow Image.
Vol. 2. Scarlet Letter, and the House with the seven Gables.

Heine's Poems, complete, from the German, by E. A. Bowring, C.B. 5s.

Hungary: its History and Revolutions; with a Memoir of Kossuth from new and authentic sources. Portrait.

Hutchinson (Colonel), Memoirs of, with the Siege of Latham House.

A CATALOGUE OF

Irving's (Washington) Life and Letters. By his Nephew, PIERRE E. IRVING. In 2 vols.

―――― **Complete Works. In 15 vols.**
Vol. 1. Salmagundi and Knickerbocker Portrait of the Author.
Vol. 2. Sketch Book and Life of Goldsmith.
Vol. 3. Bracebridge Hall and Abbotsford and Newstead.
Vol 4. Tales of a Traveller and the Alhambra.
Vol. 5. Conquest of Granada and Conquest of Spain.
Vols. 6 and 7. Life of Columbus and Companions of Columbus, with a new Index. *Fine Portrait.*
Vol. 8. Astoria and Tour in the Prairies.
Vol 9. Mahomet and his Successors
Vol. 10. Wolfert's Roost and Adventures of Captain Bonneville.
Vol. 11. Biographies and Miscellanies.
Vols. 12-15. Life of Washington. *Portrait.*
For separate Works, see Cheap Series.

James's (G. P. R.) Richard Cœur-de-Lion, King of England. *Portraits.* 2 vols.
―――― **Louis XIV.** *Portraits.* 2 vols.

Jameson's Shakespeare's Heroines: Characteristics of Women. Moral, Poetical, and Historical.

Junius's Letters, with Notes, Additions, and an Index. In 2 vols.

Lamartine's History of the Girondists. *Portraits.* In 3 vols.
―――― **Restoration of the Monarchy,** with Index. *Portraits.* In 4 vols.
―――― **French Revolution of 1848,** with a fine *frontispiece.*

Lamb's (Charles) Elia and Eliana. Complete Edition.
―――― **Dramatic Poets of the Time** of Elizabeth; including his Selections from the Garrick Plays.

Lanzi's History of Painting. Translated by ROSCOE. *Portraits.* In 2 vols.

Lappenberg's Anglo-Saxon Kings. 2 vols.

Lessing's Dramatic Works. Complete, with Memoir by HELEN ZIMMERN. *Portrait.* 2 vols.
―――― **Laokoon.** (By BEASLEY) Hamburg Dramatic Notes, Representation of Death (by Miss ZIMMERN), Frontispiece.

Locke's Philosophical Works, containing an Essay on the Human Understanding. &c., with Notes and Index by J. A. ST JOHN. *Portrait.* In 2 vols.
―――― **Life and Letters, with Extracts** from his Common-Place Books, by Lord KING.

Luther's Table Talk. Translated by WILLIAM HAZLITT. *Portrait.*

Machiavelli's History of Florence, The Prince, and other Works *Portrait.*

Martineau's, Harriet, History of England, from 1800-15.
―――― **History of the Peace,** from 1815-1846. 4 vols.

Menzel's History of Germany. *Portraits.* In 3 vols.

Michelet's Life of Luther. Translated by WILLIAM HAZLITT.
―――― **Roman Republic.** Translated by WILLIAM HAZLITT.
―――― **French Revolution,** with Index. *Frontispiece.*

Mignet's French Revolution from 1789 to 1814. *Portrait.*

Milton's Prose Works, with Index. *Portraits.* In 5 vols.

Mitford's (Mary R.) Our Village. Improved Ed., complete. *Illustrated.* 2 vols.

Molière's Dramatic Works. Translated by C. H WALL. In 3 vols. *Portrait.*

Montesquieu's Spirit of the Laws. A new Edition revised and corrected. 2 vols. *Portrait.*

Neander's Church History. Translated: with General Index. In 10 vols.
―――― **Life of Christ.** Translated.
―――― **First Planting of Christianity,** and Antignostikus. Translated. In 2 vols.
―――― **History of Christian Dogmas.** Translated. In 2 vols.
―――― **Christian Life in the Early** and Middle Ages, including his 'Light in Dark Places.' Translated.

Ockley's History of the Saracens Revised and completed. *Portrait.*

Percy's Reliques of Ancient English Poetry. Reprinted from the Original Edition, and Edited by J. V. PRICHARD. In 2 vols.

Philip de Commines, Memoirs of, containing the Histories of Louis XI. and Charles VIII., and of Charles the Bold, Duke of Burgundy. To which is added, The Scandalous Chronicle, or Secret History of Louis XI. *Portraits.* In 2 vols.

Plutarch's Lives. By G. LONG and A. STEWART. *Vols. 1 and 2 ready.*

Poetry of America. Selections from 100 American Poets, from 1776—1876. Edited by W. J. LINTON. *Portrait.*

Ranke's History of the Popes. Translated by E. FOSTER. In 3 vols.
―――― **Ranke's Servia and the Servian Revolution.**

20

Reynolds' (Sir Joshua) Literary Works. *Portrait.* In 2 vols.

Richter (Jean Paul Fr.) Levana and Autobiography. With Memoir.

—— **Flower, Fruit, and Thorn Pieces.** A Novel.

Roscoe's Life and Pontificate of Leo X., with the Copyright Notes, and an Index. *Portraits.* In 2 vols.

—— **Life of Lorenzo de Medici,** with the Copyright Notes, &c. *Portrait.*

Russia, History of, by WALTER K. KELLY. *Portraits.* In 2 vols.

Schiller's Works. Translated into English. In 6 vols.
Vol. 1. Thirty Years' War, and Revolt of the Netherlands.
Vol. 2. *Continuation of* the Revolt of the Netherlands; Wallenstein's Camp; the Piccolomini; the Death of Wallenstein; and William Tell.
Vol. 3. Don Carlos, Mary Stuart, Maid of Orleans, and Bride of Messina.
Vol. 4. The Robbers, Fiesco, Love and Intrigue, and the Ghost-Seer.
Vol. 5. Poems. Translated by EDGAR BOWRING, C.B.
Vol. 6. Philosophical Letters and Æsthetical Essays.

—— **Correspondence with Goethe,** translated by L. DORA SCHMITZ. 2 vols.

Schlegel's Philosophy of Life and of Language, translated by A. J. W. MORRISON.

—— **History of Literature, Ancient and Modern.** Now first completely translated, with General Index.

—— **Philosophy of History.** Translated by J. B. ROBERTSON. *Portrait.*

Schlegel's Dramatic Literature. Translated. *Portrait.*

—— **Modern History.**

—— **Æsthetic and Miscellaneous Works.**

Sheridan's Dramatic Works and Life. *Portrait.*

Sismondi's Literature of the South of Europe. Translated by Roscoe. *Portraits.* In 2 vols.

Smith's (Adam) Theory of the Moral Sentiments; with his Essay on the First Formation of Languages.

Smyth's (Professor) Lectures on Modern History. In 2 vols.

—— **Lectures on the French Revolution.** In 2 vols.

Sturm's Morning Communings with God, or Devotional Meditations for Every Day in the Year.

Sully, Memoirs of the Duke of, Prime Minister to Henry the Great. *Portraits.* In 4 vols.

Taylor's (Bishop Jeremy) Holy Living and Dying. *Portrait.*

Thierry's Conquest of England by the Normans. Translated by WILLIAM HAZLITT. *Portrait.* In 2 vols.

Ulrici (Dr.) Shakespeare's Dramatic Art. Translated by L. D. Schmitz. 2 vols.

Vasari's Lives of the Painters, Sculptors, and Architects. Translated by Mrs FOSTER. 5 vols.

Wesley's (John) Life. By ROBERT SOUTHEY. New and Complete Edition. Double volume. *With Portrait.* 5s.

Wheatley on the Book of Common Prayer. *Frontispiece.*

HISTORICAL LIBRARY.

21 Vols. at 5s. each.

Evelyn's Diary and Correspondence. *Illustrated with numerous Portraits, &c.* In 4 vols.

Pepys' Diary and Correspondence. Edited by Lord BRAYBROOKE. With Notes, important additions including numerous Letters. *Illustrated with many Portraits.* In 4 vols.

Jesse's Memoirs of the Reign of the Stuarts, including the Protectorate. With General Index. *Upwards of 40 Portraits.* In 3 vols.

Jesse's Memoirs of the Pretenders and their Adherents. 6 *Portraits.*

Nugent's (Lord) Memorials of Hampden, his Party, and Times. 12 *Portraits.*

Strickland's (Agnes) Lives of the Queens of England, from the Norman Conquest. From official records and authentic documents, private and public. Revised Edition. In 6 vols.

—— **Life of Mary Queen of Scots.** 2 vols.

COLLEGIATE SERIES.

6 Vols. at 5s. each.

Donaldson's Theatre of the Greeks. Illustrated with Lithographs and numerous Woodcuts.

Keightley's Classical Mythology. New Edition. Revised by Dr. L. SCHMITZ. With 12 plates.

Herodotus, Turner's (Dawson W.) Notes to. With Map, &c.

Herodotus, Wheeler's Analysis and Summary of.

Thucydides, Wheeler's Analysis of.

New Testament (The) in Greek. Griesbach's Text, with the readings of Mill and Scholz, Parallel References, a Critical Introduction and Chronological Tables. Two fac-similes of Greek MSS. 2s. 6d.; or with Lexicon, 5s. Lexicon Separately. 2s.

PHILOSOPHICAL LIBRARY.

11 Vols. at 5s. each, excepting those marked otherwise.

Comte's Philosophy of the Sciences. By G. H. LEWES.

Draper (J. W.) A History of the Intellectual Development of Europe. By JOHN WILLIAM DRAPER, M.D., LL.D. A New Edition, thoroughly Revised by the Author. In 2 vols.

Hegel's Lectures on the Philosophy of History. Translated by J. SIBREE, M.A.

Kant's Critique of Pure Reason. Translated by J. M. D. MEIKLEJOHN.

Logic; or, the Science of Inference. A Popular Manual. By J. DEVEY.

Miller's (Professor) History Philosophically considered. In 4 vols. 3s. 6d. each.

Tennemann's Manual of the History of Philosophy. Continued by J. R. MORELL.

ECCLESIASTICAL AND THEOLOGICAL LIBRARY.

15 Vols. at 5s. each, excepting those marked otherwise.

Bleek (F.) An Introduction to the Old Testament, by FRIEDRICH BLEEK. Edited by JOHANN BLEEK and ADOLF KAMPHAUSEN. Translated from the German by G. H. VENABLES, under the supervision of the Rev. E. VENABLES, Canon of Lincoln. New Edition. In 2 vols.

Chillingworth's Religion of Protestants. 3s. 6d.

Eusebius' Ecclesiastical History. With Notes.

Hardwick's History of the Articles of Religion. To which is added a Series of Documents from A.D. 1536 to A.D. 1615. Together with Illustrations from Contemporary Sources. New Edition, revised by Rev. F. PROCTER.

Henry's (Matthew) Commentary on the Psalms. *Numerous Illustrations.*

Pearson on the Creed. New Edition. With Analysis and Notes.

Philo Judæus, Works of; the contemporary of Josephus. Translated by C. D. Yonge. In 4 vols.

Socrates' Ecclesiastical History, in continuation of Eusebius. With the Notes of Valesius.

Sozomen's Ecclesiastical History, from A.D. 324-440: and the Ecclesiastical History of Philostorgius.

Theodoret and Evagrius. Ecclesiastical Histories, from A.D. 332 to A.D. 427 and from A.D. 431 to A.D. 544.

Wieseler's Chronological Synopsis of the Four Gospels. Translated by CANON VENABLES. New Edition, revised.

ANTIQUARIAN LIBRARY.
35 Vols. at 5s. each.

Bede's Ecclesiastical History, and the Anglo-Saxon Chronicle.

Boethius's Consolation of Philosophy. In Anglo-Saxon, with the A. S. Metres, and an English Translation, by the Rev. S. Fox.

Brand's Popular Antiquities of England, Scotland, and Ireland. By Sir HENRY ELLIS. In 3 vols.

Chronicles of the Crusaders. Richard of Devizes, Geoffrey de Vinsauf, Lord de Joinville.

Dyer's British Popular Customs, Present and Past. An Account of the various Games and Customs associated with different days of the year. By the Rev. T. F. THISELTON DYER, M.A. With Index.

Early Travels in Palestine. Willibald, Sæwulf, Benjamin of Tudela, Mandeville, La Brocquière, and Maundrell; all unabridged. Edited by THOMAS WRIGHT.

Ellis's Early English Metrical Romances. Revised by J. O. HALLIWELL.

Florence of Worcester's Chronicle, with the Two Continuations: comprising Annals of English History to the Reign of Edward I.

Gesta Romanorum. Edited by WYNNARD HOOPER, B.A.

Giraldus Cambrensis' Historical Works: Topography of Ireland; History of the Conquest of Ireland; Itinerary through Wales; and Description of Wales. With Index. Edited by THOS. WRIGHT.

Henry of Huntingdon's History of the English, from the Roman Invasion to Henry II.; with the Acts of King Stephen, &c.

Ingulph's Chronicle of the Abbey of Croyland, with the Continuations by Peter of Blois and other Writers. By H. T. RILEY.

Keightley's Fairy Mythology. Frontispiece by Cruikshank.

Lepsius's Letters from Egypt, Ethiopia. and the Peninsula of Sinai.

Mallet's Northern Antiquities. By Bishop PERCY. With an Abstract of the Eyrbiggia Saga, by Sir WALTER SCOTT. Edited by J. A. BLACKWELL.

Marco Polo's Travels. The Translation of Marsden. Edited by THOMAS WRIGHT

Matthew Paris's Chronicle. In 5 vols.
FIRST SECTION. Roger of Wendover's Flowers of English History, from the Descent of the Saxons to A.D. 1235. Translated by Dr. GILES. In 2 vols.
SECOND SECTION: From 1235 to 1273. With Index to the entire Work. In 3 vols.

Matthew of Westminster's Flowers of History, especially such as relate to the affairs of Britain; to A.D. 1307. Translated by C. D. YONGE. In 2 vols.

Ordericus Vitalis' Ecclesiastical History of England and Normandy. Translated with Notes, by T. FORESTER, M.A. In 4 vols.

Pauli's (Dr. R.) Life of Alfred the Great. Translated from the German. To which is appended Alfred's Anglo-Saxon version of Orosius, with a literal Translation, and an Anglo-Saxon Grammar and Glossary.

Roger De Hoveden's Annals of English History; from A.D. 732 to A.D. 1201. Edited by H. T. RILEY. In 2 vols.

Six Old English Chronicles, viz.:— Asser's Life of Alfred, and the Chronicles of Ethelwerd, Gildas, Nennius, Geoffrey of Monmouth, and Richard of Cirencester.

William of Malmesbury's Chronicle of the Kings of England. Translated by SHARPE.

Yule-Tide Stories. A Collection of Scandinavian Tales and Traditions. Edited by B. THORPE.

ILLUSTRATED LIBRARY.
84 Vols. at 5s. each, excepting those marked otherwise.

Allen's Battles of the British Navy. Revised and enlarged. Numerous fine Portraits. In 2 vols.

Andersen's Danish Legends and Fairy Tales. With many Tales not in any other edition. Translated by CAROLINE PEACHEY. 120 Wood Engravings.

Ariosto's Orlando Furioso. In English Verse. By W. S. ROSE. Twelve fine Engravings. In 2 vols.

Bechstein's Cage and Chamber Birds. Including Sweet's Warblers. Enlarged edition. Numerous plates.
*** All other editions are abridged.
With the plates coloured. 7s. 6d.

Bonomi's Nineveh and its Palaces.
New Edition, revised and considerably
enlarged both in matter and Plates.
Upwards of 300 Engravings

Butler's Hudibras. With Variorum
Notes, a Biography, and a General Index.
Edited by HENRY G. BOHN. Thirty beautiful Illustrations.

———; or, further illustrated with
62 Outline Portraits. In 2 vols. 10s.

**Cattermole's Evenings at Haddon
Hall.** 24 exquisite Engravings on Steel,
from designs by himself the Letterpress
by the BARONESS DE CARABELLA.

**China, Pictorial, Descriptive, and
Historical,** with some Account of Ava and
the Burmese, Siam, and Anam. Nearly
100 Illustrations.

Craik's (G. L.) Pursuit of Knowledge
under Difficulties, illustrated by Anecdotes and Memoirs. Revised Edition.
With numerous Portraits

**Cruikshank's Three Courses and a
Dessert.** A Series of Tales, with 50 humorous Illustrations by Cruikshank

Cruikshank's Punch and Judy.
With 24 Illustrations. 5s.

Dante. Translated by I. C. WRIGHT,
M.A. New Edition, carefully revised.
Portrait and 34 Illustrations on Steel,
after Flaxman.

Didron's History of Christian Art
in the Middle Ages. From the French.
Upwards of 150 outline Engravings.

Dyer (T. H.) The History of Pompeii;
its Buildings and Antiquities. An account
of the City, with a full description of the
Remains, and an Itinerary for Visitors.
Edited by T. H. DYER, LL.D. Illustrated with nearly 300 Wood Engravings, a large Map, and a Plan of the
Forum. A New Edition, revised and
brought down to 1874. 7s. 6d.

Gil Blas, The Adventures of. 24
Engravings on Steel, after Smirke, and
10 Etchings by George Cruikshank. 6s.

Grimm's Gammer Grethel; or, German Fairy Tales and Popular Stories.
Translated by EDGAR TAYLOR. Numerous
Woodcuts by Cruikshank. 3s. 6d.

Holbein's Dance of Death, and Bible
Cuts. Upwards of 150 subjects, beautifully engraved in fac-simile, with Introduction and Descriptions by the late
FRANCIS DOUCE and Dr. T. F. DIBDIN.
2 vols. in 1 7s. 6d

Howitt's (Mary) Pictorial Calendar
of the Seasons. Embodying the whole of
Aiken's Calendar of Nature. Upwards of
100 Engravings.

——— **(Mary and William) Stories**
of English and Foreign Life. Twenty beautiful Engravings.

**India, Pictorial, Descriptive, and
Historical,** from the Earliest Times. Upwards of 100 fine Engravings on Wood,
and a Map.

Jesse's Anecdotes of Dogs. New Edition, with large additions. Numerous fine
Woodcuts after Harvey, Bewick, and others.

———; or, with the addition of 34
highly-finished Steel Engravings. 7s. 6d.

King's Natural History of Precious
Stones, and of the Precious Metals. With
numerous Illustrations. Price 6s.

——— **Natural History of Gems**
or Decorative Stones. Finely Illustrated.
6s.

——— **Handbook of Engraved Gems.**
Finely Illustrated. 6s.

Kitto's Scripture Lands and Biblical
Atlas. 24 Maps, beautifully engraved on
Steel, with a Consulting Index.

———; with the maps coloured, 7s. 6d.

Krummacher's Parables. Translated
from the German. Forty Illustrations by
Clayton, engraved by Dalziel.

Lindsay's (Lord) Letters on Egypt,
Edom, and the Holy Land. New Edition,
enlarged. Thirty-six beautiful Engravings, and 2 Maps.

Lodge's Portraits of Illustrious Personages of Great Britain, with Memoirs.
Two Hundred and Forty Portraits, engraved on Steel. 8 vols.

Longfellow's Poetical Works.
Twenty-four page Engravings, by Birket
Foster and others, and a Portrait.

———; or, without illustrations, 3s.6d.

——— **Prose Works.** 16 page Engravings by Birket Foster, &c.

Loudon's (Mrs.) Entertaining Naturalist. Revised by W. S. DALLAS, F.L.S.
With nearly 500 Woodcuts.

Marryat's Masterman Ready; or,
The Wreck of the Pacific. 93 Woodcuts.
3s. 6d.

——— **Poor Jack.** With 16 Illustrations, after Designs by C. Stanfield,
R.A. 3s. 6d.

——— **Mission; or, Scenes in Africa.** (Written for Young People.) Illustrated by Gilbert and Dalziel. 3s. 6d.

——— **Pirate; and Three Cutters.**
New Edition, with a Memoir of the
Author. With 8 Steel Engravings, from
Drawings by C. Stanfield. R.A. 3s. 6d.

——— **Privateers-Man One Hundred** Years Ago. Eight Engravings on
Steel, after Stothard. 3s. 6d.

——— **Settlers in Canada.** New
Edition. Ten fine Engravings by Gilbert
and Dalziel. 3s. 6d.

Maxwell's Victories of Wellington
and the British Armies. *Steel Engravings.*

Michael Angelo and Raphael, their
Lives and Works. By DUPPA and QUATREMÈRE DE QUINCY. *With 13 Engravings on Steel.*

Miller's History of the Anglo-Saxons. Written in a popular style, on the basis of Sharon Turner. *Portrait of Alfred, Map of Saxon Britain, and 12 elaborate Engravings on Steel.*

Milton's Poetical Works. With a Memoir by JAMES MONTGOMERY, TODD's Verbal Index to all the Poems, and Explanatory Notes. *With 120 Engravings by Thompson and others, from Drawings by W. Harvey.* 2 vols.
  Vol. 1. Paradise Lost, complete, with Memoir, Notes, and Index.
  Vol. 2. Paradise Regained, and other Poems, with Verbal Index to all the Poems.

Mudie's British Birds. Revised by W. C. L. MARTIN. *Fifty-two Figures and 7 Plates of Eggs.* In 2 vols.
———; or, *with the plates coloured*, 7s. 6d. per vol.

Naval and Military Heroes of Great Britain; or, Calendar of Victory. Being a Record of British Valour and Conquest by Sea and Land, on every day in the year, from the time of William the Conqueror to the Battle of Inkermann. By Major JOHNS, R.M., and Lieutenant P. H. NICOLAS, R.M. *Twenty-four Portraits.* 6s.

Nicolini's History of the Jesuits: their Origin, Progress, Doctrines, and Designs. *Fine Portraits of Loyola, Lainès, Xavier, Borgia, Acquaviva, Père la Chaise, and Pope Ganganelli.*

Petrarch's Sonnets, and other Poems. Translated into English Verse. By various hands. With a Life of the Poet, by THOMAS CAMPBELL. *With 16 Engravings.*

Pickering's History of the Races of Man, with an Analytical Synopsis of the Natural History of Man. By Dr. HALL. *Illustrated by numerous Portraits.*
———; or, *with the plates coloured* 7s.6d.
. An excellent Edition of a work originally published at 3l. 3s. by the American Government.

Pictorial Handbook of Modern Geography, on a Popular Plan. 3s. 6d. *Illustrated by 150 Engravings and 51 Maps.* 6s.
———; or, *with the maps coloured*, 7s. 6d.

Pope's Poetical Works. Edited by ROBERT CARRUTHERS. *Numerous Engravings.* 2 vols.

Pope's Homer's Iliad. With Introduction and Notes by J. S. WATSON, M.A. *Illustrated by the entire Series of Flaxman's Designs, beautifully engraved by Moses (in the full 8vo. size).*

———**Homer's Odyssey, Hymns,** &c., by other translators, including Chapman, and Introduction and Notes by J. S. WATSON, M.A. *Flaxman's Designs beautifully engraved by Moses.*

———**Life.** Including many of his Letters. By ROBERT CARRUTHERS. New Edition, revised and enlarged. *Illustrations.*
The preceding 5 vols. make a complete and elegant edition of Pope's Poetical Works and Translations for 25s.

Pottery and Porcelain, and other Objects of Vertu (a Guide to the Knowledge of). To which is added an Engraved List of Marks and Monograms. By HENRY G. BOHN. *Numerous Engravings.*
———; or, *coloured*. 10s. 6d.

Prout's (Father) Reliques. Revised Edition. *Twenty-one spirited Etchings by Maclise.* 5s.

Recreations in Shooting. By "CRAVEN." New Edition, revised and enlarged. *62 Engravings on Wood, after Harvey, and 9 Engravings on Steel, chiefly after A. Cooper, R.A.*

Redding's History and Descriptions of Wines, Ancient and Modern. *Twenty beautiful Woodcuts.*

Rennie's Insect Architecture. New Edition. Revised by the Rev. J. G. WOOD, M.A.

Robinson Crusoe. With Illustrations by STOTHARD and HARVEY. *Twelve beautiful Engravings on Steel, and 74 on Wood.*
———; or, *without the Steel illustrations,* 3s. 6d.

Rome in the Nineteenth Century. New Edition. Revised by the Author. *Illustrated by 34 Steel Engravings.* 2 vols.

Sharpe's History of Egypt, from the Earliest Times till the Conquest by the Arabs, A.D. 640. By SAMUEL SHARPE. With 2 Maps and upwards of 400 Illustrative Woodcuts. Sixth and Cheaper Edition. 2 vols.

Southey's Life of Nelson. With Additional Notes. *Illustrated with 64 Engravings.*

Starling's (Miss) Noble Deeds of Women; or, Examples of Female Courage, Fortitude, and Virtue. *Fourteen Illustrations.*

Stuart and Revett's Antiquities of Athens, and other Monuments of Greece. *Illustrated in 71 Steel Plates, and numerous Woodcuts.*

A CATALOGUE OF

Tales of the Genii; or, the Delightful Lessons of Horam. *Numerous Woodcuts, and 8 Steel Engravings, after Stothard.*

Tasso's Jerusalem Delivered. Translated into English Spenserian Verse, with a Life of the Author. By J. H. WIFFEN. *Eight Engravings on Steel, and 24 on Wood, by Thurston.*

Walker's Manly Exercises. Containing Skating, Riding, Driving, Hunting, Shooting, Sailing, Rowing, Swimming, &c. New Edition, revised by "CRAVEN." *Forty-four Steel Plates, and numerous Woodcuts.*

Walton's Complete Angler. Edited by EDWARD JESSE, Esq. *Upwards of 203 Engravings.*

———; or, *with 26 additional page Illustrations on Steel*, 7s. 6d.

Wellington, Life of. From the materials of Maxwell. *Eighteen Engravings.*

Westropp's Handbook of Archæology. New Edition, revised. *Numerous Illustrations.* 7s. 6d.

White's Natural History of Selborne. With Notes by Sir WILLIAM JARDINE and EDWARD JESSE, Esq. *Illustrated by 40 Engravings.*

———; or, *with the plates coloured*, 7s. 6d.

Young, The, Lady's Book. A Manual of Elegant Recreations, Arts, Sciences, and Accomplishments. *Twelve Hundred Woodcut Illustrations, and several Engravings on Steel*, 7s. 6d.

———; or, *cloth gilt, gilt edges*, 9s.

CLASSICAL LIBRARY.

93 *Vols. at 5s. each, excepting those marked otherwise.*

Æschylus translated into English Verse by A. SWANWICK.

———. Literally Translated into English Prose by an Oxonian. 3s. 6d.

———, Appendix to. Containing the Readings given in Hermann's posthumous Edition of Æschylus. By GEORGE BURGES, M.A. 3s. 6d.

Ammianus Marcellinus. History of Rome from Constantius to Valens. Translated by C. D. YONGE, B.A. Dble. vol. 7s. 6d.

Antoninus. The Thoughts of the Emperor Marcus Aurelius. Translated by GEO. LONG, M.A. 3s. 6d.

Apuleius, the Golden Ass; Death of Socrates; Florida; and Discourse on Magic. To which is added a Metrical Version of Cupid and Psyche; and Mrs. Tighe's Psyche. *Frontispiece.*

Aristophanes' Comedies. Literally Translated, with Notes and Extracts from Frere's and other Metrical Versions, by W. J. HICKIE. 2 vols.
Vol. 1. Acharnians, Knights, Clouds, Wasps, Peace, and Birds.
Vol. 2. Lysistrata, Thesmophoriasusæ, Frogs, Ecclesiazusæ, and Plutus.

Aristotle's Ethics. Literally Translated by Archdeacon BROWNE, late Classical Professor of King's College.

——— Politics and Economics. Translated by E. WALFORD, M.A.

——— Metaphysics. Literally Translated, with Notes, Analysis, Examination Questions, and Index, by the Rev. JOHN H. M'MAHON, M.A., and Gold Medallist in Metaphysics, T.C.D.

Aristotle's History of Animals. In Ten Books. Translated, with Notes and Index, by RICHARD CRESSWELL, M.A.

——— Organon; or, Logical Treatises. With Notes, &c. By O. F. OWEN, M.A. 2 vols, 3s. 6d. each.

——— Rhetoric and Poetics. Literally Translated, with Examination Questions and Notes, by an Oxonian.

Athenæus. The Deipnosophists: or, the Banquet of the Learned. Translated by C. D. YONGE, B.A. 3 vols.

Cæsar. Complete, with the Alexandrian, African, and Spanish Wars. Literally Translated, with Notes.

Catullus, Tibullus, and the Vigil of Venus. A Literal Prose Translation. To which are added Metrical Versions by LAMB, GRAINGER, and others. *Frontispiece.*

Cicero's Orations. Literally Translated by C. D. YONGE, B.A. In 4 vols.
Vol. 1. Contains the Orations against Verres, &c. *Portrait.*
Vol. 2. Catiline, Archias, Agrarian Law, Rabirius, Murena, Sylla, &c.
Vol. 3. Orations for his House, Plancius, Sextius, Cœlius, Milo, Ligarius, &c.
Vol. 4. Miscellaneous Orations, and Rhetorical Works; with General Index to the four volumes.

——— on the Nature of the Gods, Divination, Fate, Laws, a Republic, &c. Translated by C. D. YONGE, B.A., and F. BARHAM.

Cicero's Academics, De Finibus, and Tusculan Questions. By C. D. YONGE, B.A. With Sketch of the Greek Philosopher.

――― **Offices, Old Age, Friendship,** Scipio's Dream, Paradoxes, &c. Literally Translated, by R. EDMONDS. 3s. 6d.

――― **on Oratory and Orators.** By J. S. WATSON, M.A.

Demosthenes' Orations. Translated, with Notes, by C. RANN KENNEDY. In 5 volumes.
    Vol. 1. The Olynthiac, Philippic, and other Public Orations. 3s. 6d
    Vol. 2. On the Crown and on the Embassy.
    Vol. 3. Against Leptines, Midias, Androtrion, and Aristocrates.
    Vol. 4. Private and other Orations.
    Vol. 5. Miscellaneous Orations.

Dictionary of Latin Quotations. Including Proverbs, Maxims, Mottoes, Law Terms, and Phrases; and a Collection of above 500 Greek Quotations. With all the quantities marked, & English Translations.

―――, **with Index Verborum.** 6s. Index Verborum only. 1s.

Diogenes Laertius. Lives and Opinions of the Ancient Philosophers. Translated, with Notes, by C. D. YONGE.

Epictetus. Discourses, with Encheiridion and Fragments. Translated with Notes, by GEORGE LONG, M.A.

Euripides. Literally Translated. 2 vols.
    Vol. 1. Hecuba, Orestes, Medea, Hippolytus, Alcestis, Bacchæ, Heraclidæ, Iphigenia in Aulide, and Iphigenia in Tauris.
    Vol. 2. Hercules Furens, Troades, Ion Andromache, Suppliants, Helen, Electra, Cyclops, Rhesus.

Greek Anthology. Literally Translated. With Metrical Versions by various Authors.

――― **Romances of Heliodorus,** Longus, and Achilles Tatius.

Herodotus. A New and Literal Translation, by HENRY CARY, M.A., of Worcester College, Oxford.

Hesiod, Callimachus, and Theognis. Literally Translated, with Notes, by J. BANKS, M.A.

Homer's Iliad. Literally Translated.

――― **Odyssey, Hymns, &c.** Literally Translated.

Horace. Literally Translated. by SMART. Carefully revised by an OXONIAN. 3s. 6d.

Justin, Cornelius Nepos, and Eutropius. Literally Translated, with Notes and Index, by J. S. WATSON, M.A.

Juvenal, Persius, Sulpicia, and Lucilius. By L. EVANS, M.A. With the Metrical Version by Gifford. *Frontispiece*

Livy. A new and Literal Translation. By Dr. SPILLAN and others In 4 vols.
    Vol. 1. Contains Books 1—8.
    Vol. 2. Books 9—26
    Vol. 3. Books 27—36.
    Vol. 4. Books 37 to the end; and Index.

Lucan's Pharsalia. Translated, with Notes, by H. T. RILEY

Lucretius. Literally Translated, with Notes, by the Rev. J. S. WATSON, M.A. And the Metrical Version by J. M. GOOD.

Martial's Epigrams, complete. Literally Translated. Each accompanied by one or more Verse Translations selected from the Works of English Poets, and other sources. With a copious Index. Double volume (660 pages). 7s. 6d.

Ovid's Works, complete. Literally Translated 3 vols.
    Vol. 1. Fasti, Tristia, Epistles, &c.
    Vol. 2. Metamorphoses.
    Vol. 3. Heroides, Art of Love, &c.

Pindar. Literally Translated, by DAWSON W. TURNER, and the Metrical Version by ABRAHAM MOORE.

Plato's Works. Translated by the Rev. H. CARY and others. In 6 vols.
    Vol. 1. The Apology of Socrates, Crito, Phædo, Gorgias, Protagoras, Phædrus, Theætetus, Euthyphron, Lysis.
    Vol. 2. The Republic, Timæus, & Critias.
    Vol. 3. Meno, Euthydemus, The Sophist, Statesman, Cratylus, Parmenides, and the Banquet.
    Vol. 4. Philebus, Charmides, Laches, The Two Alcibiades, and Ten other Dialogues.
    Vol. 5. The Laws.
    Vol. 6. The Doubtful Works. With General Index.

――― **Dialogues,** an Analysis and Index to. With References to the Translation in Bohn's Classical Library. By Dr DAY.

Plautus's Comedies. Literally Translated, with Notes, by H. T. RILEY, B.A. In 2 vols.

Pliny's Natural History. Translated, with Copious Notes, by the late JOHN BOSTOCK, M.D., F.R.S., and H. T. RILEY, B.A In 6 vols

Pliny the Younger, The Letters of. MELMOTH's Translation revised. By the Rev. F. C. T. BOSANQUET, M.A.

Propertius, Petronius, and Johannes Secundus, and Aristænetus Literally Translated, and accompanied by Poetical Versions, from various sources.

Quintilian's Institutes of Oratory. Literally Translated, with Notes, &c., by J. S. WATSON, M.A. In 2 vols.

Sallust, Florus, and Velleius Paterculus. With Copious Notes, Biographical Notices, and Index, by J. S. WATSON.

Sophocles. The Oxford Translation revised.

Standard Library Atlas of Classical Geography. Twenty-two large coloured Maps according to the latest authorities. With a complete Index (accentuated) giving the latitude and longitude of every place named in the Maps. Imp. 8vo. 7s. 6d.

Strabo's Geography. Translated. with Copious Notes, by W. FALCONER, M.A., and H. C. HAMILTON, Esq. With Index, giving the Ancient and Modern Names. In 3 vols.

Suetonius' Lives of the Twelve Cæsars, and other Works. Thomson's Translation, revised, with Notes, by T. FORESTER.

Tacitus. Literally Translated, with Notes. In 2 vols.
Vol. 1. The Annals.
Vol. 2. The History, Germania, Agricola. &c. With Index.

Terence and Phædrus. By H. T. RILEY. B.A.

Theocritus, Bion, Moschus, and Tyrtæus. By J. BANKS, M.A. With the Metrical Versions of Chapman.

Thucydides. Literally Translated by Rev. H. DALE. In 2 vols. 3s. 6d. each.

Virgil. Literally Translated by DAVID-SON. New Edition, carefully revised. 3s. 6d.

Xenophon's Works. In 3 Vols.
Vol. 1. The Anabasis and Memorabilia. Translated, with Notes, by J. S. WATSON, M.A. And a Geographical Commentary, by W. F. AINSWORTH, F.S.A., F.R.G.S., &c.
Vol. 2. Cyropædia and Hellenics. By J. S. WATSON, M.A., and the Rev. H DALE.
Vol. 3. The Minor Works. By J. S. WATSON, M.A.

SCIENTIFIC LIBRARY.

57 Vols. at 5s. each, excepting those marked otherwise.

Agassiz and Gould's Comparative Physiology. Enlarged by Dr. WRIGHT. Upwards of 400 Engravings.

Bacon's Novum Organum and Advancement of Learning. Complete, with Notes, by J. DEVEY, M.A."

Bolley's Manual of Technical Analysis. A Guide for the Testing of Natural and Artificial Substances. By B. H. PAUL. 100 Wood Engravings.

BRIDGEWATER TREATISES.—

——— **Bell on the Hand.** Its Mechanism and Vital Endowments as evincing Design. Seventh Edition Revised.

——— **Kirby on the History, Habits,** and Instincts of Animals. Edited with Notes, by T. RYMER JONES. Numerous Engravings, many of which are additional. In 2 vols.

——— **Kidd on the Adaptation of** External Nature to the Physical Condition of Man. 3s. 6d.

——— **Whewell's Astronomy and** General Physics, considered with reference to Natural Theology. 3s. 6d.

——— **Chalmers on the Adaptation** of External Nature to the Moral and Intellectual Constitution of Man.

BRIDGEWATER TREATISES—cont.

——— **Prout's Treatise on Chemistry,** Meteorology, and Digestion. Edited by Dr. J. W. GRIFFITH.

——— **Buckland's Geology and** Mineralogy. 2 vols. 15s.

——— **Roget's Animal and Vegetable** Physiology. Illustrated. In 2 vols. 6s. each.

Carpenter's (Dr. W. B.) Zoology. A Systematic View of the Structure, Habits, Instincts, and Uses, of the principal Families of the Animal Kingdom, and of the chief forms of Fossil Remains. Revised by W. S. DALLAS. F.L.S. Illustrated with many hundred Wood Engravings. In 2 vols. 6s. each.

——— **Mechanical Philosophy, Astronomy,** and Horology. A Popular Exposition. 18s Illustrations.

——— **Vegetable Physiology and** Systematic Botany. A complete Introduction to the Knowledge of Plants. Revised, under arrangement with the Author, by E. LANKESTER, M.D., &c. Several hundred Illustrations on Wood. 6s.

——— **Animal Physiology.** In part re-written by the Author. Upwards of 300 capital Illustrations. 6s.

Chevreul on Colour. Containing the Principles of Harmony and Contrast of Colours, and their application to the Arts. Translated from the French by CHARLES MARTEL. Only complete Edition. Several Plates. Or, with an additional series of 16 Plates in Colours. 7s. 6d.

Ennemoser's History of Magic. Translated by WILLIAM HOWITT. With an Appendix of the most remarkable and best authenticated Stories of Apparitions, Dreams, Table-Turning, and Spirit-Rapping, &c. In 2 vols.

Hogg's (Jabez) Elements of Experimental and Natural Philosophy. Containing Mechanics, Pneumatics, Hydrostatics, Hydraulics, Acoustics, Optics, Caloric, Electricity, Voltaism, and Magnetism. New Edition, enlarged. Upwards of 400 Woodcuts.

Hind's Introduction to Astronomy. With a Vocabulary, containing an Explanation of all the Terms in present use. New Edition, enlarged. Numerous Engravings. 3s. 6d.

Humboldt's Cosmos; or, Sketch of a Physical Description of the Universe. Translated by E. C. OTTÉ and W. S. DALLAS, F.L.S. Fine Portrait. In five vols. 3s. 6d. each; excepting Vol. V., 5s.

*** In this edition the notes are placed beneath the text, Humboldt's analytical Summaries and the passages hitherto suppressed are included, and new and comprehensive Indices are added.

—— **Travels in America.** In 3 vols.

—— **Views of Nature;** or, Contemplations of the Sublime Phenomena of Creation. Translated by E. C. OTTÉ and H. G. BOHN. With a complete Index.

Hunt's (Robert) Poetry of Science; or, Studies of the Physical Phenomena of Nature. By Professor HUNT. New Edition, enlarged.

Joyce's Scientific Dialogues. By Dr. GRIFFITH. Numerous Woodcuts.

—— **Introduction to the Arts and Sciences.** With Examination Questions. 3s. 6d.

Knight's (Chas.) Knowledge is Power. A Popular Manual of Political Economy.

Lectures on Painting. By the Royal Academicians. With Introductory Essay, and Notes by R. WORNUM, Esq. Portraits.

Lilly's Introduction to Astrology. With numerous Emendations, by ZADKIEL.

Mantell's (Dr.) Geological Excursions through the Isle of Wight and Dorsetshire. New Edition, by T. RUPERT JONES, Esq. Numerous beautifully executed Woodcuts, and a Geological Map.

—— **Medals of Creation;** or, First Lessons in Geology and the study of Organic Remains; including Geological Excursions. New Edition, revised. Coloured Plates, and several hundred beautiful Woodcuts. In 2 vols., 7s. 6d. each.

—— **Petrifactions and their Teachings.** An Illustrated Handbook to the Organic Remains in the British Museum. Numerous Engravings. 6s.

—— **Wonders of Geology;** or, a Familiar Exposition of Geological Phenomena. New Edition, augmented by T. RUPERT JONES, F.G.S. Coloured Geological Map of England, Plates, and nearly 200 beautiful Woodcuts. In 2 vols., 7s. 6d. each.

Morphy's Games of Chess. Being the Matches and best Games played by the American Champion, with Explanatory and Analytical Notes, by J. LÖWENTHAL. Portrait and Memoir.

It contains by far the largest collection of games played by Mr. Morphy extant in any form, and has received his endorsement and co-operation.

Richardson's Geology, including Mineralogy and Palæontology. Revised and enlarged, by Dr. T. WRIGHT. Upwards of 400 Illustrations.

Schouw's Earth, Plants, and Man; and Kobell's Sketches from the Mineral Kingdom. Translated by A. HENFREY, F.R.S. Coloured Map of the Geography of Plants.

Smith's (Pye) Geology and Scripture; or, The Relation between the Holy Scriptures and Geological Science.

Stanley's Classified Synopsis of the Principal Painters of the Dutch and Flemish Schools.

Staunton's Chess-player's Handbook. Numerous Diagrams.

—— **Chess Praxis.** A Supplement to the Chess-player's Handbook. Containing all the most important modern Improvements in the Openings, illustrated by actual Games; a revised Code of Chess Laws; and a Selection of Mr. Morphy's Games in England and France. 6s.

A CATALOGUE OF

Staunton's Chess-player's Companion. Comprising a new Treatise on Odds, Collection of Match Games, and a Selection of Original Problems.

―――― **Chess Tournament of 1851.** *Numerous Illustrations.*

Stockhardt's Principles of Chemistry, exemplified in a series of simple experiments. Based upon the German work of Professor STOCKHARDT, and Edited by C. W. HEATON, Professor of Chemistry at Charing Cross Hospital. *Upwards of 270 Illustrations.*

Ure's (Dr. A.) Cotton Manufacture of Great Britain, systematically investigated; with an introductory view of its comparative state in Foreign Countries. New Edition, revised by P. L. SIMMONDS. *One hundred and fifty Illustrations.* In 2 vols.

―――― **Philosophy of Manufactures;** or, An Exposition of the Factory System of Great Britain. Continued by P. L. SIMMONDS. 7s. 6d.

REFERENCE LIBRARY.

25 Vols. at various prices.

Blair's Chronological Tables, Revised and Enlarged. Comprehending the Chronology and History of the World, from the earliest times. By J. WILLOUGHBY ROSSE. Double Volume. 10s.; or, half-bound, 10s. 6d.

Clark's (Hugh)' Introduction to Heraldry. *With nearly* 1000 *Illustrations.* 18th *Edition.* Revised and enlarged by J. R. PLANCHE, Rouge Croix. 5s. Or, with all the Illustrations coloured, 15s.

Chronicles of the Tombs. A Collection of Remarkable Epitaphs. By T. J. PETTIGREW, F.R.S., F.S.A. 5s.

Handbook of Domestic Medicine. Popularly arranged. By Dr. HENRY DAVIES. 700 pages. With complete index. 5s.

―――― **Games.** By various Amateurs and Professors. Comprising treatises on all the principal Games of chance, skill, and manual dexterity. In all, above 40 games (the Whist, Draughts, and Billiards being especially comprehensive). Edited by H. G. BOHN. *Illustrated by numerous Diagrams.* 5s.

―――― **Proverbs.** Comprising all Ray's English Proverbs, with additions; his Foreign Proverbs; and an Alphabetical Index. 5s.

Humphrey's Coin Collector's Manual. A popular introduction to the Study of Coins. *Highly finished Engravings.* In 2 vols. 10s.

Index of Dates. Comprehending the principal Facts in the Chronology and

History of the World, from the earliest time, alphabetically arranged. By J. W. ROSSE. Double volume, 10s.; or, half-bound, 10s. 6d.

Lowndes' Bibliographer's Manual of English Literature. New Edition, enlarged, by H. G. BOHN. Parts I. to X. (A to Z). 3s. 6d. each. Part XI. (the Appendix Volume). 5s. Or the 11 parts in 4 vols, half morocco, 2l. 2s.

Polyglot of Foreign Proverbs. With English Translations, and a General Index, bringing the whole into parallels, by H. G. BOHN. 5s.

Political Cyclopædia. In 4 vols. 3s. 6d. each.

―――― Also in 2 vols. bound. 15s.

Smith's (Archdeacon) Complete Collection of Synonyms and Antonyms. 5s.

The Epigrammatists. Selections from the Epigrammatic Literature of Ancient Mediæval, and Modern Times. With Notes, Observations, Illustrations, and an Introduction. By the Rev. HENRY PHILIP DODD, M.A., of Pembroke College, Oxford. Second Edition, revised and considerably enlarged; containing many new Epigrams, principally of an amusing character. 6s.

Wheeler's (W. A., M.A.) Dictionary of Noted Names of Fictitious Persons and Places. 5s.

Wright's (T.) Dictionary of Obsolete and Provincial English. In 2 vols. 5s. each; or half-bound in 1 vol, 10s. 6d.

www.ingramcontent.com/pod-product-compliance
Lightning Source LLC
Chambersburg PA
CBHW020306240426
43673CB00039B/719